LITERACY IN WITHDRAWN
AMERICAN SCHOOLS

LITERACY IN AMERICAN SCHOOLS

Learning to Read and Write

Edited by Nancy L. Stein

The University of Chicago Press

Chicago and London

The essays in this volume originally appeared in *American Journal of Education*, November 1984, Volume 93, No. 1.

The University of Chicago Press, Chicago 60637
The University of Chicago Press, Ltd., London

Library of Congress Cataloging-in-Publication Data
Main entry under title:

Literacy in American schools.

"The essays in this volume originally appeared in
American journal of education, November 1984, volume 93,
no. 1"—T.p. verso.
  Bibliography: p.
  Includes index.
  1. Reading—United States—Addresses, essays,
lectures. 2. English language—Composition and
exercises—Addresses, essays, lectures. I. Stein,
Nancy L.
LB1050.L499   1986   428.4'07'1073   85-24625
ISBN 0-226-77177-6
ISBN 0-226-77178-4 (pbk.)

The paper used in this publication meets the
minimum requirements of American National Standard
for Information Sciences—Permanence of Paper for
Printed Library Materials, ANSI Z39.48-1984.

Contents

Introduction: The Development of Literacy in the American Schools

In the last few years, the emergence of a national concern about the quality of education in America has assumed center stage. Witness the Carnegie Foundation's report on education and the state of American schools. Read any one of the handful of books that have followed the foundation's report. The consensus seems to be growing that our schools are in deep trouble and that substantial reform must be considered at all levels of the educational enterprise.

The critics have been extremely vocal about every aspect of education, but two areas have received more than their share of criticism: the physical and mathematical sciences and the development of reading and writing skills. The latter, which we will term "the development of verbal literacy," has loomed as an ominous problem because the success of instructional programs in the sciences are thought to depend directly on the knowledge and skills acquired in learning how to read and write. For that matter, the development of reading skill is believed to be central to almost every aspect of intellectual pursuit in the American schools.

Given the importance of reading and writing, why is it that we are experiencing difficulty teaching our children the prerequisite skills necessary to understand and produce text? What are the problems? Why has such an important area of education become so problematic? This volume is devoted to answering some of these questions.

The collection of essays is divided into four sections. The first section concerns the definition of literacy and how literacy is valued in our society. Two contributors have addressed these issues: Sylvia Scribner and Henry Jay Becker. Scribner's paper is devoted to an analysis of how literacy is valued in our society. She uses three different metaphors associated with the development of literacy to show the different and sometimes contrasting set of values that underlie the meaning and definition of literacy. More important, Scribner begins to question the implications for learning and curriculum development when any one metaphor is used to define what is meant by literacy. In short, she shows the potential conflicts in curriculum evaluation when people have differing viewpoints on what constitutes literacy education.

Becker also focuses on the definition of literacy in the American schools. His concerns, however, are unique because he addresses the importance of the computer in advancing literacy education in the school system. Two issues are discussed in his article: (1) whether the expense and usefulness of computers warrant the degree of attention that has been given to the introduction of computers in the school system, and (2) what degree and level of knowledge should be acquired by children who use the computer.

As Becker shows, the computer can be thought of as a tool to facilitate learning and instruction across a variety of domains. In this regard, the computer is often viewed as a substitute for the teacher and is seen as an instrument that can contend with the differing levels of ability and knowledge that students bring to any new learning situation. Becker evaluates the success of this approach in increasing instructional efficiency in the schools at the present time.

He also shows, however, that the computer can be studied in its own right. The machinery underlying its operation can be analyzed, its capacity to handle different types of programs can be evaluated, and students can be taught about computers and computer programming. Thus, the computer's capabilities with respect to its hardware and software limitations can be explored. Again, Becker evaluates this role with respect to the development of literacy in the American schools.

The second section of this collection is devoted to specific concerns about the development of reading skill. Both decoding and comprehension aspects are considered. Charles A. Perfetti focuses on issues related to decoding. Isabel L. Beck and Margaret G. McKeown are concerned with issues underlying comprehension instruction.

Perfetti considers two definitions of the reading process. The first considers reading as akin to thinking guided by print. The second views reading as the translation of written elements into language. Perfetti shows that both definitions are of value. Controversy over the nature of reading instruction has occurred because many people attempt to adopt one definition to the exclusion of the other. Perfetti illustrates the need for both definitions. He also points out that defining reading as the translation of written elements into language is essential, especially in the early stages of learning to read. He alerts us that children need to acquire knowledge about the phonetic and linguistic aspects of the written code and that this knowledge, as well as semantic knowledge, is used in word recognition skill. Perfetti then argues that multiple pathways to word recognition are the preferred mode and guarantee that a reader will develop a fair amount of skill in decoding and understanding text.

Beck and McKeown focus on comprehension processes that occur during reading and discuss certain factors that are known to influence whether or not a text will be comprehended. The role of prior knowledge and the organization and structure of text material are highlighted in this article. These investigators illustrate the significant effects that both of these factors have on comprehension processes. Additionally, they illustrate how a teacher or investigator can take a "poorly formed" text and reconstruct the text so that it is more comprehensible. The major point they make about the reconstruction of text materials is that there are usually *many* different types of changes that should be made in constructing materials to improve them, ranging from the linguistic level (e.g., disambiguating pronominal references, putting in correct rhetorical markers) to the semantic and structural level of the text. Concentrating on one factor will not necessarily improve the comprehensibility of the text. Considering a multidimensional approach to text construction, however, appears to be effective.

The third section of the collection focuses on both reading and writing achievement in the American schools. Alan C. Purves and Judith A. Langer raise some general issues that concern almost all aspects of literacy education, and George Hillocks, Jr., presents an overview of instructional studies. Purves addresses the issue of the difference between the potential and real achievement of students in American schools. First, he shows that the development of reading skill depends on many different types of knowledge and that this knowledge is used in an interactive fashion during the comprehension process. Purves's assumptions are similar to Perfetti's and Beck and McKeown's beliefs. He clearly acknowledges the complex nature of the reading process and shows how comprehension depends on several different types of knowledge.

Purves also discusses the results of the National Assessment of Educational Progress's evaluation of reading achievement in this country, with respect both to the implicit definition of literacy underlying the construction of items on the NAEP test and to levels of reading achievement attained in this and other countries. He also examines the role of instruction in promoting the growth of literacy skills, showing that schools are successful in teaching certain skills related to the development of literacy and not so successful at teaching other types of skills. However, as Purves points out, the United States fares no worse than other countries that are attempting to educate their students through schooling. He then raises the question of whether we should maintain the same standards of literacy for all students.

Judith Langer's essay is similar in nature to Purves's in that she considers certain factors that influence the development of literacy

3

education in this country. However, she is more concerned with how traditional ways of evaluating reading and writing skills have interfered with an accurate assessment of comprehension and writing skills. She also focuses on the nature of instructional strategies in teaching certain literacy skills such as writing in the classroom.

One of Langer's main concerns is that tests of reading and writing skill often provide the teacher with incorrect information about student achievement. Also, these tests are sometimes difficult to use for diagnostic purposes because they rarely include items that allow an accurate diagnosis of what the student does not understand. In fact, she proposes that it is often impossible to gain insight from standardized tests into what children do and do not know about text material.

A second focus of her essay concerns the type of model that should be used in instructional settings, especially those that focus on the acquisition of writing skills. Langer outlines several principles that she considers important if instruction is to be successful in a classroom devoted to literacy instruction.

In the final essay of this section, George Hillocks presents a meta-analysis of a large number of instructional studies that have been completed in the field of writing. His basic question concerns the effectiveness of different types of instruction on students' skill at producing written prose.

Two factors are identified as important in analyzing the effectiveness of instructional strategies: the mode of instruction and the focus of instruction. The mode refers to how a teacher (or experimenter) chooses to transmit information (e.g., through presenting a lecture, through a socratic dialogue, through student interchange). The focus refers to the general types of materials and content used in each study (e.g., focus on the mechanics of writing, the structure, or the content of written material).

The results of Hillocks's analysis are important in that the data challenge some of the more common assumptions associated with effective writing instruction. In particular, his meta-analysis shows that the naturalistic mode of instruction, used by many of the well-known writing instruction programs, is the least effective in promoting improvement in written prose. A mode where information is presented in a lecture-type fashion is also not very effective. Hillocks shows that certain types of interactions between students and teachers during instruction are the most effective for improving writing skill.

The last section of the volume is devoted to an analysis of some of the critical issues in literacy instruction. In this essay, I attempt to identify the major themes inherent in the seven papers collected here. My charge as editor, however, was not only to identify the issues in

4

the field of literacy education. Rather, the goal was to develop suggestions and means for studying these issues further. Thus, I attempted an integrated discussion of the critical (and sometimes controversial) issues raised in individual papers. Additionally, I included specific suggestions for further research in the area of literacy education, providing examples and drawing on the ongoing research of several investigators.

Of primary importance in this discussion is the development of a model of both learning and instruction. To this extent, a beginning model is proposed and distinctions are made between the process of instructing a student and the process of learning new material. In addition, suggestions are made concerning the development of a theory of literacy that takes into account different definitions and functions of literacy. At the present time, most school systems have an ideal view of the literate student. This view is often quite narrow and based on a set of very specific skills, mostly in the area of verbal proficiency. It is suggested that a common core of skills be established in the verbal domain, but that the definition of literacy used by school systems take into account the development of skill in other domains that does not necessarily relate to or depend on the development of complex literacy skills in the verbal domain.

Finally, a call for more interdisciplinary communication is made. The areas of reading and writing research are not only the domain of educators. The process of comprehension and composition is being studied by philosophers, linguists, anthropologists, psychologists, cognitive scientists, and computer scientists. As my overview indicates, the assumptions underlying the approaches in each of these domains are often very different and frequently contradictory. Each approach has a strong tendency to believe only in the validity of its own assumptions. I show, by an analysis and review of specific data, that some of the basic assumptions held by each group have proven to be inaccurate. A necessary step in the direction of more binding research requires a definite integration of several approaches to the study of literacy. No one approach has been accurate or comprehensive enough to warrant the strong support and beliefs that are adopted by the majority of educators. Only through an active attempt at understanding the assumptions underlying different approaches to the problems of literacy will the field progress.

NANCY L. STEIN

Literacy in Three Metaphors

SYLVIA SCRIBNER
City University of New York

Although literacy is a problem of pressing national concern, we have yet to discover or set its boundaries. This observation, made several years ago by a leading political spokesman (McGovern 1978), echoes a long-standing complaint of many policymakers and educators that what counts as literacy in our technological society is a matter "not very well understood" (Advisory Committee on National Illiteracy 1929).

A dominant response of scholars and researchers to this perceived ambiguity has been to pursue more rigorously the quest for definition and measurement of the concept. Many approaches have been taken (among them, Adult Performance Level Project 1975; Bormuth 1975; Hillerich 1976; Kirsch and Guthrie 1977–78; Miller 1973; Powell 1977), and at least one attempt (Hunter and Harman 1979) has been made to put forward an "umbrella definition." Each of these efforts has identified important parameters of literacy, but none has yet won consensual agreement (for a thoughtful historical and conceptual analysis of shifting literacy definitions, see Radwin [1978]).

The definitional controversy has more than academic significance. Each formulation of an answer to the question "What is literacy?" leads to a different evaluation of the scope of the problem (i.e., the extent of *il*literacy) and to different objectives for programs aimed at the formation of a literate citizenry. Definitions of literacy shape our perceptions of individuals who fall on either side of the standard (what a "literate" or "nonliterate" is like) and thus in a deep way affect both the substance and style of educational programs. A chorus of clashing answers also creates problems for literacy planners and educators. This is clearly evident in the somewhat acerbic comments of Dauzat and Dauzat (1977, p. 37), who are concerned with adult basic education: "In spite of all of the furor and the fervor for attaining literacy . . . few have undertaken to say what they or anyone else means by literacy.

Those few professional organizations, bureaus and individuals who have attempted the task of explaining 'what is literacy?' generate definitions that conflict, contradict but rarely complement each other. . . . These 'champions of the cause of literacy' crusade for a national effort to make literacy a reality without establishing what that reality is."

What lies behind the definitional difficulties this statement decries? The authors themselves provide a clue. They suggest that literacy is a kind of reality that educators should be able to grasp and explain, or, expressed in more classical terms, that literacy has an "essence" that can be captured through some Aristotelian-like enterprise. By a rational process of discussion and analysis, the "true" criterial components of literacy will be identified, and these in turn can become the targets of education for literacy.

Many, although by no means all, of those grappling with the problems of definition and measurement appear to be guided by such a search for the "essence"—for the "one best" way of conceptualizing literacy. This enterprise is surely a useful one and a necessary component of educational planning. Without denigrating its contribution, I would like to suggest, however, that conflicts and contradictions are intrinsic to such an essentialist approach.

Consider the following. Most efforts at definitional determination are based on a conception of literacy as an attribute of *individuals;* they aim to describe constituents of literacy in terms of individual abilities. But the single most compelling fact about literacy is that it is a *social* achievement; individuals in societies without writing systems do not become literate. Literacy is an outcome of cultural transmission; the individual child or adult does not extract the meaning of written symbols through personal interaction with the physical objects that

---

SYLVIA SCRIBNER is professor of psychology at the Graduate School and University Center of the City University of New York and was formerly associate director of the National Institute of Education. She has studied the social organization and cognitive implications of literacy in traditional societies and in work settings in the United States and has a long-term interest in the continuities and discontinuities between learning in school and in nonacademic environments. Her recent publications include *The Psychology of Literacy* (with Michael Cole), a special issue of the journal *Cognitive Studies of Work,* and chapters on practical thinking and working intelligence. She is a member of the steering committee of Psychologists for Social Responsibility (New York) and a fellow of the American Association for the Advancement of Science.

embody them. Literacy abilities are acquired by individuals only in the course of participation in socially organized activities with written language (for a theoretical analysis of literacy as a set of socially organized practices, see Scribner and Cole [1981]). It follows that individual literacy is relative to social literacy. Since social literacy practices vary in time (Resnick [1983] contains historical studies) and space (anthropological studies are in Goody [1968]), what qualifies as individual literacy varies with them. At one time, ability to write one's name was a hallmark of literacy; today in some parts of the world, the ability to memorize a sacred text remains the modal literacy act. Literacy has neither a static nor a universal essence.

The enterprise of defining literacy, therefore, becomes one of assessing what counts as literacy in the modern epoch in some given social context. If a nation-society is the context, this enterprise requires that consideration be given to the functions that the society in question has invented for literacy and their distribution throughout the populace. Grasping what literacy "is" inevitably involves social analysis: What activities are carried out with written symbols? What significance is attached to them, and what status is conferred on those who engage in them? Is literacy a social right or a private power? These questions are subject to empirical determination. But others are not: Does the prevailing distribution of literacy conform to standards of social justice and human progress? What social and educational policies might promote such standards? Here we are involved, not with fact but with considerations of value, philosophy, and ideology similar to those that figure prominently in debates about the purposes and goals of schooling. Points of view about literacy as a social good, as well as a social fact, form the ground of the definitional enterprise. We may lack consensus on how best to define literacy because we have differing views about literacy's social purposes and values.

These differing points of view about the central meaning of literacy warrant deeper examination. In this essay, I will examine some of them, organizing my discussion around three metaphors: literacy as adaptation, literacy as power, and literacy as a state of grace. Each of these metaphors is rooted in certain assumptions about the social motivations for literacy in this country, the nature of existing literacy practices, and judgments about which practices are critical for individual and social enhancement. Each has differing implications for educational policies and goals. I will be schematic in my discussion; my purpose is not to marshal supporting evidence for one or the other metaphor but to show the boundary problems of all. My argument is that any of the metaphors, taken by itself, gives us only a partial grasp of the many and varied utilities of literacy and of the complex social and psychological factors sustaining aspirations for and achievement of individual literacy. To illustrate this theme, I will draw on the literacy experiences of a Third World people who, although remaining at an Iron Age level of technology, have nevertheless evolved varied functions for written language; their experience demonstrates that, even in some traditional societies, literacy is a "many-meaninged thing."

Literacy as Adaptation

This metaphor is designed to capture concepts of literacy that emphasize its survival or pragmatic value. When the term "functional literacy" was originally introduced during World War I (Harman 1970), it specified the literacy skills required to meet the tasks of modern soldiering. Today, functional literacy is conceived broadly as the level of proficiency necessary for effective performance in a range of settings and customary activities.

This concept has a strong commonsense appeal. The necessity for literacy skills in daily life is obvious; on the job, riding around town, shopping for groceries, we all encounter situations requiring us to read or produce written symbols. No justification is needed to insist that schools are obligated to equip children with the literacy skills that will enable them to fulfill these mundane situational demands. And basic educational programs have a similar obligation to equip adults with the skills they must have to secure jobs or advance to better ones, receive the training and benefits to which they are entitled, and assume their civic and political responsibilities. Within the United States, as in other nations, literacy programs with these practical aims are considered efforts at human resource development and, as such, contributors to economic growth and stability.

In spite of their apparent commonsense grounding, functional literacy approaches are neither as straightforward nor as unproblematic as they first appear. Attempts to inventory "minimal functional competencies" have floundered on lack of information and divided perceptions of functionality. Is it realistic to try to specify some uniform set of skills as constituting functional literacy for all adults? Two subquestions are involved here. One concerns the choice of parameters for defining a "universe of functional competencies." Which literacy tasks (e.g., reading a newspaper, writing a check) are "necessary," and which are "optional"? The Adult Performance Level Project test (1975), one of the best conceptualized efforts to specify and measure competencies necessary for success in adult life, has been challenged on the grounds that it lacks content validity: "The APL test fails to meet this [validity] criterion . . . not necessarily because test development procedures were technically faulty, but because it is not logically possible to define this universe of behaviors [which compose functional competence] without respect to a value position which the test developers have chosen not to discuss" (Cervero 1980, p. 163).

An equally important question concerns the concept of uniformity. Do all communities and cultural groups in our class-based and heterogeneous society confront equivalent functional demands? If not, how do they differ? Some experts (e.g., Gray 1965; Hunter and Harman 1979) maintain that the concept of functional literacy makes sense only with respect to the proficiencies required for participation in the actual life conditions of particular groups or communities. But how does such a relativistic approach mesh with larger societal needs? If we were to consider the level of reading and writing activities carried out in small and isolated rural communities as the standard for functional literacy, educational objectives would be unduly restricted. At the other extreme, we might not want to use literacy activities of college teachers as the standard determining the functional competencies required for high school graduation. Only in recent years has research been undertaken on the range of literacy activities practiced in different communities or settings within the United States (e.g., Heath 1980, 1981; Scribner 1982a), and we still know little about how, and by whom, required literacy work gets done. Lacking such knowledge, public discussions fluctuate between narrow definitions of functional skills pegged to immediate vocational and personal needs, and sweeping definitions that virtually reinstate the ability to cope with college subject matter as the hallmark of literacy. On the other hand, adopting different criteria for different regions or communities would ensure the perpetuation of educational inequalities and the differential access to life opportunities with which these are associated.

Adapting literacy standards to today's needs, personal or social, would be shortsighted. The time-limited nature of what constitutes minimal skills is illustrated in the "sliding scale" used by the U.S. Bureau of Census to determine literacy. During World War I, a fourth-grade education was considered sufficient to render one literate; in 1947, a U.S. Census sample survey raised that figure to five years; and by 1952 six years of school was considered the minimal literacy threshold. Replacing the school-grade criterion with a functional approach to literacy does not eliminate the time problem. Today's standards for functional competency need to be considered in the light of tomorrow's requirements. But not all are agreed as to the nature or volume of literacy demands in the decades ahead. Some (e.g., Naisbitt 1982) argue that, as economic and other activities become increasingly subject to computerized techniques of production and information handling, even higher levels of literacy will be required of all. A contrary view, popularized by McLuhan (1962, 1964) is that new technologies and communication media are likely to reduce literacy requirements for all. A responding argument is that some of these technologies are, in effect, new systems of literacy. The ability to use minicomputers as information storage and retrieval devices requires mastery of symbol systems that build on natural language literacy; they are second-order literacies as it were. One possible scenario is that in coming decades literacy may be increased for some and reduced for others, accentuating the present uneven, primarily class-based distribution of literacy functions.

From the perspective of social needs, the seemingly well-defined concept of functional competency becomes fuzzy at the edges. Equally as many questions arise about functionality from the individual's point of view. Functional needs have not yet been assessed from the perspective of those who purportedly experience them. To what extent do adults whom tests assess as functionally illiterate perceive themselves as lacking the necessary skills to be adequate parents, neighbors, workers? Inner-city youngsters may have no desire to write letters to each other; raising one's reading level by a few grades may not be seen as a magic ticket to a job; not everyone has a bank account that requires the mastery of unusual forms (Heath 1980). Appeals to individuals to enhance their functional skills might founder on the different subjective utilities communities and groups attach to reading and writing activities.

The functional approach has been hailed as a major advance over more traditional concepts of reading and writing because it takes into account the goals and settings of people's activities with written language. Yet even tender probing reveals the many questions of fact, value, and purpose that complicate its application to educational curricula.

We now turn to the second metaphor.

Literacy as Power

While functional literacy stresses the importance of literacy to the adaptation of the individual, the literacy-as-power metaphor emphasizes a relationship between literacy and group or community advancement.

Historically, literacy has been a potent tool in maintaining the hegemony of elites and dominant classes in certain societies, while laying the basis for increased social and political participation in others (Resnick 1983; Goody 1968). In a contemporary framework, expansion of literary skills is often viewed as a means for poor and politically powerless groups to claim their place in the world. The International Symposium for Literacy, meeting in Persepolis, Iran (Bataille 1976), appealed to national governments to consider literacy as an instrument for human liberation and social change. Paulo Freire (1970) bases his influential theory of literacy education on the need to make literacy a resource for fundamental social transformation. Effective literacy education, in his view, creates a critical consciousness through which a community can analyze its conditions of social existence and engage in effective action for a just society. Not to be literate is a state of victimization.

Yet the capacity of literacy to confer power or to be the primary impetus for significant and lasting economic or social change has proved problematic in developing countries. Studies (Gayter, Hall, Kidd, and Shivasrava 1979; United Nations Development Program 1976) of UNESCO's experimental world literacy program have raised doubts about earlier notions that higher literacy rates automatically promote national development and improve the social and material conditions of the very poor. The relationship between social change and literacy education, it is now suggested (Harman 1977), may be stronger in the other direction. When masses of people have been mobilized for fundamental changes in social conditions—as in the USSR, China, Cuba, and Tanzania—rapid extensions of literacy have been accomplished (Gayter et al. 1979; Hammiche 1976; Scribner 1982*b*). Movements to transform social reality appear to have been effective in some parts of the world in bringing whole populations into participation in modern literacy activities. The validity of the converse proposition—that literacy per se mobilizes people for action to change their social reality— remains to be established.

What does this mean for us? The one undisputed fact about illiteracy in America is its concentration among poor, black, elderly, and minority-language groups—groups without effective participation in our country's economic and educational institutions (Hunter and Harman 1979). Problems of poverty and political powerlessness are, as among some populations in developing nations, inseparably intertwined with problems of access to knowledge and levels of literacy skills. Some (e.g., Kozol 1980) suggest that a mass and politicized approach to literacy education such as that adopted by Cuba is demanded in these conditions. Others (e.g., Hunter and Harman 1979) advocate a more action-oriented approach that views community mobilization around practical, social, and political goals as a first step in creating the conditions for effective literacy instruction and for educational equity.

The possibilities and limits of the literacy-as-power metaphor within our present-day social and political structure are not at all clear. To what extent can instructional experiences and programs be lifted out of their social contexts in other countries and applied here? Do assumptions about the functionality and significance of literacy in poor communities in the United States warrant further consideration? Reder and Green's (1984) research and educational work among West Coast immigrant communities reveals that literacy has different meanings for members of different groups. How can these cultural variations be taken into account? How are communities best mobilized for literacy—around local needs and small-scale activism? or as part of broader political and social movements? If literacy has not emerged as a priority demand, should government and private agencies undertake to mobilize communities around this goal? And can such efforts be productive without the deep involvement of community leaders?

Literacy as a State of Grace

Now we come to the third metaphor. I have variously called it literacy as salvation and literacy as a state of grace. Both labels are unsatisfactory because they give a specific religious interpretation to the broader phenomenon I want to depict—that is, the tendency in many societies to endow the literate person with special virtues. A concern with preserving and understanding scripture is at the core of many religious traditions, Western and non-Western alike. As studies by Resnick and Resnick (1977) have shown, the literacy-as-salvation metaphor had an almost literal interpretation in the practice of post-Luther Protestant groups to require of the faithful the ability to read and remember the Bible and other religious material. Older religious traditions—Hebraic and Islamic—have also traditionally invested the written word with great power and respect. "This is a perfect book. There is no doubt in it," reads a passage from the Qur'an. Memorizing the Qur'an—literally taking its words into you and making them part of yourself—is simultaneously a process of becoming both literate and holy.

The attribution of special powers to those who are literate has its ancient secular roots as well. Plato and Aristotle strove to distinguish the man of letters from the poet of oral tradition. In the perspective of Western humanism, literateness has come to be considered synonymous with being "cultured," using the term in the old-fashioned sense to refer to a person who is knowledgeable about the content and techniques of the sciences, arts, and humanities as they have evolved historically. The term sounds elitist and archaic, but the notion that participation in a literate—that is, bookish—tradition enlarges and develops a person's essential self is pervasive and still undergirds the concept of a liberal education (Steiner 1973). In the literacy-as-a-state-of-grace concept, the power and functionality of literacy is not bounded by political or economic parameters but in a sense transcends them; the literate individual's life derives its meaning and significance from intellectual, aesthetic, and spiritual participation in the accumulated creations and knowledge of humankind, made available through the written word.

The self-enhancing aspects of literacy are often given a cognitive interpretation (Greenfield and Bruner 1969; Olson 1977). For centuries, and increasingly in this generation, appeals have been made for increased attention to literacy as a way of developing minds. An individual who is illiterate, a UNESCO (1972) publication states, is bound to concrete thinking and cannot learn new material. Some teachers of college English in the United States (e.g., Farrell 1977) urge greater prominence for writing in the curriculum as a way of promoting logical reasoning and critical thinking. Literate and nonliterate individuals presumably are not only in different states of grace but in different stages of intellectual development as well. Although evidence is accumulating (Scribner and Cole 1981) refuting this view, the notion that literacy per se creates a great divide in intellectual abilities between those who have and those who have not mastered written language is deeply entrenched in educational circles of industrialized countries.

The metaphor of literacy-as-grace, like the others, has boundary problems. For one thing, we need to know how widely dispersed this admiration of book knowledge is in our society. To what extent are beliefs about the value of literateness shared across social classes and ethnic and religious groups? How does book culture—more accurately, how do book cultures—articulate with the multiple and diverse oral cultures flourishing in the United States? Which people value literacy as a preserver of their history or endow their folk heroes with book learning? Are there broad cultural supports for book learning among wide sectors of the population? McLuhan and others have insisted that written literacy is a vestige of a disappearing "culture." Is this point of view defensible? And if so, what implications does it pose for our educational objectives?

I have described some current views of the meaning of literacy in terms of three metaphors. I have tried to indicate that each metaphor embraces a certain set of, sometimes unexamined, values; moreover, each makes assumptions about social facts in our society—the utilities of literacy and the conditions fostering individual attainment of literacy status. These metaphors are often urged on us as competitive; some choice of one or the other does in fact seem a necessary starting point for a definitional enterprise. But for purposes of social and educational planning, none need necessarily become paramount at the expense of the others; all may have validity. To illustrate this argument, I will briefly describe research on the social meaning of literacy among a West African people. Learning how literacy functions among a people far removed from us culturally and geographically may help us take a new look at its functions here at home.

Social Meaning of Literacy: A Case Study

My own consideration of the question "What is literacy?" was prompted by research experiences in a traditional West African society. Together with colleagues, I spent five years studying the social and intellectual consequences of literacy among the Vai people of West Africa (Scribner and Cole 1981). The material conditions of Vai life are harsh. Rural villages lack electricity and public water supplies; clinics and schools are scarce; dirt roads, often impassable in the rainy season, restrict social and economic exchanges. To the casual observer, Vai society is the very prototype of traditional nonliterate subsistence farming societies. Yet the Vai have practiced literacy for over 150 years, initially in a syllabic writing system of their own invention. The Vai script has been passed on from one generation to another in tutorial fashion without benefit of a formal institution such as a school and without the constitution of a professional teacher group. In addition to this indigenous script, literacy in the Arabic and Roman alphabets also flourishes in the countryside. The Vai are a Muslim people, and the Arabic script is the literacy for religious practice and theological learning. Missionaries and, more recently, the Liberian government have been disseminating English literacy, the official government literacy, through the establishment of Western-style schools. About one-third of the Vai male population is literate in one of these scripts, the majority in the Vai script. Many read and write both Vai and Arabic, and some outstanding scholars are literate in all three scripts. Since each writing system has a different orthography, represents a different language, and is learned in a different setting, becoming literate in two or more scripts is an impressive intellectual accomplishment. Why do people take the trouble to do it?

Certain obvious answers are ruled out. Literacy is not a necessity for personal survival. As far as we could determine, nonliteracy status does not exclude a person from full participation in economic activities or in town or society life. As we look around Vai country and see major activities and institutions continuing to function in the traditional oral mode, we are at a loss to define the literacy competencies that might be useful in everyday life. But Vai literates have not been at such a loss and have found no end of useful functions for writing.

16

Commonly they engage in extensive personal correspondence, which for some involves the composition of 30–40 letters per month. Since Vai society, like other traditional societies, maintains an effective oral grapevine system, reasons for the popularity of letter writing are not self-evident, especially since all letters must be personally sent and hand-delivered. Yet literates find the advantage of secrecy and guarantee of delivery more than compensation for the time and trouble spent in writing. Scholars (Hair 1963; Holsoe 1967) speculate that the usefulness of the Vai script in protecting secrets and allowing clandestine resistance to the central governing machinery of Liberia, whose official literacy was English, were important factors in its invention and longevity.

On closer study, we find that Vai script literacy also serves many personal and public record-keeping functions. Household heads keep albums for family births, deaths, and marriages; some maintain lists of dowry items and death feast contributions that help to regulate kinship exchanges. Records also enlarge the scope and planful aspects of commerical transactions. Artisans maintain lists of customers; farmers record the yield and income from cash-crop farming. The script also serves a variety of administrative purposes such as recording house tax payments and political contributions. Some fraternal and religious organizations maintain records in Vai script. All of these activities fit nicely into the metaphor of literacy as functional adaptation; the only surprising aspect is that so many varieties of pragmatic uses occur in an economic and social milieu in which modern institutions (schools, cash markets) still play a limited role.

Not all literacy uses are devoted to practical ends. Although the Vai script has not been used to produce public books or manuscripts, in the privacy of their homes, many Vai literates engage in creative acts of composition. Almost everyone keeps a diary; some write down maxims and traditional tales in copybooks; others maintain rudimentary town histories; some record their dreams and tales of advice to children; a few who might qualify as scholars produce extended family and clan histories. Townspeople, when questioned about the value of the script, will often cite its utilitarian functions, but will equally as often speak about its importance for self-education and knowledge. Vai script literates are known in the community, are accorded respect, and are sought out for their information and help as personal scribes or as town clerks. A Vai parable about the relative merits of money, power, and book learning for success in this world concludes with the judgment that the "man who knoweth book passeth all."

Why this excursion into a case of African literacy after our metaphoric discussion of the goals of literacy education in a technological society? Perhaps because Vai society, much simpler than ours in the range of literacy functions it calls for, nonetheless serves to highlight unnecessary simplicities in our attempts to define the one best set of organizing principles for literacy education. If we were called on as experts to devise literacy education programs for the Vai people, which metaphor would dominate our recommendations? Would we emphasize the spread of functional competencies, urging all farmers to keep crop records and all carpenters to list customers? This would be an effective approach for some, but it would neglect the interests and aspirations of others. Should we appeal to the cultural pride of the populace, suggesting Vai script literacy be extended as an instrument for group cohesion and social change? We might count on support for this appeal, but resistance as well; Qur'anic schools and the network of Muslim teachers and scholars are a powerful counterforce to the Vai script and a countervailing center for cultural cohesion. Moreover, families participating in the Vai script tradition do not necessarily repudiate participation in English literacy; some find it prudent to have one or more children in English school as well as Qur'anic school. As for literacy as a state of grace, aspirations for self-improvement and social status clearly sustain many aspects of Vai literacy both in the Arabic religious and Vai secular traditions. A diversity of pragmatic, ideological, and intellectual factors sustains popular literacy among the Vai.

The sociohistorical processes leading to multiple literacies among the Vai are not unique. In their research in Alaska, Reder and Green (1983) found community members practicing literacy in any one (or, occasionally, a combination) of three languages. Some used the Cyrillic script, introduced by the Russian Orthodox Church, for reading and writing Russian; others used that script for literacy activities in their native Eskimo language; and still others participated in English literacy. Each of these literacies, they report, occurred through distinct socialization processes and in well-defined, nonoverlapping domains of activity, and each had a distinctive social meaning. Wagner (in press) similarly documents the multiple meanings of literacy in contemporary Moroccan society, and other reports might be cited.

This is not to suggest, of course, that all cultural groups have elaborated rich functions for literacy, nor that all groups strive for participation in the official literacy of their state (as, for example, English in Alaska and throughout the United States). The value of the growing body of ethnographic studies for the "What is literacy?" question is twofold. First, it promotes skepticism of the "one best answer" approach to the improvement of literacy in our society. Second, it urges the need for understanding the great variety of beliefs and aspirations that various people have developed toward literacy in their particular historical and current life circumstances.

What implications does this analysis have for literacy policy and education? This is a question that calls for the continued, sustained, and thoughtful attention of educators and others in our society. One implication that I find compelling is the need to "disaggregate" various levels and kinds of literacy. If the search for an essence is futile, it might appropriately be replaced by serious attention to varieties of literacy and their place in social and educational programs. In this disentangling process, I would place priority on the need to extricate matters of value and policy from their hidden position in the definitional enterprise and to address them head on. The International Symposium for Literacy, closing UNESCO's Experimental World Literacy Program, declared that literacy is a fundamental human right (Bataille 1976). Literacy campaigns need no other justification. Setting long-range social and educational goals, however, pushes us farther toward an inquiry into the standard of literacy that is a desirable (valued) human right in our highly developed technological society, whose policies have such a powerful impact on the world's future. What is *ideal* literacy in our society? If the analysis by metaphor presented here contributes some approach to that question, it suggests that ideal literacy is simultaneously adaptive, socially empowering, and self-enhancing. Enabling youth and adults to progress toward that ideal would be a realization of the spirit of the symposium in Persepolis reflective of the resources and literacy achievements already available in our society. This suggests that long-term social and educational policies might be directed at maximal literacy objectives; minimal literacy standards would serve a useful function, not as goals but as indicators of our progress in equipping individuals and communities with the skills they need for "takeoff" in continuing literacy careers.

Recognition of the multiple meanings and varieties of literacy also argues for a diversity of educational approaches, informal and community-based as well as formal and school-based. As ethnographc research and practical experience demonstrate, effective literacy programs are those that are responsive to perceived needs, whether for functional skills, social power, or self-improvement. Individual objectives may be highly specific: to qualify for a promotion at work, to help children with their lessons, to record a family history. Anzalone and McLaughlin (1982) have coined the term "specific literacies" to designate such special-interest or special-purpose literacy skills. The road to maximal literacy may begin for some through the feeder routes of a wide variety of specific literacies.

These are speculative and personal views; others will have different conceptions. The notions offered here of ideal and specific literacies do not simplify the educational issues nor resolve the definitional dilemmas. I hope, however, that these concepts and the metaphoric analysis from which they flowed suggest the usefulness of "dissecting literacy" into its many forms and, in the process, clarifying the place of fact and value in discussions of the social meaning of literacy.

Note

This paper is based on a planning document for research on literacy that I prepared when associate director of the National Institute of Education. Eugene Radwin made many helpful comments on that document and contributed a number of bibliographic references cited here.

References

Adult Performance Level Project. *Adult Functional Competency: A Summary.* Austin: University of Texas, Division of Extension, 1975.

Advisory Committee on National Illiteracy. "Report." *School and Society* 30 (1929): 708.

Anzalone, S., and S. McLaughlin. *Literacy for Specific Situations.* Amherst: University of Massachusetts, Center for International Education, 1982.

Bataille, L., ed. *A Turning Point for Literacy: Proceedings of the International Symposium for Literacy, Persepolis, Iran, 1975.* Oxford: Pergamon Books, 1976.

Bormuth, J. R. "Reading Literacy: Its Definition and Assessment." In *Toward a Literate Society: The Report of the Committee on Reading of the National Academy of Education,* edited by J. B. Carroll and J. S. Chall. New York: McGraw-Hill Book Co., 1975.

Cervero, R. M. "Does the Texas Adult Performance Level Test Measure Functional Competence?" *Adult Education* 30 (1980): 152–65.

Dauzat, S. J., and J. Dauzat. "Literacy in Quest of a Definition." *Convergence* 10 (1977): 37–41.

Farrell, L. J. "Literacy, the Basics, and All that Jazz." *College English* 38 (1977): 443–59.

Freire, P. *Cultural Action for Freedom* (Monograph Series no. 1). Cambridge, Mass.: Harvard Educational Review, 1970.

Gayter, M., B. Hall, J. R. Kidd, and V. Shivasrava. *The World of Literacy: Policy, Research and Action.* Toronto: International Development Centre, 1979.

Goody, J., ed. *Literacy in Traditional Societies.* Cambridge: Cambridge University Press, 1968.

Gray, W. *The Teaching of Reading and Writing: An International Survey.* Chicago: Scott, Foresman & Co./UNESCO, 1965.

Greenfield, P. M., and J. S. Bruner. "Culture and Cognitive Growth." In *Handbook of Socialization: Theory and Research,* edited by D. A. Goslin. New York: Rand McNally & Co., 1969.

Hair, P. E. H. "Notes on the Discovery of the Vai Script." *Sierra Leone Language Review* 2 (1963): 36–49.

Hammiche, B. "Functional Literacy and Educational Revolution." In *A Turning Point for Literacy: Proceedings of the International Symposium for Literacy, Persepolis, Iran, 1975,* edited by L. Bataille. Oxford: Pergamon Press, 1976.

Harman, D. "Review of *The Experimental World Literacy Program.*" *Harvard Educational Review* 47 (1977): 444–46.

Heath, S. B. "The Functions and Uses of Literacy." *Journal of Communication* 30 (1980): 123–33.

Heath, S. B. "Toward an Ethnohistory of Writing in American Education." In *Writing: The Nature, Development and Teaching of Written Communication,* vol. 1, edited by M. F. Whiteman. Hillsdale, N.J.: Lawrence Erlbaum Associates, 1981.

Hillerich, R. L. "Toward an Assessable Definition of Literacy." *English Journal* 65 (1976): 50–55.

Holsoe, S. E. "Slavery and Economic Response among the Vai." In *Slavery in Africa: Historical and Anthropological Perspectives,* edited by S. Miers and I. Kopytoff. Madison: University of Wisconsin Press, 1977.

Hunter, C. S. J., and D. Harman. *Adult Illiteracy in the United States.* New York: McGraw-Hill Book Co., 1979.

Kirsch, I., and J. T. Guthrie. "The Concept and Measurement of Functional Literacy." *Reading Research Quarterly* 13 (1977–78): 485–507.

Kozol, J. *Prisoners of Silence: Breaking the Bonds of Adult Illiteracy in the United States.* New York: Continuum Publishing Corp., 1980.

McGovern, G. *Congressional Record* (September 1978), p. 14,834.

McLuhan, M. *The Gutenberg Galaxy.* Toronto: University of Toronto Press, 1962.

McLuhan, M. *Understanding Media: The Extensions of Man.* New York: McGraw-Hill Book Co., 1964.

Miller, G. A., ed. *Linugistic Communication: Perspectives for Research.* Newark, Del.: International Reading Association, 1973.

Naisbett, J. *Megatrends: Ten New Directions Transforming Our Lives.* New York: Warner Books, 1982.

Olson, D. R. "From Utterance to Text: The Bias of Language in Speech and Writing." *Harvard Educational Review* 47 (1977): 257–81.

Powell, W. R. "Levels of Literacy." *Journal of Reading* 20 (1977): 488–92.

Radwin, E. "Literacy—What and Why." Unpublished manuscript, Harvard University, 1978.

Reder, S., and K. R. Green. "Literacy as a Functional Component of Social Structure in an Alaska Fishing Village." *International Journal of the Sociology of Language* 42 (1983): 122–41.

Resnick, D. P., ed. *Literacy in Historical Perspective.* Washington, D.C.: Library of Congress, 1983.

Resnick, D. P., and L. B. Resnick. "The Nature of Literacy: An Historical Exploration." *Harvard Educational Review* 47 (1977): 370–85.

Scribner, S. "Industrial Literacy" (Final Report to the Ford Foundation). New York: CUNY, Graduate School and University Center, 1982. (*a*)

Scribner, S. "Observations on Literacy Education in China." *Linguistic Reporter* 25 (1982): 1–4. (*b*)

Scribner, S., and M. Cole. *The Psychology of Literacy.* Cambridge, Mass.: Harvard University Press, 1981.

Steiner, G. "After the Book." In *The Future of Literacy,* edited by R. Disch. Englewood Cliffs, N.J.: Prentice-Hall, Inc., 1973.

United Nations Development Program. *The Experimental World Literacy Programme: A Critical Assessment.* Paris: UNESCO, 1976.

UNESCO. *Regional Report on Literacy.* Teheran: UNESCO, 1972.

Wagner, D. A., B. M. Messick, and J. Spratt. "Studying Literacy in Morocco." In *The Acquisition of Literacy: Ethnographic Perspectives,* edited by B. B. Schieffelin and P. Gilmore. Norwood, N.J.: Ablex, in press.

Computers in Schools Today: Some Basic Considerations

HENRY JAY BECKER
Johns Hopkins University

There may be no topic in education today that gets the attention of so many people as computers. At least six nationally circulated monthly publications on the subject are targeted at school teachers and administrators.[1] Newspapers and general-interest magazines regularly contain stories about individual schools or school districts using computers in some unique and exciting way. A recently published directory provides annotated descriptions of more than 5,000 computer programs for classroom use ranging from exploration of number concepts for 5-year-olds to simulations of international trade for high school students (Educational Products Information Exchange 1984).

The development that has generated this fever is the introduction into schools of "microcomputers"—self-contained desktop units costing from about $300 to $3,000 each and providing the computational power equivalent to much bulkier and less easily used computers costing 30 times as much only a decade ago. Between mid-1981 and the fall of 1983, the percentage of elementary schools with one or more microcomputers jumped from 10 percent to over 60 percent. During that same period, the percentage of secondary schools with five or more microcomputers grew from 10 percent to well over 50 percent (Center for Social Organization of Schools 1983a).[2] Schools financed these acquisitions in a variety of ways, but most commonly by spending large portions of discretionary funds, including state and federal block grants, money that would have been spent on other ways of assisting the instructional process (Center for Social Organization of Schools 1984). The total amount spent by schools on computers and related software and hardware in 1983 may have been as much as one-third the amount they spent on books for instruction in all subjects and all grade levels combined.

Why this movement has taken hold so rapidly and so broadly has little to do with any clear and demonstrable instructional advantage of using computers in a school setting. It has more to do with the general society-wide interest in the applicability of computers that has blossomed across a wide range of institutional contexts from small businesses and voluntary associations to religious study and family life.

For schools in particular, several motives seem apparent: Parents worry that their children will be unemployable unless they know how to use computers in ways their future employers might like. Since computers are not yet within the easy reach of most families, and since many parents feel incapable of guiding their children's learning through a medium with which they have had little experience, schools are widely seen as the most appropriate setting in which to confront this problem.

Many teachers and school administrators fear that they, too, need to know something about how to use computers. A number who have tried programming or using computer programs on their own find it intellectually stimulating and possibly even cost-effective. Like adventurous computerists in other professional domains, many become proselytizers for their use by others in their workplace. This happens first and most often in high schools and among mathematics teachers, for whom computers, as objects to be programmed, are most easily integrated into other instructional responsibilities.

By virtue of their nature—interactive, colorful, manipulable, and logical—the new breed of personal microcomputers appears to have attractive features for providing instruction and intellectual challenge for adults, adolescents, and children. Many people, having access to computers for the first time and recognizing a plausible concordance of computers and education, write and market programs with manifest instructional content. They do this for a variety of reasons, not the least of which is that they enjoy doing it. As profitability becomes apparent, development projects become more highly capitalized, and a high proportion of costs become allocated to product design, marketing, and advertising. More effort is directed at the lower grades, where there is less curriculum differentiation, where the instructional

---

HENRY JAY BECKER is director of the School Uses of Microcomputers project at the Center for Social Organization of Schools, Johns Hopkins University. He received his Ph.D. in sociology from Johns Hopkins in 1973. His most recent work has been conducting and analyzing a national survey of how schools use microcomputers.

content is less complex, and where the unique attributes of the computer—dynamic and interactive color graphics—make it relatively more attractive than alternative instructional media.

Schools and school systems, with varying degrees and emphases, either accept the plausibility of the instructional value of computers and invest in a major way, or, acting with more reservation, find that, with some sacrifice, they can afford to purchase one or two microcomputers in order to explore for themselves what the excitement is all about. In just a few years, an entire industry has grown up, much of it focused on selling schools on the value of their products for improving the content of school life through the use of computers.

With such a sudden emergence of "computers" in the instructional repertoire of schools, it is not surprising that an intellectual and empirical rationale for their educational value has barely begun to develop. At the same time that schools invest much energy and resources in developing computer-related curricula and in purchasing computer-based instructional materials, scholars and researchers are still addressing critical questions whose answers, by all rights, should precede, not follow, the actions of practitioners—questions such as the following:

1. Compared with the clearly important goals of developing broad verbal and mathematical fluency among students, including writing and problem-solving skills, and compared with the importance of teaching other culturally valued knowledge, such as that from scientific, historical, and literary domains, how necessary is it that schools spend valuable instructional time teaching students about computers, and specifically, about how to program them in general-purpose computer programming languages like BASIC or Pascal?
2. Are there other nontraditional skills, such as information storage and retrieval techniques or testing quantitative models, that are appropriate in today's secondary school curriculum because, in the near future, many adults will want or need to use similar computer capabilities in their work or in family or recreational activities?
3. For which types of students and for what portion of the traditional curriculum, if any, are computers a cost-effective way of improving student skills and competencies? That is, with the best available (or even the best possible) educational computer programs, are there some students (e.g., slow learners or the gifted and talented) for whom some skills or competencies (e.g., decoding skills, scientific principles, or basic concepts of arithmetic) are most cost-effectively learned through using computers instead of alternative media or methods?

4. Even if computers are theoretically better for the instruction of individual students, can most schools appropriately allocate and use the relatively few microcomputers they own when they are accountable to hundreds of variably prepared and diversely talented students grouped in classrooms where each teacher must simultaneously and independently teach 25 or more children?

At the most basic level, discussion about computers in schools often treats the subject as if it were a unitary issue, ignoring that there are three completely different ways in which computers might be seen as relevant to instruction in schools—as an administrative tool for the human providers of instruction, as a medium through which instruction in other subject matter is provided, and as an object of instruction—a focus of the students' learning itself. The value of computers for any one of these functions may be quite independent of their value for any other.

As administrative tools, computers may be used by teachers to prepare dittos and other instructional materials, to keep records, grades, and test scores, and to manage individualized instructional programs—including using them to analyze student performance and route students to different instructional or practice activities.

Under the term "medium of instruction," we subsume a number of different uses of computers: computer-assisted-instruction in both its drill-and-practice and tutorial modes; simulations and other ways of providing students with a risk-free, inexpensive, structured environment for exploring a particular content domain; and productivity tools, content-free programs like word processors, planners, mathematical problem solvers, and information retrieval systems that may be used as tools for studying new or traditional subject matter or for producing an intellectual product.

As an object of instruction, the computer is treated as an area of the curriculum itself, regardless of its value as a means of learning other subject matter. The term "computer literacy," as it is most commonly used, is synonymous with "computers as the object of instruction," but its precise meaning varies according to the writer's beliefs about the instructional content that is appropriate for students of a given grade level to learn. It may include instruction in computer programming or in how to use existing programs (for their value in learning how to manipulate the computer rather than for their immediate instructional value), and it may include instruction in social and historical aspects of processing and communicating information by machines.

The application of the term "literacy" to computers seems to have arisen as a linguistic ploy to support a suggestion that computer-related skills are as universally valuable for adults today as reading and writing came to be at an earlier time. The argument may have been most succinctly stated by Luehrmann (1972/1980). In this paper, Luehrmann tells a parable about a society that passed along information solely by oral means. He relates the sequence of events that occurred when the society invented the techniques of reading and writing. Reading and writing technologies were first used in business and government, where the capacities to read and write were most easily translated into economic profit. Eventually, however, the "vendors of reading and writing" looked to education as a new market to explore. They developed a system where scribes wrote down the words of master teachers, and then professional readers read these lectures to students, at a cost far lower than when solely master teachers were employed.

As Luehrmann describes it, this was the "sad ending." However, he provides an alternate ending in which small groups of isolated master teachers began trying to understand the new reading/writing technology themselves and a few tried to teach it to their students. Their philosophical rationale was that "reading and writing constitute a new and fundamental intellectual resource. To use that resource as a mere delivery system for instruction, but not to give a student instruction in how he might use the resource himself, was the chief failure of the W.A.I. [writing-assisted-instruction] effort. . . . What a loss of opportunity . . . if the skill of reading and writing were to be harnessed for the purpose of turning out masses of students who were unable to read and write!" (Luehrmann 1972/1980, pp. 132–33). In Luehrmann's "happy ending," this new skill gradually became more and more acceptable, even to school administrators, some of whom "became competent and imaginative users of the skill" themselves (p. 133).

For Luehrmann, it is computing that "constitutes a new and fundamental intellectual resource" (p. 133), and the loss of opportunity arises if computers are "harnessed for the purpose of turning out masses of students" (p. 134) who are unable to use computing for their own chosen ends.

The appeal of computers for both mechanical and ideational aspects of children's and adolescents' education derives not only from the personal stakes of the creators and distributors of computer-related products but also from computers having theoretical capacities that directly address broadly shared visions or ideals for children's education. What are some of these capacities and visions?

First is the ability to engage students in a highly motivating and intellectually active dialogue, to provide appropriate instructional stimuli on an individualized basis, and to provide diagnoses and feedback both to the student and to the teacher. Computers clearly have the capacity to do these things, perhaps as well as an average human tutor—but only if the computer programming "bottleneck" can be surmounted.

Second is the ability to create intellectually stimulating environments for students to explore subject matter generally foreign to the current curriculum, perhaps beyond the competency of the teacher, but important and useful preparation for the student's future life. Imagine children creating music and art on a highly sophisticated machine that integrates instruction in the physics and physiology of the subject while it encourages creative play.

Third is the ability to provide each student with the resources of a library, a librarian, a typewriter, and a personal editorial assistant—convenient, accessible, and easily used—that teaches students skills that may be necessary for their subsequent adult responsibilities.

Fourth is the ability to provide learning experiences and opportunities through simulations—experiences that would be otherwise too costly, too risky, too time consuming, or not possible. People often learn best by participating in a system rather than merely being a spectator. Computers provide a way to get close to actual participation without the costs or risks of actual participation.

Finally, there is the ability to foster in a generation of young adults the capacity to perform analytic tasks and solve important organizational problems involving information far better than older generations because they receive an early and continuous exposure to concepts and specific tools for computer-assisted problem solving.

Whether computers can actually help schools achieve these outcomes for large numbers of students depends on many factors. Perhaps the most basic requirement—one that holds regardless of how the computer might be used—is that schools must have enough computers so that each student can use one for a sufficient duration to accomplish a significant outcome. Although schools have made major investments in microcomputers during the last two years, the typical school still has more than one hundred students enrolled for each computer owned. The inevitable result is either that very few students get a substantial exposure and benefit from using computers or the typical computer-using student gets little more than a cursory exposure.

In elementary schools, this description is particularly apt. During the 1982–83 school year, I conducted a national survey that examined how schools use microcomputers (Center for Social Organization of Schools 1983*a*, 1983*b*, 1983*c*, 1984). The survey found that, during an average week, only about one-eighth of the students in elementary schools that owned microcomputers had an opportunity to use one. More significantly, the students who did use a microcomputer spent on the average only 20 minutes at the computer during the week, some of this in a paired or group situation. Only one out of 50 elementary school students who used a microcomputer for practicing math or language skills during the week spent more than one hour at the task— that is, about 12 minutes each day. At many schools, different students were given a turn at the computer in different weeks. Elementary schools that had a few more microcomputers than the typical school gave exposure to more students, but each computer-using student at those schools got no more time per week at the computer than did students at elementary schools with only one or two computers.

Schools with fewer than 30 computers not only suffer from having to divide computer time among hundreds of eager students. They also must make important organizational adjustments in the allocation of adult supervisors to student classrooms. It is extremely expensive for schools to allocate the presence of a single adult to a classroom with less than 20 or so students. Yet most schools with microcomputers have enough computers for simultaneous use by less than one-fourth of the students in a single classroom. This means that schools must assign to a single teacher the supervisory and instructional responsibility for only a small number of students at once—perhaps 10 students at a time sharing the use of five computers; or regular classroom teachers, responsible for 30 students, must organize additional appropriate tasks for the 25 or so students who otherwise would spend five-sixths of their time waiting for their turn at the computer.

Having fewer computers than is organizationally feasible is a problem that affects the value of computers regardless of how schools might want to use them. Other problems are more specific to particular applications, where they are used as a medium of instruction, object of instruction, or administrative tool. In the remainder of this paper, we will examine the problems and possibilities associated with two applications of computers that are particularly relevant to issues of verbal literacy in children and adolescents. These two applications are computer-assisted instruction (both the drill-and-practice type and direct instructional tutorials) and productivity tools for instruction in com-position.

Computer-assisted Instruction: Drills and Tutorials

Schools today use computers primarily as an object of instruction— to provide students with a cursory computer literacy exposure and to teach a minority of high school students to program microcomputers in the general computer language called BASIC. Apart from these uses, though, by far the most common way that schools use their computers is with commercial and locally produced programs that give students math and language-arts skill-building drills and that test their knowledge of social studies and science facts (Center for Social Organization of Schools 1983*a*).

This drill-and-practice application differs substantially from the infinitely patient and directly instructive tutor imagined in our dreams about computer-assisted instruction (CAI). Most existing drill-and-practice computer programs do include some elements of good instruction—for example, moving students rapidly through many short problems ordered according to difficulty, providing immediate reinforcement (cognitive and affective feedback regarding performance), and using information about the student's prior performance to guide subsequent testing and practice.

Some existing programs go beyond drill, presenting and trying to explain concepts and selecting successive screens of information according to whether the student's answer to a multiple-choice question indicates understanding of the concept. These programs are referred to as "tutorials." However, it is extremely rare to find, in current tutorial CAI, sophisticated diagnoses of incorrect performance or elaborate routing systems providing individualized concept remediation. In addition, existing tutorial programs mainly cover individual "lessons" rather than entire curricula.

Although drill-and-practice programs have so much more limited goals, they constitute the dominant form of computer-assisted instruction in schools today. Why is this so?

First, traditional beliefs about the most effective ways of learning math, reading, and language include the importance of repetitious practice of skills and memorization of facts and relationships. The most limited resource in the classroom—the teacher's attention and response to individual student needs—is often taken up directing and monitoring this practice activity. Having a computer present problems, accept student responses, provide feedback, and measure student attainment is an easily conceived model that would be one way to free the teacher for more uniquely "human" functions of instruction. Computer-based drills, then, require little change in the mental imagery of teachers and others about who is supposed to do what in school.

Computer-based programmed drills hold several advantages over less automated forms. Their interactive nature and their flexible and visually appealing display formats make them more enjoyable experiences. Student time is likely to be more on-task than in traditional seat-work activities. Student feedback is direct and immediate; this may enable students to make better adjustments in their conceptual understanding. Automated management can be built in to give the teacher a summary of the student's achievement. And tasks and problems may be quite heavily individualized, with little administrative effort, and can be based on precise patterns of student performance on prior exercises. Of course, not every drill-and-practice program builds in all these capabilities.

Another reason that schools use drill-and-practice programs is that many schools have begun their involvement with computers without a systematic plan for how computers might improve the educational enterprise. They have obtained equipment and then tried to find appropriate ways to use it with their students. One plausible use, as suggested above, is drill and practice. Parallelling this receptivity by schools is the fact that drill and-practice programs are among the easiest to write; often they have been written by teachers who themselves are novice programmers looking for ways to exercise and improve their programming skills. Not only are they easy to write but, because the curriculum is so standardized in areas of basic math and language for which drills seem most relevant, producers have sensed a profitable market for products here that they have not seen for other subjects and uses of computers. Thus, although seemingly circular, it is truly the case that schools use drill-and-practice programs because they are there, and they are there because producers can produce them and because producers believe that schools are likely to buy them.

Drill and practice may also be attractive because most of the limited evaluation research that has been done has found computer-based drills to be responsible for increased student achievement on standardized tests in comparison with prior cohorts or control groups. These positive research results have been found often in mathematics instruction and less frequently in language learning (Jamison, Suppes, and Wells 1974; Ragosta, Holland, and Jamison 1981).

However, most of this research has been done under organizational conditions that allowed many computers to be in use at one time, and most have been heavily monitored and well-managed implementations. Research under conditions more typical of schools that use drill-and-practice programs with their several recently purchased microcomputers and research that evaluates the more commonly used drill-and-practice materials is just beginning.

Nevertheless, the existence of favorable research results is likely to have some impact on school practices in this area, regardless of the appropriateness of generalizing existing findings. On the other hand, even if replicated under typical current conditions, the research results will only have limited direct influence on how schools use their computer equipment. School practice, on the whole, is based more on subcultural traditions and values than on systematic, empirical evidence.

Many people feel, for example, that drill and practice is already overused by teachers and, even if done more efficiently by using computers, should not be encouraged. After all, repetitive drill is most useful only when the student already knows the relevant principles and procedures and when the skill to be mastered is merely applying the principles and procedures accurately and speedily. If children mistakenly think they understand how to do a math or grammar exercise, or if they do not know how to attack the problem and are "just guessing," repetitive drill on similar problems will reveal at most the level of understanding the children have; that is, it serves as a testing instrument, not a way of teaching understanding.

A related philosophical criticism of drill-and-practice programs is that they may exaggerate an existing overemphasis on learning facts. Facts, after all, are more easily translated into computer programs than are conceptual ideas. The student, according to this view, is already too often called on to provide the "right" answer to someone else's question, while little emphasis is placed on encouraging students to ask questions, organize their ideas, apply their understanding to new situations, learn to work productively with their peers to accomplish planned goals, and learn how to improve their learning skills (Garson 1980). Drill and practice on the computer, rather than helping students expand their intellects, conditions them to regard the computer as a rather boring tool of the teacher over which they have little control.

Why, then, has most CAI to date been limited to drill and practice? Why do we not have programs that actually engage students in conversation, not just present concepts to be ingested or problems to be solved; that diagnose the cause of students' errors, not just report that they were wrong; and that provide frameworks to assist students in asking productive questions and in organizing their thinking? In other words, where is the computer-based instruction that deals with thinking and understanding?

The most problematic aspect of this type of computer-assisted instruction is that it is hard to do well. Using computers successfully to direct appropriate sequences of stimuli to the student requires a clear understanding of how people acquire skills and knowledge. The program may need to know, for example, the optimum point at which to offer hints, what kinds of hints to provide, and how much to emphasize concepts relative to examples. For computer-based instruction to be effective, the programs must incorporate into their procedures the sequences of material, response-contingent alternatives, user-controlled options, and feedback mechanisms that promote learning for the greatest number of students. Yet, as Ellis (1974, p. 62) points out, "Even the best teacher does not know completely what it is that makes him a good teacher." Therefore, our ability to create computerized interactive intellectual environments is limited. The scholarly and programming effort required to improve tutoring abilities of computers could involve lifelong careers in and of themselves.

In contrast, minimal tutorial dialogue can be written using a limited number of programming statements that display information and questions, accept the student's response, compare the response with the "right" answer, and branch to a remedial information display or the next sequential information display depending on the appropriateness of the student's answer. The tutorial programs now being marketed resemble these simple dialogues more than they do an "intelligent computer tutor." Yet even these simple tutorial CAI programs are few in number. Uttal, Rogers, Heironymous, and Pasich (1969) believe that the most limiting aspect of "canned tutorials" is their dependence on a large dictionary of material. First, the task of entering dialogue into the computer specific to particular vocabulary and problem sequences is time-consuming. Second, it is "remarkably tedious" to anticipate all the dialogue needed to carry out an instructional conversation based on all combinations of prior and current student responses. To keep to a reasonable size, tutorial programs must be limited to "understanding" only a fraction of possible student verbal responses, or the program must cover a narrow range of material.

The problem of creating instructional material is less severe in subjects such as math, science, and music, where the number of concepts are fewer and represent greater levels of generality than do those of everyday linguistic discourse and the verbal symbols used in studying subjects such as history and literature.

But, overall, the problems of successfully emulating the instructional model used by a human tutor are massive. Many people feel that basic research in artificial intelligence and cognitive psychology will soon yield results that will make computer-based tutorial systems effective. Others doubt that the work will yield a practical methodology. Even if it does, applying these principles to produce computer-based teaching programs for elementary and secondary school subjects may cost far more than society is willing to invest to find alternatives to direct instruction by human teachers in classroom settings.

Although it sounds crass, cost effectiveness is a central—perhaps the central—criterion on which CAI must be judged. If there are other means of producing similar ends at lower cost and at roughly the same level of student time and effort, CAI must yield.

With tutorial CAI, the major financial questions relate to the cost of developing the instructional programs. But even then the cost of the computers themselves is still significant. A typical computer costs a school from about $1,000 to $1,500. Although this is of the same order of magnitude as other traditionally purchased audio-visual equipment such as movie projectors, television sets, and film strip and overhead projectors, the use of the computer is distinctly different. The computer shares with the far less expensive textbook—and not with these others—the characteristic of usually being used with an individual student rather than a classroom of students at any one time. Thus, like books, computers are needed in numbers similar to the number of students to be served rather than the number of classrooms.

At some point, the decision must be made about how much money more efficient progress in math or language achievement is worth. Clearly, for example, individual human tutors would produce increments in student achievement higher than that obtained by traditional classroom teaching. Just as clearly, school systems do not have the money to provide a tutor for every child. If the value of microcomputer-based instruction is judged solely by its role as a tool to deliver subject-matter learning to students, its use must be put to the same test. The computer must show a magnitude in improved learning efficiency that justifies the financial investment and the investment of time and effort. For students whose alternative educational delivery system is relatively expensive and labor-intensive (e.g., students taught in small classes and with "individual education programs") such cost-effectiveness may be more easily demonstrated.

Drill-and-practice and computer-based tutorials dominate most discussions of instructional uses of the computer primarily because they promise to help educators perform functions that have become central elements in the school curriculum—teaching computational procedures in arithmetic and teaching the components and pieces of written English. Another reason, as we have suggested, is that these learning activities are so easily modeled on the computer. Thus, computer-based products for schools tend to be developed to address those learning activities rather than to address some others for which computer applications may in fact be more suited.

Licklider (1979) suggests that applying information technology to education can be dangerous because what is easiest and most profitable to do is often not what is best for the benefit of society and mankind. It is important, he says, to "exploit" opportunities offered by technology without letting organizations responding to narrower interests "exploit" people's naive understanding about how technology can be used.

One opportunity that may be worth exploiting, but around which few schools have developed programs, is using computers in writing instruction.

Computers and Writing Instruction

The value of having students use computers to compose and produce written text derives from a more general proposition that computers serve people best when they have been programmed to be special-purpose tools to help accomplish similar, often-performed, goal-related tasks. That is how adults use computers. Engineers use them to perform calculations needed to design products or structures; business people use them to keep necessary records on customers, suppliers, and inventory; artists, musicians, and writers use them—at least, some of them do—also as tools of their respective crafts. Students, according to this view, should use computers in those contexts where using them helps them to be more productive at school—to accomplish the tasks they acknowledge to be part of the job of student.

Writing is certainly one of the most important tasks that students have. How can writing through the use of a computer enable them to be more productive? By far, the most significant advantage of computer-based writing systems is the minimal effort required to make changes in one's text. With handwritten or even typed text, if writers decide, after some consideration, that the first words, sentences, and paragraphs that they commit to paper are not the best possible ordering of words, sentences, and paragraphs to convey their ideas, their choice is between making rough notes on the text and then rewriting or retyping the entire draft or making a shamefaced compromise with reality and leaving the text in its current condition.

If, as one writing teacher recently said, writing is a means of clarifying thought by "coaxing what one means to the surface through writing words on paper" (Workman 1983, p. 203), then clearly any method that gets students to make repeated attempts to improve the precision of their expressed thoughts must assist their productivity and sense of accomplishment. Computer word-processing programs undoubtedly have the capacity to do this.

Outside of the educational market—that is, among home and business computer buyers—programs for composing and revising text ("word processors") have been among the most widely sold programs for the same microcomputers that schools have bought. For example, one of the three most widely purchased computer programs in the history of computers is WordStar, a word-processing program that, like most others, contains a facility for typing and revising text and a formatting package that enables users, for example, to obtain printed output in multiple columns or to merge information selectively from one "file" (e.g., bibliographic references) with that of another.

Like WordStar, most word-processing programs have been written for an adult audience, and, until recently, most were written without much regard for a novice computer user. This may explain why the national survey of the Center for Social Organization of Schools (1983*a*, 1983*b*, 1983*c*, 1984), conducted in January 1983, found that only about 7 percent of the secondary schools with computers, and even fewer elementary schools, used computers regularly for student writing. Of those that did use word processing, many used it in business education classes (along with accounting and budgeting programs) rather than as part of English instruction or for writing for other subjects.

Since the survey was done, a number of word-processing programs have appeared designed specifically for schools and less sophisticated home markets, and word processing by children and adolescents is likely to have become somewhat more common since then.

However, computers, particularly in secondary schools, are overwhelmingly managed by math and math-science department personnel (except where the business education department has some); English teachers are only beginning to demand access to computers for their instructional program. When they do, they will face the same problems of trying to use a small number of computers with a large number of students that teachers using computers for other instructional functions have been facing. Even if word processing improves student writing immensely, the same kinds of issues discussed earlier concerning the cost-effectiveness of the effort must be considered.

It is also important to know whether (or under what conditions) the theoretical advantage of using computer-based writing is actually achieved by school-aged children in school settings. To begin with, to use any mechanical system of written communication effectively, one must have—or easily be able to develop—the mechanical skills required to operate the equipment. Traditionally, students have not been taught typing skills—in the computer milieu, they are called "keyboarding skills"—until late junior high or high school, and then it has always been an elective rather than a required subject.

Relatively few of the students who now use computers in schools are proficient typists. For example, in our survey of schools, a majority of secondary school computer-using teachers reported that 10 percent or fewer of the students who used computers for drill and practice had "already learned some 'touch-typing' skills."

There is a disagreement among those who have observed and trained students to use word-processing programs about whether touch-typing skills are prerequisite to effective use of the computer for writing instruction. On the one hand, having to use conscious energy to locate letters on the keyboard must certainly distract the thinking process of these novice writers—just as an absence of penmanship ability would interfere with children being able to express their thoughts on paper. However, others believe that, because relatively little of the time that students spend writing is actually spent putting words down on paper (or on a computer keyboard)—most time is spent thinking, formulating ideas, and mentally constructing sentences—keyboard inefficiency is relatively unimportant. As of now, we have little evidence to decide this issue besides the strong (and conflicting) opinions of teachers, researchers, and developers.

In addition, the potential opportunities for painlessly making changes in text that word processors provide are irrelevant if students are not motivated to improve their text or if teachers do not use instructional practices that get students to do so. Initial research being done on writing with word processors suggests that, although students write *more* text with a word processor, they may not do any more editing and rewriting, and the quality of their writing is not significantly improved (Riel 1983). Of course, what may be required is a systematic teaching method that changes how students do writing so that the capabilities of the word-processing tool are exploited.

These initial research results, though, remind us that other skills are necessary to produce good writing besides the capacity to modify text effortlessly. Although word-processing programs can assist students to overcome a reluctance to write because of a fear of making "errors" or because of having to rewrite large portions of text, by themselves they cannot get students to overcome a reluctance to "face a blank page"—that is, to organize their thoughts into coherent and systematic text. Students need prewriting skills for organizing their initial ideas and to give them confidence that they have something to say. And they need self-checking skills for finding syntactical and structural errors and errors of content in material as they write and while editing previously written text.

Many students are not intrinsically motivated to optimize their writing. In the absence of such intrinsic motivation, a powerful alternative is having pressure from valued peers. Researchers at the Human Cognition Laboratory at the University of California, San Diego, have found that computer-based writing stimulates collaborative writing among children because of the more publicly visible and legible computer screen, and this in turn motivates the students to take a greater interest in their writing (Riel 1983). The importance of writing for a personally meaningful audience is also widely recognized, and computer-based writing projects are able to address this motive more realistically because of the computer's ability to produce easily read and easily distributed text.

Researchers at Bolt, Beranek, and Newman, a firm in Cambridge, Massachusetts, are developing a series of computer-based writing activities that relate to nearly all of the points made above (Rubin and Bruce 1983). Their project, "Quill," is based on six pedagogical goals for which computers might be seen as a helpful tool: planning prior to writing, the integration of reading and writing, writing for a real audience, two-way written communication, cooperative writing efforts, and understanding that revision—including stylistic and structural changes—is a basic element in the production of text. Their project has been attempting to produce and use prototype computer programs to address each of these goals.

For example, their "Planner" program helps students to structure their initial notes on a subject into a guide for composing complete text. It provides a variety of questions about the text from which students may select several in order to summarize the things they feel should be included in their composition. A second program, "Publisher," simplifies the mechanics of classroom newspaper and book projects by relieving the teacher and students of many of the technical aspects of fitting together text into appropriately designed pages. Also, the group's electronic message system is a means of encouraging writing by providing a ready audience of classroom readers, and it may enable participating classrooms in different cities, for example, to exchange writing and information on a topic of common effort.

In another program, called "Story Maker Maker," students build a story on an assigned theme by selecting sentences or paragraphs from alternatives presented to them, and then they add their own text, thus taking direct control over the course of the story. The theory is that students write faster initially because they do not have to compose nor type text themselves, but, in time, students become motivated to put their own imprint on the course of the story. One way of using "Story Maker Maker" has children take turns contributing successive parts to the story.

The Quill project suggests that computers may be profitably used in writing instruction in other ways than simply as word-processing machines. Nevertheless, we must continue to be cognizant of the relative cost and relative efficiency of computer-based means for improving writing in comparison with less technologically sophisticated ones. Development of computer-based writing tools may lead to a better understanding of how to improve student motivation to write, writing habits, and writing styles. However, this knowledge, in turn, might lead to other programs that implement these principles without the costs associated with technologically sophisticated means.

On the other hand, specialized computer programs, including word processors, developed and used with an understanding of the processes by which children and adolescents are able to learn to write in classroom settings, may become important tools in writing instruction. Such tools would not replace the didactic and explanatory functions of teachers — as would the ideal intelligent computer tutors. Nor would they be machines that train students to use reflexively the basic skills of language and number, as do the many drill-and-practice and simple tutorial programs that are now being sold. They are, instead, a possible means of enabling students to express better the vague thoughts and feelings that abound inside each of them and to translate their ideas into a publicly visible, defensible, intellectual product. In contrast with their use of drills and tutorials, students would not use such programs as consumers of knowledge and ideas, but as producers. In other words, computer-based writing tools may not only be a means for students to become literate, but to use literacy to make a productive contribution to their surroundings.

Notes

1. Even where their editorial policies try to show restraint, these publications tend to project support for the activities of developers and distributors of currently marketed computer products. The publications accept the basic premise that, generally speaking, these products have instructional value and can be effective in typical classroom situations. Products are judged in terms of standards that enable most to be favorably received, being based on technical considerations such as the ability to provide "on-screen" assistance for users and on their method of presenting and testing students' knowledge of their instructional content. See, for example, the magazines *Electronic Learning, Classroom Computer Learning, Electronic Education,* and *Educational Computer.*

2. These estimates are drawn from two sources: the national survey, entitled "School Uses of Microcomputers," conducted in January 1983 by the author (Center for Social Organization of Schools 1983*a*, 1983*b*, 1983*c*, 1984), and published reports from Market Data Retrieval, an educational marketing research firm, based on their census of schools in September 1983.

References

Center for Social Organization of Schools. *School Uses of Microcomputers: Reports from a National Survey,* no. 1. Baltimore: Johns Hopkins University, April 1983. (*a*)

Center for Social Organization of Schools. *School Uses of Microcomputers: Reports from a National Survey,* no. 2. Baltimore: Johns Hopkins University, June 1983. (*b*)

Center for Social Organization of Schools. *School Uses of Microcomputers: Reports from a National Survey,* no. 3. Baltimore: Johns Hopkins University, October 1983. (*c*)

Center for Social Organization of Schools. *School Uses of Microcomputers: Reports from a National Survey,* no. 4. Baltimore: Johns Hopkins University, February 1984.

Ellis, A. B. *The Use and Misuse of Computers in Education.* New York: McGraw-Hill Book Co., 1974.

EPIE Institute. *T.E.S.S.: The Educational Software Selector.* New York: Teachers College Press, 1984.

Garson, J. "The Case against Multiple Choice Test." *Computing Teacher* 7 (1980): 29–34.

Jamison, D., P. Suppes, and S. Wells. "The Effectiveness of Alternative Instructional Media: A Survey." *Review of Educational Research* 44 (1974): 1–35.

Licklider, J. C. R. "Impact of Information Technology on Education in Science and Technology." In *Technology in Science Education: The Next Ten Years: Perspectives and Recommendations.* Washington, D.C.: National Science Foundation, 1979.

Luehrmann, A. "Should the Computer Teach the Student, or Vice-versa?" In *The Computer in the School: Tutor, Tool, Tutee,* edited by R. P. Taylor. New York: Teachers College Press, 1980. (Reprinted from *AFIPS Joint Computer Conference Proceedings* 40 [1972].)

Ragosta, M., P. Holland, and D. Jamison. *Computer-assisted Instruction and Compensatory Education: The ETS/LAUSD Study.* Princeton, N.J.: Educational Testing Service, 1981.

Reil, M. "Education and Ecstasy: Computer Chronicles of Students Writing Together." *Quarterly Newsletter of the Laboratory of Comparative Human Cognition* 3 (1983): 59–67.

Rubin, A., and B. Bruce. *Quill: Reading and Writing with a Microcomputer* (Report no. 5410). Cambridge, Mass.: Bolt, Beranek, and Newman, Center for the Study of Reading, September 1983.

Uttal, W. R., M. Rogers, R. Heironymous, and T. Pasich. *Generative C.A.I. in Analytic Geometry.* Ann Arbor: University of Michigan, November 1969.

Workman, B. "Teaching Writing." In *Computers in Education: Realizing the Potential* (Report of a Research Conference). Washington, D.C.: Department of Education, Office of Educational Research and Improvement, November 1982.

Reading Acquisition and Beyond: Decoding Includes Cognition

CHARLES A. PERFETTI
University of Pittsburgh

The definition of literacy is a tricky business, but it is important for the study of the development of reading skill. My intention in this paper is to discuss the importance of decoding in reading acquisition and beyond. There is good evidence to conclude that decoding is important to the development of reading skill. However, what this means in detail is an interesting question, and this is where the definition issue comes in. So, although my primary concern lies with the development of reading skill, I begin with some issues concerning the definition of literacy that affect how the development of reading skill is viewed.

Definitions

Reading can be considered a higher-level mental activity in which print plays a role. This understanding of reading has fairly strong traditions in research on reading and in teaching reading. Edward L. Thorndike (1917) and, much later, Robert L. Thorndike (1973) exemplified the view that reading was essentially thinking. The meaning-emphasis approaches to teaching reading seem to reflect this understanding. So does the "psycholinguistic guessing game" approach to reading (Goodman 1967). These approaches are in the spirit of definition 1.

Definition 1: Reading is thinking guided by print. Call this the "thinking definition."

There are many versions of the thinking definition, but their differences are minor. In some respects, modern cognitive psychology in general has added prestige to this definition of reading. Our science has emphasized the importance of higher-level cognitive structures as a focus of study and as a pervasive influence on even lower-level cognitive processes. This focus reflects the increased methodological and theoretical ability to deal with complex processes and follows a period that lacked these abilities. Examples of this focus on complex processes are wide-ranging—the study of problem solving (Newell and Simon 1972), planning (Hayes-Roth and Hayes-Roth 1979), scripts (Schank 1982). In the case of reading, the examples include both the influence of higher-level cognitive structures on word reading and the demonstration that higher-level structures (schemata) organize comprehension and memory processes (Anderson, Spiro, and Anderson 1978; Bransford and Johnson 1973). In such a context, reading is seen as a special kind of complex higher-level activity. It has elements of problem solving and its essential characteristic is schema construction.

An alternative definition is that the essential characteristic of reading is decoding print.

Definition 2: Reading is the translation of written elements into language. Call this the "decoding definition."

This is a definition with its own tradition and one not entirely without support. Still, it is hard to find anyone today who defines reading this narrowly. Among psychologists, Crowder (1982) and Liberman and Shankweiler (1979) are among those who seem to take the decoding definition. However, they are in the minority.

One problem with this narrower definition is specifying what the result of decoding is—that is, whether print is decoded into meaning, sound, speech, or something else. Part of the unpopularity of the decoding definition is probably a result of its lack of emphasis on meaning. However, in the decoding definition, meaning is taken to be a product of the spoken language system, so that decoding into speech is the critical reading event from which meaning will follow. This decoding is not merely translating print into sound, however. It is translating print into language. The entire complexity of spoken language is entailed by this definition, and the units of language involved

---

CHARLES A. PERFETTI is a professor of psychology and a senior scientist in the Learning Research and Development Center at the University of Pittsburgh. His research broadly has been in psycholinguistics and, in recent years, especially on the cognitive processes that underlie reading ability. His forthcoming book, *Reading Ability,* published by Oxford Press, discusses the conclusions to be drawn from much of this research.

may include words, morphemes (including morphophonemes), and phonemes.

This definition seems to suggest that written elements are not language. Indeed, strings of letters do not constitute a language until they have been connected, through a primary language system, to semantic, syntactic, and word formation structures. However, the internal structure of written elements does constitute part of the language, once it is learned. In an alphabetic orthography, the rule-governed generation of an innumerably large set of word symbols is made possible by a handful of elements (26 letters in English, 24 in Greek, 32 in Russian). Although, once it is learned, the orthographic system may allow the reader to reduce reliance on speech units, the initial acquisition of this system requires decoding.

This last point raises the possibility that there are two different relevant definitions of reading. Definition 2, the decoding definition, applies to learning to read; definition 1, the thinking definition, applies to skilled reading. This in fact seems quite reasonable. In the acquisition of fundamental literacy, the decoding definition is predominant. In the acquisition of intelligent literacy, the thinking definition becomes central.

An integrated view of these definitions would be commonplace as well as reasonable were it not for the insistence of some that the thinking definition applies to reading acquisition as well as to skilled reading. Making "thinking" central even to beginning reading may be partly the result of overgeneralizing the cognitive studies of complex processes.[1]

These cognitive studies have been devoted to *demonstrating* the important role of higher-level cognitive structures in all sorts of memory and problem solving tasks. For example, the interpretation of words and sentences depends on relevant schemata. The translation of such demonstrations into both reading "theory" and reading instruction has been to elevate schemata to a place of fundamental causality; that is, schemata enable (cause) reading comprehension.

However, cognitive studies have had less to say about learning. Studies of cognitive processes have provided descriptions of representations and demonstrations of representation effects, but, so far, much less about how representations are acquired and how a learner comes to use them. As such work on learning progresses, there is little reason to assume that descriptions of learning will be particularly simple in the way that, for example, demonstrations of schema effects in comprehension are simple. Likewise, there is little justification for promoting schemata to a privileged position in the acquisition of reading skills.

Are these definitional issues important for any substantive issues in literacy? Indeed, they are significant for how reading is taught and how reading research is viewed in relation to instruction. The reading-as-thinking definition implies that there is no distinction between learning how to read and learning how to think. It puts great demands on the teaching of reading, and it assures reading failure by defining reading at such a high level.

Since the reading-as-decoding definition does not identify reading with thinking, it leaves a piece of the "reading" process to other areas of instruction. Its narrowness, which is seen as a disadvantage in some respects, provides a clearer instructional objective. Both success and failure at reading are more detectable.

Finally, consider the possibility that the processes of word recognition are important in skilled reading comprehension as well as in initial reading. In that case, even the reading-as-thinking definition has to make room for decoding. Only a reader with skilled decoding processes can be expected to have skilled comprehension processes. Thus, in a sense, decoding is important no matter which definition of reading is accepted. The only thing that depends on the definition is whether decoding is merely what needs to be learned (the decoding definition) or is, in addition, instrumental to thinking (the thinking definition).

Acquisition and Use of Word Representations

There are many ways to learn how to read, at least superficially. The same is true of teaching reading, of course. Children who begin to learn to read at home before entering school have a different course of acquisition from children who have their first meaningful print encounters in school. Children who learn to read in a meaning-emphasis program may have a different course of acquisition from children in a phonics program. More clearly, children learning to read Arabic have a different course of acquisition from children learning to read Chinese. And both cases are very different from children learning to read English. Thus it appears, at least superficially, that the acquisition of literacy is specific to culture, orthography, and instructional method.

One of the major concerns of cognitive psychology has been the distinction between outward appearance (surface structures) and underlying realities (deep structures). This distinction has had a significant impact on reading research—for example, in the development of text models that represent underlying text meaning rather than text surfaces (e.g., Kintsch and van Dijk 1978) and in the prominence given to underlying schemata as mental structures that organize text material (e.g., Rumelhart 1975; Stein and Glenn 1979). The general import of this kind of work is to make clear that cognitive processes, including reading, work on mental representations. For some reason, this emphasis on representation has not had as much impact on the way decoding is understood. However, word representations are the structures on which processes of decoding and word identification operate. It is these underlying word representations structures that are used in skilled reading. And it is these same structures that must be acquired by children who learn to read. Thus, although there may be many routes to acquisition, it is not necessarily the case that each acquisition route leads to a different type of word representation. It may be that, within a given orthographic system, the underlying word representation systems of different readers are more similar than they are different *at a given level of skill.* The question of whether different acquisition routes lead to a common representation system is one in need of further research. Meanwhile, we can at least suggest what the general form of representation is for readers of English. This we do in the next section. The question for reading acquisition then becomes, How does a child come to have such a representation?

What Makes Lexical Access So Important?

In some approaches to reading, problems of word representation and word processing are matters mainly of inconvenience. If it were possible to assume that reading can occur without reading words, then these problems could safely be ignored. As things stand, such an assumption is counterfactual. Thus, attention to word representation and word processes is required by the facts of reading.

Lexical access is important in reading because it is the central recurring reading process. Cognitive research has been very helpful on this point: The idea that a skilled reader processes a text by skipping over lots of words has been shown to be false. Studies of eye movements show that, in reading texts, the reader's eyes fixate on most words, one estimate being about 70–80 percent of all "content" words (Carpenter and Just 1981). The frequency of fixation is lower for function words, but the clear conclusion is that most words in a text are directly fixated when a college student reads a text. The type of the text, whether it is a scientific text or a story, for example, does not seem to exert a profound influence on the word sampling rate (Just, Carpenter, and Masson 1982). The intentions of readers, however, do make an obvious difference. A reader intending to skim a passage makes fewer fixations than a reader trained in speed reading. Although skimmers and speed readers make fewer fixations, they are not able to answer questions about material that they have not fixated (Just et al. 1982).

This rather dense sampling rate in normal reading is a result of the limitations of the perceptual span. Readers do not obtain much information beyond the center of fixation. Rayner (1975) found that information sufficient to identify a word is not available beyond three or four spaces to the right of a fixation. Information about the shape of words and letters was available farther to the right of the fixation (12 spaces), but such information is not sufficient for identification of a specific word.

Thus the span of perception is quite narrow, and this dictates frequent fixations. The role of context is important in lexical access, but it does not exert the profound influence on fixations that one might expect. Zola (1979; reported in McConkie and Zola 1981) found that readers did *not* skip words that were highly predictable because of context. The effect of contextual constraint was to reduce the duration of a fixation (by 14 milliseconds) rather than the probability of a fixation. On the other hand, Ehrlich and Rayner (1981) did find that the probability of fixation can be reduced by context under the right circumstances. If the word is short enough, there is a reduction in fixation probability for a word that is highly predictable. However, even then the probability of fixation remained very high, 54 percent and 70 percent in two different experiments. Furthermore, Ehrlich and Rayner (1981) found that, when words were misspelled, such misspellings were detected 64 percent of the time, even when the word was very predictable because of context. This implies that visual analysis was carried out on the word even when, in some sense, it was not necessary.

All of this argues for a reading process in skilled reading that is driven by frequent, rapid access to printed words. The overall rate of word sampling is clearly set by the reader's purpose. Once set, it remains sensitive to local text conditions, such as word predictability, but to a limited degree. Fixation probabilities are only modestly affected. This then is what makes lexical access so important. Basic constraints on visual analysis dictate a narrow perceptual span, which in turn dictates frequent lexical access operations. Context is important, but it does not change the nature of the reading process very much. It is hard to imagine a more misleading metaphor for reading than the one that invites us to think of it as a guessing game.

Basic Features of the Lexical Representation System

Given the recurrence of lexical processes in reading, the questions become how these processes work and how learning readers make progress toward achieving high levels of skill. The general theoretical understanding of the lexical problem is that the skilled reader has accessible *representations* of many specific words and a system of implicit rules for word formations. "Word identification" is the process by which visually encoded letters are used to access these representations. The history of research on word identification and word recognition is too long and too rich to review here. However, there are a few recurring problems that have seemed especially important for reading in general. These are whether word identification is holistic, whether it uses a level of orthographic representation, and whether it uses alevel of speech representation. Some understanding of these problems is useful for understanding the importance of decoding. Although there is room for some disagreement on these issues, I take what follows to be theoretically reasonable and reflective of evidence.

Lexical access is interactive.—The issue of whether we perceive words as wholes or as strings of letters has remained alive for a long time. (Compare an early discussion by Huey [1908/1968] with more recent reviews by Baron [1978] and Vellutino [1982].) Another perspective on this question is whether word identification is primarily "top-down" or "bottom-up." "Top-down" implies not only holistic perception of words but strong influences from context on word perception. The word superiority effect, in which a letter is identified more readily in a word than in a letter string, has been the main empirical result in favor of a holistic hypothesis.

It has become clear, however, that simple ideas such as "holistic" word identification are inadequate. The identification of words is mediated by the perception of letters. Cues of word shape and word length are of some significance, but clearly carry only a small portion of the burden of word identification compared with letter perception. The only serious question among researchers is exactly *how* letter perception makes its contribution. There are several different descriptions of word identification that are consistent with the basic constraint that letter perception occurs as part of the process (Adams 1979; LaBerge and Samuels 1974; Massaro 1975; Rumelhart and McClelland 1981).

The model of Rumelhart and McClelland (1981) is more strongly interactive than the other models. "Strongly interactive" means that it allows a free flow of information between higher-level structures (words) and lower-level structures (letters) in both directions. It is instructive to consider what such a strongly interactive model implies about reading words. The basic features of the model are its *representation* structure and its *activation* process. Words and letters are represented as units that are connected by activation links. The word-level representation is accessed only after letter perception has been initiated from the visual features. Activation spreads from letters, as they are perceived, up to words that contain these letters in the right positions. However, as soon as "evidence" for a given word begins to accumulate, activation spreads down to all letters that the word contains. This increases the activation level of the letters, which in turn increases the activation level of the word, which then feeds back down again to the letters, and so forth, in bidirectional activation cycles that very quickly lead to word identification. Thus, top-down and bottom-up activation (and inhibition) accumulate to produce word identification.

The Rumelhart and McClelland model provides a good account for a wide range of facts of word recognition. Still it is not completely clear that other models that are only weakly interactive cannot do as well in accounting for the data. Such models would allow the word representation to receive activation from multiple sources, thus allowing word identification to be assisted by information other than from the letter level; however, weakly interactive models would not allow direct influences from the word level to the letter level. What is instructive for a consideration of general and practical issues of reading is to realize that even a strongly interactive model must give a significant role to letter perception. Letter perception begins the process, and most of the letters of a word are eventually perceived.

Orthographic structure.—The Rumelhart and McClelland model does not have a level of representation between the letter and the word. However, the knowledge a reader has about permissible letter patterns (i.e., well-formed grapheme strings) is a potentially important level of knowledge. The skilled reader has acquired from experience countless two- and three-letter sequences that occur in printed English. In addition, more complex patterns defined over longer strings and letter categories (vowels vs. consonants), rather than specific letters, further enrich this knowledge source. Readers' implicit understanding of orthographic rules (Venezky 1970), which grows out of the large number of patterns that they encounter, is a part of the representation system used in reading. For example, the representation of words includes the knowledge that *tr* is well-formed as a word-initial string but not as a word-final string. Such facts can be represented *indirectly*, as they are in the Rumelhart and McClelland model, by the fact that there are many words of one type (*tr*-initial) and few or none of the other (*tr*-final). But the important point is that such intermediate infra-word knowledge is part of the knowledge to be represented at some level. Similarly, the knowledge about how such infra-word units map onto speech patterns allows decoding of novel word forms.

Speech processes in lexical access.—The final issue of word identification is whether speech recoding occurs during lexical access. That is, do skilled readers use a speech-based representation of a word during silent reading? This has proved to be a difficult issue scientifically, but it has *seemed* to have some practical implications. If speech processes occur only when words are to be pronounced—that is, oral reading— and not when words are read silently, then is it not possible that reading instruction and reading practice should similarly ignore the speech part of reading to focus on the meaning part? However, it is important to see that this implication does not follow from the speech recoding issue. Whether speech processes occur during skilled silent reading has no logical bearing on whether oral reading practices should be encouraged or discouraged. That is, beginning readers, for whom oral reading practice is often used, are still learning and practicing print to speech mappings.

As for skilled reading, it appears that recoding print into speech prior to lexical access is not necessary in normal silent reading (Coltheart 1978; for a review, see McCusker, Bias, and Hillinger 1981). However, it is clear that speech information is part of the lexical representation system. Perfetti and McCutchen (1982) have proposed that this information is routinely activated as an automatic component of lexical access, in much the same way as the word itself and its constituent letters are activated. Depending on factors that influence the speed of lexical access, this speech activation sometimes occurs early and sometimes late relative to word identification. In either case it is available for subsequent comprehension processes. It is these comprehension processes, including verbatim memory but not restricted to it, that are really served by speech activation during reading.

Summary

Word representations and the processes of word identification that operate on these representations are a critical part of reading. Indeed, skilled readers access most words during reading because the span of perception is relatively narrow. This establishes word identification as the central recurring event during normal text reading, even in rich contexts. Thus, theories of representation and identification take on some importance. Important questions that arise in models of representation and identification were identified. Representations of words, letters, orthographic patterns, and speech components seem to be necessary as part of the overall representation system. Identification of words is interactive, involving input from different levels of representation. However the details of the process are understood, word identification is not holistic. Also, although identification may not depend on speech recoding, this has no bearing on learning to read. Indeed, it remains likely that speech processes play a significant role in reading.

Acquisition of the Word Representation System

There is much to be learned about how a child acquires the kind of lexical representation system just described. Cognitive studies have informed us about how skilled lexical processes work and countless educational studies have been directed at how to teach reading. But what is missing is some model of how the child's word representation system moves in the direction of a skilled reader. Such a model, as Glaser (1976, 1982) points out, is a necessary part of scientifically motivated design of instruction. It actually includes two submodels — one of the learner's knowledge at any given point in acquisition and one of the conditions that promote acquisition. There is not much in the way of detailed examples to offer here. It seems fair to say that, although quite a bit is known about selected aspects of a child's progress in learning to read, there is no model that approaches the level of detail needed.

Nevertheless, there is quite a bit to say about parts of the acquisition process, even if it is difficult to be detailed about it. In what follows, I use the case of learning to read in an alphabetic orthography.

The Alphabetic Principle

Learning to read in an alphabetic system entails discovery of the alphabetic principle. This principle is that the elementary units of print map onto units of speech rather than units of meaning. A written symbol, a letter, is associated with a meaningless unit of speech, a phoneme. Of course, logographic scripts produce mappings between print units and word meanings, so literacy does not depend on the alphabetic principle. But reading in an alphabetic system, and even in a syllabary system, requires this mapping of meaningless symbols to meaningless segments.

The obstacles to discovering the alphabetic principle are well known (Gleitman and Rozin 1973; Liberman and Shankweiler 1979). One obstacle is that the phonemes, especially the consonants, are abstract. Acoustically, this means that a given consonant will not be quite the same in one environment as in another. The *t* in "time" is not the same acoustically as the *t* in "cat."

The second obstacle is the failure of alphabets to provide unique letter codes for vowels. Whereas the first obstacle is intrinsic to speech, this second obstacle is extrinsic to speech and depends only on properties of the script. Thus, a writing system can be more or less explicit in this regard, trading economy against explicitness. Thus, the English version of the Roman alphabet is fairly economical (26 letters) and somewhat less than fully explicit. "Cat," "can," and "cake" each use the letter *a* to code a different vowel sound. The system can easily be made more explicit, as it has in alternative teaching alphabets (Pitman and St. John 1969), by creating a different grapheme or diacritical element for each vowel and consonant.

These obstacles are, of course, not insurmountable. The value of the alphabet principle is enormous. Once it is mastered, it allows even the learning reader to read (and write) words never seen before. Only a writing system that has an intermediate level of speech between print and meaning can allow this. The obstacles to acquiring the principle are overcome by everyone who really learns how to read. And even children who have trouble learning to read can be helped to discover the mapping principle (Gleitman and Rozin 1973).

Linguistic Knowledge

Before they begin to read, children have developed communicative control of language. They are able to use language in its pragmatic functions to initiate and sustain conversations, make requests, and so forth. However, this functional language competence does not fully prepare children for the new uses of language that they will need. What is needed is an appreciation of the formal structures of language in addition to control of the pragmatic structures. This need is quite clear in the case of learning to read an alphabetic language by associating letter with phonemes. Both of these elements are abstract formal structures, not functional ones. They are not interpreted within a meaning system.

The issue here is children's awareness of language forms. Prereading children have a rather dim awareness of the phonetic structures of speech, in particular. The phonetic level of language has remained rather transparent during the earlier uses of language, but becomes less transparent with learning to read. That is, children will come to notice the phonetic level as they try to make sense of reading. If the teacher calls their attention to the /ae/ sound in the letter *a* in "apple," the children must attend to a meaningless speech segment as well as a meaningless print segment. Of course, this is even more difficult if

51

the phoneme is a consonant, since a consonant is more abstract than a vowel, lacking clear context-free acoustic duration.

All of this has been the subject of much research and discussion under the label of "phonemic awareness" (or, the more general case, "linguistic awareness"; for a review, see Ehri 1979). Prior to learning to read, children show low levels of phonemic awareness, as evidenced by simple tasks designed to get the children to indicate the number of segments in a word (Liberman, Shankweiler, Fischer, and Carter 1974). Furthermore, the ability to demonstrate explicit phonemic knowledge is highly predictive of early reading achievement (Liberman and Shankweiler 1979).

The exact relationship between phonemic awareness and the development of reading skill is somewhat less certain. On the one hand, a training study by Bradley and Bryant (1983) strongly suggests that children improve this reading ability following training on phonemic segmentation. On the other hand, Perfetti, Beck, and Hughes (1981) have shown that progress in the acquisition of some phonemic abilities follows, rather than precedes, progress in learning to read. It is likely that both of these relationships hold—that a child learning to read is helped by the early emergence of some levels of phonemic awareness and that deeper levels of phonemic awareness may be a consequence of learning to read.

The implication of these awareness considerations is that they pose another obstacle to children's learning to read; or, more specifically, to their learning the alphabetic principle. Indeed, the lack of fully explicit phonemic knowledge by young children may appear to justify a focus on "meaningful wholes" in reading. Ignoring the code may seem justified by the difficulty of teaching it. However, the alternative to not learning the code is not attractive, if the child is to advance to a stage of true reading. (Note that this is not the same as saying the code must be taught in some particular way.) Lack of explicit phoneme knowledge is not an obstacle to learning to read if, as seems to be the case, it can be acquired right along with learning to read.

Ways to Acquire the Code

In the course of learning to read, the learner acquires representations of specific word forms. Many of these specific forms will be short, frequently encountered words such as "the," "of," and "you." They are learned as specific unique patterns. However, this acquisition of specific word forms can also apply to longer words, including words that are more "regular"—that is, more reflective of context-free decoding rules.

Word identification occurs for these words when a string of visually encoded letters triggers the word representation constructed from frequent encounters with the word.

In the course of learning specific word forms, the learner acquires a vast vocabulary of printed letter sequences. Thus, letter patterns that occur in many different words or letter patterns that occur in highly frequent words can acquire a representation status, either directly as a level of representation between single letters and words or indirectly as reflected in the frequency counts of actual words. Thus there is an inductive learning mechanism that detects that, in printed English, 26 graphemes recycle through a few hundred two- and three-letter patterns. In addition it is likely that this mechanism induces the abstract principles that organize these patterns. This mechanism induces the generalization that *str* is a possible word-initial pattern but not a possible word-final pattern. At a still higher level, it induces the generalization that a triple occurrence of a given consonant letter is nonoccurring.

A third acquisition, in addition to specific word forms and induced letter patterns, is the phonemic mappings. Somehow children learn that, in nearly all contexts, b → /b/ and k → /k/. And they learn that *a, e,* and *i* have variable context-sensitive mappings. They also learn that context-sensitive mappings rules are fairly complex. Of course, all of this learning is implicit, or at least it can be.

Both the orthographic patterns and the phonemic mappings are essential if the learner is to become a skilled reader. They enable new words to be identified and unfamiliar words to be decoded into speech form. An overlooked benefit from these acquisitions is that they provide *redundant* representation systems. Specific word forms provide a technically sufficient representation system. But it is possible, although not yet demonstrated, that it is redundancy in the word representation systems that allows fluent word identification to occur. A word can be accessed from single letters, orthographic patterns, and speech-coded representations. These multiple representations may be important for achieving accuracy and fluency in word identification.

How does the learner achieve these multiple representations? Or, more directly, how is the code learned? Is there an order in which the different representations are acquired? The most plausible scenario is that, depending in part on instructional practices, the learner acquires all three representation systems at the same time. Gough and Hillinger (1980) have suggested that the first stage of reading, at least for many children, is a stage of specific word learning. However, this is word learning in which the features of the representation are unsystematic. For example, a reader may "recognize" a word based on its length or its strong contextual association, such as a stop sign. However, this is more a stage of prereading than actual reading. The representation in a true reading stage must at least reflect position-sensitive grapheme information. Learners may acquire this mapping system through repeated encounters with print. It is probably helpful for most learners, however, to have some of the system brought directly to their attention.

Induction and direct teaching.—Human beings are prolific pattern learners. This fact suggests a most powerful mechanism for learning how to read. Exposure to printed words, at least active exposure, provides a powerful condition for learning the orthographic patterns in reading. This has been demonstrated many times for adults and children (Brooks 1977; Pick, Unze, Brownell, Drozdal, and Hopmann 1978).

There is a paradoxical problem for the learner, however. Pattern induction is a powerful mechanism for learning to read, but it is only available to the child through reading. It helps the pattern induction process if the learner has part of the representation system. Clearly, the mapping system would be a tremendous advantage to the learner. It is the one representation system that allows the acquisition of the other representation systems.

This mapping system, indeed, can be taught successfully in a very direct manner with *no known negative consequences* and some obvious advantages. The conclusion of Chall (1967) and others (e.g., Williams 1979) concerning the advantage of code-emphasis programs over meaning-emphasis programs seems beyond dispute, even though the advantage may be slight. Advocacy for specific teaching methods is a complex problem and beyond the scope of this essay. There are many *superficially* different ways to learn to read. However, only those that lead to learning of speech mappings and orthographic patterns will be successful in an alphabetic system.

Consequences of Not Learning the Code

I began this essay by discussing two possible definitions of literacy. Thus far, I have pointed out some of the implications of the narrower reading-as-decoding definition, especially the need to understand printed word representations and how they are acquired. Now I raise the issue of decoding in the context of the broader reading-as-thinking definition. My claim is that, if children do not learn the code to a high degree of skill, their ability to read with comprehension will be at risk.

The general cognitive framework for this claim is provided by verbal efficiency theory (Perfetti, in press; Perfetti and Lesgold 1977; Perfetti and Roth 1981). This theory is grounded in the assumption that some of the higher-level mental processes of comprehension require a share of limited resources. If word identification also requires a significant share of these resources, then comprehension will be at risk. Verbal efficiency theory correctly predicts that comprehension skill will be related to word identification speed and short-term memory (Perfetti and Lesgold 1977). It also predicts correctly that readers of low skill will be more dependent on context for word identification than readers of high skill (Perfetti and Roth 1981). This last point is also made by the interactive-compensatory theory of Stanovich (1980), which is fully compatible with verbal efficiency theory.

Despite the large body of evidence consistent with verbal efficiency theory, the evidence has been largely correlational, and a certain amount of skepticism has been understandably generated. For example, it is a prediction of verbal efficiency theory that, ceteris paribus, increasing the word identification speed of low-skill readers will increase their comprehension. Negative results from experiments that have trained decoding speed of low-skill readers have appeared to count against this hypothesis (Fleisher, Jenkins, and Pany 1979). However, neither the Fleisher et al. study nor unpublished studies of my research group have done more than short-term superficial increases of speed. There is no evidence concerning readers who have had their identification speed *permanently* increased. This can result only from serious long-term training.

The main issue here is the theoretical status of word identification speed. What is the significance of being relatively fast or relatively slow at identifying words? There has sometimes been a lack of explicitness on this question, both in some discussions of verbal efficiency and in its applications to instruction and training. To be clear about it, the speed of word identification, by any measure, is assumed to reflect the accessibility of lexical representations. There are several possibilities for further understanding of "accessibility" in this context. One possibility is that a word representation is more accessible if the processes of access are automatic. This is probably the most common interpretation, and it follows the spirit of the argument by LaBerge and Samuels (1974) that automaticity of identification processes can result from extended practice.

However, the exact status of automatic processes has been a difficult theoretical issue in general, not just for reading. Automatic processes normally have been understood as processes that can occur without attention. The demonstration of automaticity has logically required that a subject's performance on some primary task be unaffected by the simultaneous performance of a secondary task. If this demonstration is successful, then the processes of the secondary task can be said to be attention-free or automatic. It has never been clear that all the processes of word identification can meet this test of automaticity. In fact, careful investigations of automaticity have involved much simpler processes, and even such processes as comparing one letter with another seem not to be automatic (Posner and Boies 1971). It is likely that "automaticity of word identification" can only be an approximation. Skill at word identification can be conceptualized along a continuum of effort, where effort is the expenditure of processing resources. In any case, the speed of word identification cannot be taken as a demonstration of automaticity. More clearly, an increase in speed cannot be taken as the achievement of automaticity without some additional evidence. Word identification speed reflects the accessibility of word representations from graphic inputs.

There is, however, a second way of understanding accessibility. The accessibility of a word may depend on the quality of its representation. The mental representation of words, as I suggested earlier, includes word-, letter-, phoneme-, and orthographic-level information. Accessibility applies rather naturally to the representation system. A reader who really "knows" words has precise representation of specific word spellings, a large set of orthographic patterns or an equivalent orthographic rule system, and a full complement of context-sensitive speech-print representations. It is the precision of these representations, and perhaps their interconnectedness and redundancy, that enables rapid word identification.

These two interpretations of accessibility are not mutually incompatible. One emphasizes a *process* description, and the other emphasizes a *representation* description. There may be no logical grounds for choosing one over the other. However, there is a heuristic value, at least, to the representation description. It makes it easier to notice that, to improve reading efficiency, the reader's knowledge of words and orthographic patterns should be increased. Speed of identification should be thought of as a reflection of this kind of knowledge. *Speed of access is not necessarily something to train independently of the representation system it works on.*

This conclusion by no means should be taken to say that speed training in lexical processes is not a good idea. Indeed, John Frederiksen and his colleagues have demonstrated some specific benefits from training low-ability readers to process words more rapidly (Frederiksen, Weaver, Warren, Gillotte, Rosebery, Freeman, and Goodman 1983). It can be taken to suggest that instruction that fosters word knowledge and orthographic knowledge is better than instruction that does not and that training for speed alone will not compensate for not training for knowledge.

It is not necessary, of course, to improve word identification skill only by practice with single words. For example, the method of repeated reading, proposed by Samuels (1979), seems to provide word identification practice in text. It is especially not necessary to choose between teaching comprehension and teaching decoding. Text materials can be designed to give practice at word identification and comprehension at the same time, or, as Beck (1981, 1983) has proposed, different levels of text difficulty can be used, an easier one to practice word identification skills and a more difficult one to challenge comprehension processes.

Overall, it is correct to say that verbal efficiency theory makes a strong practical prediction that has not been given a clear test. It predicts that extended instruction sufficient to increase permanently the accessibility of words will have effects on comprehension. Although this prediction has not been tested, there is supportive indirect evidence from a longitudinal study of Lesgold and Resnick (1982). They found that gains in children's word identification speed preceded gains in comprehension rather than vice versa. This seems to add a bit to the substantial circumstantial evidence linking coding facility to comprehension.

It is fair to ask how verbal efficiency theory differs from alternative accounts of reading skill that emphasize higher-level cognitive structures as causal in reading skill. The first thing to emphasize is that verbal efficiency theory accords a significant place for such concepts as schemata. These higher-level knowledge structures play a crucial role in how understanding of texts, or the understanding of anything for that matter, works. Schemata allow the reader to organize text propositions into mental models of the text (see Perfetti [in press] for a fuller account of this process). The critical difference between verbal efficiency theory and schema theory is that the latter attaches privileged status to schemata. Schema theory seems to assume that schemata are the central causal elements in comprehension, whereas verbal efficiency theory assumes they are one of several necessary causal components. It is not surprising, accordingly, that training studies motivated by schema-theory ignore the basic word identification processes of children who are trained. It is a generally secure assumption that a low level in one skill (reading) can be compensated to some extent by an increased level in complementary skill.

The point is not that all comprehension problems are traceable to word identification or coding problems. Such a claim is clearly absurd. Rather, it remains a very credible hypothesis that comprehension in reading takes place within limits provided by word identification skills.

A consequence of not acquiring fluent word identification is that the reader's comprehension processes are at risk.

Summary

Acquisition of the alphabetic code is a critical component—indeed, the definitive component—of reading in an alphabetic language. Although reading research and reading instruction have been ambivalent about the definition of reading—whether it is inclusive of thinking or more restricted to printed word identification—this conclusion regarding the code is correct. The heart of reading is the access of word representations, the central recurring process of reading. In normal reading, most individual words are read, and this requires word processes, including decoding, to be an important part of reading. There are obstacles to learning the code, including the child's functional approach to language and the abstractness of the phoneme. Research is needed to understand how a learner moves forward through stages of incomplete learning to a high level of coding skill. However, it is clear that various learning mechanism of pattern induction and explicit associative learning can lead to the level of skilled representation. This includes three types of representation—word forms, letter patterns, and mapping. Instruction must provide conditions that promote the learner's achievement of these representations. The consequences of not gaining word coding fluency are reading comprehension processes that are at risk. Instruction for word coding fluency may involve speed training but increases in the accessibility of word representations are the key objective. This implies knowledge instruction rather than mere speed. Although higher-level components of reading (schemata) are very important, they have no privileged status in explaining overall reading skill. Coding remains the central acquisition for reading skill, the one component unique to reading.

Notes

Preparation of this manuscript and the author's research cited in it are supported in part by the Learning Research and Development Center, which is supported in part by the National Institute of Education.
1. However, it is equally clear that this thinking emphasis predates modern cognitive psychology. The latter has probably had no more than a mildly reinforcing role in the development of attitudes toward literacy.

References

Adams, M. J. "Models of Word Recognition." *Cognitive Psychology* 11 (1979): 133–76.

Anderson, R. C., R. J. Spiro, and M. C. Anderson. "Schemata as Scaffolding for the Representation of Information in Connected Discourse." *American Education Research Journal* 15 (1978): 433–40.

Baron, J. "The Word-Superiority Effect." In *Handbook of Learning and Cognitive Processes,* vol. 6, edited by W. K. Estes. Hillsdale, N.J.: Lawrence Erlbaum Associates, 1978.

Beck, I. L. "Reading Problems and Instructional Practices." In *Reading Research: Advances in Theory and Practice,* vol. 2, edited by T. G. Waller and G. E. MacKennon. New York: Academic Press, 1981.

Beck, I. L. "Developing Comprehension: The Impact of the Directed Reading Lesson." In R. Anderson, R. Tierney, and J. Osborn (Ed.), *Learning to Read in American Schools.* Hillsdale, N.J.: Lawrence Erlbaum Associates, 1983.

Bradley, L., and P. E. Bryant. "Categorizing Sounds and Learning to Read— A Causal Connection. *Nature* 301 (1983): 419–21.

Bransford, J. D., and M. K. Johnson. "Consideration of Some Problems of Comprehension." In *Visual Information Processing,* edited by W. G. Chase. New York: Academic Press, 1973.

Brooks, L. R. "Visual Pattern in Fluent Word Identification." In *Toward a Psychology of Reading,* edited by A. Reber and D. Scarborough. Hillsdale, N.J.: Lawrence Erlbaum Associates, 1977.

Carpenter, P. A., and M. A. Just. "Cognitive Processes in Reading: Models Based on Readers' Eye Fixations." In *Interactive Processes in Reading,* edited by A. M. Lesgold and C. A. Perfetti. Hillsdale, N.J.: Lawrence Erlbaum Associates, 1981.

Chall, J. *Learning to Read: The Great Debate.* New York: McGraw-Hill, 1967.

Coltheart, M. "Lexical Access in Simple Reading Tasks." In *Strategies of Information Processing,* edited by G. Underwood. London: Academic Press, 1978.

Crowder, R. G. *The Psychology of Reading.* New York: Oxford University Press, 1982.

Ehri, L. C. "Linguistic Insight: Threshold of Reading Acquisition." In *Reading Research: Advances in Theory and Practice,* edited by T. Waller and G. E. MacKinnon. New York: Academic Press, 1979.

Ehrlich, S. F., and K. Rayner. "Contextual Effects on Word Perception and Eye Movements during Reading." *Journal of Verbal Learning and Verbal Behavior* 20 (1981): 641–55.

Fleisher, L. S., J. R. Jenkins, and D. Pany. "Effects on Poor Readers' Comprehension of Training in Rapid Decoding." *Reading Research Quarterly* 14 (1979): 30–48.

Frederiksen, J. R., P. A. Weaver, B. M. Warren, H. P. Gillotte, A. S. Rosebery, B. Freeman, and L. Goodman. *A Componential Approach to Training Reading Skills* (Report No. 5295). Cambridge, Mass.: Bolt Beranek and Newman, Inc., 1983.

Glaser, R. "Components of a Psychology of Instruction: Toward a Science of Design." *Review of Educational Research* 46 (1976): 1–24.

Glaser, R. "Instructional Psychology: Past, Present, and Future." *American Psychologist* 37 (1982): 292–305.

Gleitman, D. M., and P. Rozin. "Teaching Reading by the Use of Syllabary." *Reading Research Quarterly* 8 (1973): 447–83.

Goodman, K. S. "Reading: A Psycholinguistic Guessing Game." *Journal of Reading Specialist* 6 (1967): 126–35.

Gough, P. B., and M. L. Hillinger. "Learning to Read: An Unnatural Act." *Bulletin of the Orton Society* 20 (1980): 179–96.

Hayes-Roth, B., and F. Hayes-Roth. "A Cognitive Model of Planning." *Cognitive Science* 3 (1979): 275–310.

Huey, E. B. *The psychology and pedagogy of reading.* Cambridge, Mass.: MIT Press, 1968. (Originally published, 1908.)

Just, M. A., P. A. Carpenter, and M. E. J. Masson. "What Eye Fixations Tell Us about Speed Reading and Skimming" (Technical Report). Pittsburgh: Carnegie-Mellon University, 1982.

Kintsch, W., and T. A. van Dijk. "Toward a Model of Text Comprehension and Production." *Psychological Review* 85 (1978): 363–94.

LaBerge, P., and S. J. Samuels. "Toward a Theory of Automatic Information Processing in Reading." *Cognitive Psychology* 6 (1974): 293–323.

Lesgold, A. M., and L. B. Resnick. "How Reading Disabilities Develop: Perspectives from a Longitudinal Study." In *Theory and Research in Learning Disability,* edited by J. P. Das, R. Mulcahy, and A. E. Wall. New York: Plenum Publishing Corp., 1982.

Liberman, I. Y., and D. Shankweiler. "Speech, the Alphabet, and Teaching to Read. In *Theory and Practice of Early Reading,* vol. 2, edited by L. Resnick and P. Weaver. Hillsdale, N.J.: Lawrence Erlbaum Associates, 1979.

Liberman, I. Y., D. Shankweiler, F. W. Fischer, and B. Carter. "Explicit Syllable and Phoneme Segmentation in the Young Child." *Journal of Experimental Child Psychology* 18 (1974): 201–12.

Massaro, D. W. *Understanding Language: An Information-processing Analysis of Speech Perception, Reading, and Psycholinguistics.* New York: Academic Press, 1975.

McConkie, G., and D. Zola. "Language Constraints and the Functional Stimulus in Reading." In *Interactive Processes in Reading,* edited by A. M. Lesgold and C. A. Perfetti. Hillsdale, N.J.: Lawrence Erlbaum Associates, 1981.

McCusker, L. X., R. G. Bias, and M. L. Hillinger. "Phonological Recoding and Reading." *Psychological Bulletin* 89 (1981): 217–45.

Newell, A., and H. A. Simon. *Human Problem Solving.* Englewood Cliffs, N.J.: Prentice-Hall, Inc., 1972.

Perfetti, C. A. *Reading Ability.* New York: Oxford University Press, in press.

Perfetti, C. A., I. L. Beck, and C. Hughes. "Phonemic Knowledge and Learning to Read." Paper presented at the biennial meeting of the Society for Research in Child Development, Boston, 1981.

Perfetti, C. A., and A. M. Lesgold. "Discourse Comprehension and Sources of Individual Differences." In *Cognitive Processes in Comprehension,* edited by M. A. Just and P. A. Carpenter. Hillsdale, N.J.: Lawrence Erlbaum Associates, 1977.

Perfetti, C. A., and D. McCutchen. "Speech Processes in Reading." In *Speech and Language: Advances in Basic Research and Practice,* vol. 7, edited by N. Lass. New York: Academic Press, 1982.

Perfetti, C. A., and S. F. Roth. "Some of the Interactive Processes in Reading and Their Role in Reading Skill." In *Interactive Processes in Reading,* edited by A. M. Lesgold and C. A. Perfetti. Hillsdale, N.J.: Lawrence Erlbaum Associates, 1981.

Pick, A. D., M. G. Unze, C. A. Brownell, J. G. Drozdal, Jr., and M. R. Hopmann. "Young Children's Knowledge of Word Structure." *Child Development* 49 (1978): 669–80.

Pitman, J., and J. St. John. *Alphabets and Reading.* Belmont, Calif.: Pitman Learning, Inc., 1969.

Posner, M. I., and S. J. Boies. "Components of Attention." *Psychological Review* 78 (1971): 391–408.

Rayner, K. The perceptual span and peripheral cues in reading. *Cognitive Psychology* (1975): 65–81.

Rumelhart, D. E., and J. L. McClelland. "Interactive Processing through Spreading Activation." In *Interactive Processes in Reading,* edited by A. M. Lesgold and C. A. Perfetti. Hillsdale, N.J.: Lawrence Erlbaum Associates, 1981.

Rumelhart, D. W. Notes on schema for stories. In *Representation and Understanding: Studies in Cognitive Science,* edited by D. Bobrow and A. Collins. New York: Academic Press, 1975.

Samuels, S. J. "The Method of Respected Readings." *Reading Teacher* 32 (1979): 403–8.

Schank, R. C. *Reading and Understanding: Teaching from the Perspective of Artificial Intelligence.* Hillsdale, N.J.: Lawrence Erlbaum Associates, 1982.

Stanovich, K. E. "Toward an Interactive-Compensatory Model of Individual Differences in the Development of Reading Fluency." *Reading Research Quarterly* 16 (1980): 32–71.

Stein, N. L., and C. G. Glenn. "An Analysis of Story Comprehension in Elementary School Children." In *Advances in Discourse Processing,* vol. 2: *New Directions in Discourse Processing,* edited by R. Freedle. Norwood, N.J.: Ablex, Inc., 1979.

Thorndike, E. L. "Reading as Reasoning: A Study of Mistakes in Paragraph Reading." *Journal of Educational Psychology* 8 (1917): 323–32.

Thorndike, R. L. "Reading as Reasoning." *Reading Research Quarterly* 2 (1973): 135–47.

Vellutino, F. R. "Theoretical Issues in the Study of Word Recognition: The Unit of Perception Controversy Reexamined." In *Handbook of Applied Psycholinguistics,* edited by S. Rosenberg. Hillsdale, N.J.: Lawrence Erlbaum Associates, 1982.

Zola, D. "The Perception of Words in Reading." Paper presented at the annual meeting of the Psychonomic Society, Phoenix, Arizona, 1979.

Application of Theories of Reading to Instruction

ISABEL L. BECK and MARGARET G. McKEOWN
University of Pittsburgh

Our role in this volume is to discuss the application of theory to reading instruction. The relationship between theory and instructional practice is not necessarily straightforward (Kintsch 1979; Resnick 1975; Weaver and Resnick 1979). One of the reasons there is not always a direct link is that the development of theory is not necessarily pursued for the purpose of influencing practice. At the most basic level, scientists are concerned with explaining how phenomena work and may not have as a primary goal that such explanations be directly applicable to practical concerns. Another reason that the link between theory and practice is sometimes problematic is that even when there is concern to relate theory to practice, it may not be transparent how such a relationship should be drawn. Often, when theory is discussed, suggestions for applying it take the form of general recommendations rather than concrete demonstrations.

Yet theory can be enormously helpful to the instructional process. In the case of our own work, the richness of some recent theory motivated us to pursue its practical application with vigor. Hence, in this chapter, we will take aspects of theory, illustrate how we applied these aspects to instructional design, and discuss the results of this application. The aspects to be considered are those of a reader's *background knowledge* and the *organization of text events and ideas*. These two aspects have been prominent in recent literature on text processing and have been shown to play important roles in how well text is comprehended.

Our demonstration of theoretical applications to instruction will be based on two experiments that we carried out and reported in the literature (Beck, McKeown, Omanson, and Pople 1984; Beck, Omanson, and McKeown 1982). For these experiments we drew on theory and research on text processing to revise lessons found in elementary basal reading programs (Beck et al. 1982) and to revise the texts themselves (Beck et al. 1984). In both cases, the children who received the revised materials exhibited greater comprehension, as measured by recall and questions, than those who received the lessons or stories in their original forms.

For the reports of the studies just mentioned, our results were presented in traditional experimental ways, based on summaries of group data, statistical analyses, and tests of significance. In this chapter, the evidence we present about the relationship between comprehension and aspects of knowledge and text organization will be in the form of samples of what children told us in recalling stories they had read. This qualitative look at aspects of children's recall protocols will illustrate in very concrete ways the consequences for comprehension of certain instructional and text conditions. We now turn to a discussion of the first of the two theoretical aspects to be considered, a reader's background knowledge.

Background Knowledge: Theory and Research

Recently there has been a great amount of research about the background knowledge a reader brings to text and its role in comprehension. This new work has greatly enhanced understanding of how one's background knowledge about text concepts functions in the reading process. The theoretical notion of schemata, abstract knowledge structures that provide frameworks for related concepts, plays a major role in the view of how knowledge affects reading comprehension. (For a fuller discussion of the conceptualization of schemata, see Anderson, Spiro, and Anderson 1978; Rumelhart 1980; Rumelhart and Ortony

---

Isabel L. Beck is a professor of education at the University of Pittsburgh and a senior scientist at the Learning Research and Development Center, University of Pittsburgh, where she is co-director of the Reading and Comprehension unit. Margaret G. McKeown is a postdoctoral fellow at the Learning Research and Development Center, University of Pittsburgh. She received her Ph.D. in education from the University of Pittsburgh in 1983. The research interests of each include vocabulary development, reading comprehension, and computer-assisted reading instruction.

1977; Thorndyke and Yekovitch 1980; Stein and Trabasso 1982.) Within the reading task, a schema functions as a framework that contains slots to be filled by incoming text information. Consider, for example, a text about preparing for dinner guests. An adult's "dinner guest schema" would probably contain a slot for setting the table. Text references to linens, silverware, and wine glasses would then be interpreted as part of setting the table for dinner guests. If a reader's dinner guest schema lacked a "setting the table slot," text references about items for the table might not be readily understood.

Of course, the fundamental notion that the knowledge brought to a reading task helps to determine what the reader will understand from reading was realized before this period of current research. For example, Nila Banton Smith (1963) cited studies from the 1930s that gave evidence of the role of background knowledge in reading comprehension. Toward enhancing comprehension, Smith recommended that teachers strive to build their students' background knowledge.

The notion of building background to enhance comprehension has been institutionalized in basal reading texts, which are the traditional materials for reading instruction across the country. The format of the basal reading lesson begins with a teacher-led discussion that is intended to provide background information for the upcoming story. Often included in this discussion are a story setting, new concepts to be encountered in the story, and any personal experiences the children may be able to share that are relevant to the upcoming story.

Although the concern with the topic of background knowledge in reading is not new, the approach to the topic being taken currently is different. Previously, recognition of the role of background knowledge in comprehension involved more general, intuitive notions. Knowledge was assumed to contribute to comprehension, and efforts to enrich children's knowledge were assumed to be sound instructionally. But the extent of the involvement of prior knowledge in comprehension and its specific effects were not investigated, nor was inadequate background knowledge typically targeted as an important cause of reading failure. In the present period, prior knowledge is seen to have much deeper implications for comprehension than were previously assumed. Recent research has revealed how specific knowledge affects comprehension and explored strategies to boost knowledge toward facilitating comprehension.

Voss and his associates (Chiesi, Spilich, and Voss 1979; Spilich, Vesonder, Chiesi, and Voss 1979) investigated the interaction of knowledge and text information and its effect on comprehension. These investigators analyzed comprehension of text by people with high and low knowledge in a specific context area, the game of baseball.

Subjects were presented with a passage about a baseball game and then asked to recall the text. In addition to differences in amount of recall between high- and low-knowledge groups, there were qualitative differences as well. First, high-knowledge subjects were more likely to recall information that was more relevant to the game, whereas low-knowledge subjects were more likely to recall information about such peripheral matters as the weather or what the crowd was thinking. Second, although both high- and low-knowledge subjects recalled setting information, the initial event, and outcomes, only high-knowledge subjects were likely to recall the sequence of events that developed the theme of the text. Third, high-knowledge subjects were better able to integrate the events and construct a representation of the game described in the text.

Related results were obtained in a study with second-grade children. Pearson, Hansen, and Gordon (1979) tested the comprehension of second graders with high and low knowledge about spiders on a passage about spiders. The children differed on spider knowledge, but not on test scores of IQ and reading achievement. Both explicit and implicit questions were asked to assess comprehension. Although the high-knowledge group performed significantly better overall, an examination of the two question types showed that the high-knowledge group was significantly better on the implicit questions but not on the explicit questions. This result points to the importance of the role of strong knowledge of a content topic in deriving inferences.

It is very important to point out that all subjects in the studies just discussed had *some* knowledge about the content subject being investigated. That is, comparisons were not between knowledge and lack of knowledge but between high and low levels of knowledge. The results then lead to the conclusion that not merely the presence of specific knowledge but also the extent and quality of that knowledge is a factor in how well a text is comprehended.

Applying Background Knowledge: A Demonstration

Before undertaking the experimental studies in which we revised reading lessons and stories, we analyzed basal reading programs to identify aspects that seemed problematic for enhancing comprehension (Beck, McKeown, McCaslin, and Burkes 1979). One of our findings was that the knowledge required for understanding text selections was not always handled well instructionally. Text selections often introduced concepts that were likely unfamiliar to target-age readers. Yet efforts to establish and activate these concepts in a way that would be useful to story comprehension often seemed inadequate.

Based on what we learned from the analysis work, the introduction and activation of background knowledge became a major focus in revising lessons to improve comprehension. The structure of our lesson revisions was tied to that of the directed reading lesson, the traditional format found in the basal readers. The lesson begins, as mentioned earlier, with a general introduction to the story, which includes the introduction of new concepts and setting a purpose for reading. In the primary grades the teacher then prepares children to read a small segment of text, one to three pages in length, by introducing information specific to that segment, or silent reading unit (SRU). Pictures that accompany the text are then typically discussed. After children read the first SRU, they are asked questions about it. Then preparation for the next SRU is presented, and the cycle continues until the entire story is read. In our lesson revisions, we worked with four components of the directed reading lesson—story preparation, SRU preparation, pictures, and after-reading questions.

The redesigned components for the Beck et al. (1982) study were based on two notions that were believed to facilitate comprehension. The first is the activation or establishment of relevant background knowledge prior to reading, and the second is the highlighting of events that are central to the story. In the redesign of the lessons, the intention was to use the pre-story preparation and the pre-SRU preparation to provide relevant background knowledge and the post-SRU questions to highlight the events that were most important to the development of the story. While it is impossible to determine that there was no overlap, it is reasonable to suggest that the background knowledge made available came mostly from the preparation components.

In the rest of this section, we take the reader through the process of applying notions about background knowledge to reading lessons and demonstrate how knowledge functions in a comprehension task by examining protocols of children's story recalls. The basis of the discussion will be the story preparation component for one of the two stories used in our experiments, "The Raccoon and Mrs. McGinnis" (Clymer et al. 1976), which was drawn from a late second-grade text.

First we will describe the knowledge requirements we identified for this story and how the revised activities fulfilled these requirements in contrast to the original lesson activities. Then specific instances of interference in comprehension that can be traced to a lack of appropriate background knowledge will be presented.

67

We begin with a summary of the McGinnis story. The plot of the story involves a woman who wishes on a star for a barn for her animals, a raccoon who comes to her doorstep each night to look for food, and some bandits intent on stealing Mrs. McGinnis's animals. The raccoon, in its nightly search for food, follows the bandits and eventually climbs a tree to be safe from them. The bandits see the raccoon and mistake its masked appearance for another bandit. Frightened, the men release the animals, flee, and drop a bag of money. The raccoon picks up the moneybag and eventually drops it on Mrs. McGinnis's doorstep while looking for food. Mrs. McGinnis finds the money, attributes her good fortune to her wish on the star, and uses the money to build a barn.

In consideration of the knowledge needed to comprehend the story, the key concepts we identified were coincidence, since Mrs. McGinnis's wish comes true through a series of coincidences, and habit, since the raccoon's habitual behavior allows the coincidences to occur. The revised story preparation component was designed to introduce the concepts of coincidence and habit and to set up conditions to help children identify and interrelate story events that bring about the coincidences. These conditions include the general idea that animals behave in a routine manner and focus on seeking food and avoiding danger. More specific notions discussed were that raccoons tend to pick up objects found in their path and that bandits and raccoons share the physical characteristic of a masked face.

Although a great deal of information was presented to the child, care was taken to insure that the child's role was an active one. Throughout the preparation component the child was called on to interact with the notions being developed.

The following outlines the revised story preparation component of the Mrs. McGinnis lesson:

1. A picture of a raccoon from the story was pointed out, and the idea that raccoons appear as if they are wearing a mask was elicited. The child was asked about kinds of *people* that might wear masks, toward establishing that bandits are often masked.
2. The behavior of raccoons was discussed, including the facts that raccoons frequently live near people as a convenient food source and that they hunt for food at night.
3. The concept of habit, "when people or animals always do things exactly the same way," was introduced. Examples of habits that people have were presented, and the children were asked to contribute a habit of their own.

4. The concept of habit was specifically linked to raccoons. Introduced here was the raccoon habit of picking up and carrying off objects that lie in its path.
5. The concept of coincidence, "when two things happen just by chance, but they fit together . . . like they were supposed to happen that way," was introduced by way of an example in which a stuck Thermos lid was loosened by being accidentally knocked to the floor. The child was questioned about what two events from the example "fit together." Then a scenario was set up that the child was guided to complete by telling about a coincidence that could occur. The scenario involved waking up late and rushing off to school hungry, but without breakfast.
6. The experimenter concluded by telling the child that, in the story they are going to read, Mrs. McGinnis, as well as the raccoon, exhibits some habits and that some coincidences occur.

The revisions contrast with the original pre-story preparation component provided by the commercial lesson, which focused on a brief discussion of raccoons as clever, playful animals. It does not include information about raccoons that we judged as most useful for story comprehension, such as raccoons' habitual behavior and masked appearance. Nor is the notion of coincidence included. The original preparation component consists of the following activities:

1. Children are told that the story is about Mrs. McGinnis and a raccoon.
2. The meaning of the word "tame" is discussed.
3. Several characteristics of raccoons are presented: raccoons are curious, clever, intelligent, and mischievous; raccoons can remove garbage can covers; and raccoons rinse their food.
4. Children are told that the story is to be read for enjoyment.
5. Children are to note unusual things that happen to Mrs. McGinnis because of the raccoon.

Some evidence of the effect of the background knowledge we identified on comprehension of the McGinnis story can be gleaned from children's protocols of the lesson. The key to comprehending the story is realizing that the raccoon is just going about his habitual nocturnal business when it happens into some coincidental events that result in Mrs. McGinnis's wish appearing to come true. If readers do not understand the coincidental nature of the plot, they are likely to interpret the story as a fanciful tale of a heroic raccoon whose planful actions save the day. Indeed, interpretation of intentionality is apparent in some of the protocols of children who received the original lesson.

Each of the following is an excerpt from protocols of children who received this lesson and presents a child's account of how the raccoon ends up scaring off the bandits and leaving a moneybag on Mrs. McGinnis's steps: "The raccoon had to get [Mrs. McGinnis's cow and pigs] back"; "The raccoon stopped them from stealing her stuff. It wanted her to have her stuff back"; "He made his tail look like a gun"; "He scared them away, and he got the money back and the cow and pigs back"; "He returned the animals"; "The raccoon gave the money to Mrs. McGinnis."

Only one child in the revised lesson group made a statement that similarly attributed the outcome to intentional behavior: "The raccoon left [the moneybag] for her to buy a barn."

Not only did the revised group's story recalls virtually lack this faulty interpretation of the story but they also gave some indications of an awareness of coincidence. Several children in the revised group described Mrs. McGinnis's wish fulfillment by contrasting what *she thought* had happened with how the event actually occurred, thus capturing the essence of coincidence as "two things that happen just by chance, but fit together": "She thought her wish came true, but it didn't, because the raccoon done it all"; "In the morning she thought it was a wish that came true, but the raccoon done it"; "Mrs. McGinnis thought her wish came true. She didn't know the raccoon put it on her steps."

Similar descriptions do not occur in the original lesson group's recalls.

Applying Background Knowledge: Recommendations

In the remainder of this section we put forth our notions about how a teacher can deal with the problem of background knowledge. As we have noted, the notion that one should prepare children to read a story by providing some background information is well-accepted and has been long followed in the reading field. The issue of interest is how to provide an effective background that will guide children to comprehend the story better. We will discuss the issue under two general categories. The first concerns the selection of the content, and the second concerns how that content is introduced and discussed.

The process of selecting concepts to highlight is a matter of giving the story a close, careful reading and continually asking, "What's here that the children won't know or won't have firmly in control?" and "What content and concepts that my judgment suggests children won't know are particularly important for comprehension?" In making these considerations, one needs to avoid both errors of omission and errors of inclusion. Errors of omission occur when a concept that is important to story comprehension is not introduced or activated prior to reading. The opposite of the omission problem is errors of inclusion, which occur when concepts and content irrelevant to the upcoming text, or only tangentially related, are introduced. Discussion of such issues is costly in terms of time that could be better spent preparing children for more crucial story concepts. Even worse, discussion of irrelevant or tangential material can distract children from the main points of the story and cause them to set up inappropriate expectations.

As our discussion implies, there is no precise recipe to follow in selecting content for prereading attention. Yet, if one has a deep understanding of how fundamental background knowledge is to reading comprehension, our suggestions are not as mystical as they may sound. In university classes, after presenting theory and data associated with the role of background knowledge, we have had students redesign the prereading component of several basal lessons, and the results are virtually always a better selection of the content to be presented in the prereading component than the original. We are convinced that, if teachers are sensitized to the issues, they will better select useful content for inclusion in prereading components. When teachers take the time to be reflective, they can bring the greatest amount of insight to bear regarding what their own students know and what they may have difficulty with.

The second issue associated with developing useful prereading components concerns how the content is presented—that is, the engineering of the activities to communicate the concepts. There are more and less effective ways of presenting the same concepts. For example, in the second story we worked with, entitled "The Donkey Egg," both the revised and original versions included the fact that donkeys do not hatch from eggs. Yet many children in the original lesson group stated in their story recalls that a donkey indeed hatched from what one of the characters believed to be a donkey egg. This seems to highlight the notion that the prereading activities must aim toward creating an understanding of concepts being introduced rather than merely mentioning them. A reason that this distinction is crucial is that reading is a complex process involving the workings of simultaneous subprocesses. For young children the control of lower-level processes, such as decoding, and the coordination of the various subprocesses are not yet well developed. If, in addition to getting through the words to construct meaning, children are called on to bring to bear knowledge that has been only weakly established, a breakdown in comprehension can easily occur. Thus, to aid comprehension, concepts must be established strongly enough to be easily accessed during reading.

To prepare an effective prereading plan for a story, one must develop ways to introduce and exemplify the target concepts. This can be done through defining the concepts, presenting examples, and eliciting children's reactions to the concepts in ways that test their understanding of them. This is done toward establishing a framework into which children can fit story events as they read. For example, in the prereading activity for the revised lesson of "The Raccoon and Mrs. McGinnis," children were introduced to habit as "something animals or people always do in exactly the same way," and then presented with several examples of habits and opportunities for the children to discuss their own habits. Thus when the children met an event such as the raccoon's nightly trip to Mrs. McGinnis's steps, they might be likely to fit that into the concept of habit and use it to help interpret the story's unusual outcome.

Another technique to help make important concepts available during reading, in addition to presenting information before the story is begun, is to reinforce important concepts during the brief discussion prior to each SRU. Traditionally this pre-SRU preparation component has a variety of functions, including bringing in issues tangential to the story, as well as alerting children to what is coming up in the text. Since these activities occur in the midst of reading, they seem most appropriately used to help children focus on important concepts just before they are reached in text.

The point of this discussion is that the goal of facilitating comprehension through background knowledge is not fulfilled by the mere mention of story-related information. Rather, prereading activities must be carefully crafted to add to the child's knowledge in such a way that the information is readily available from memory as the child reads.

Text Organization: Theory and Research

In the instructional world, a major concern has been with sorting and ordering texts according to their ease of comprehensibility. Traditionally, the comprehensibility of texts has been assessed by the use of readability formulas that use vocabulary difficulty and sentence length to index text difficulty. Although sentence length and word difficulty are generally predictive of comprehensibility, they do not influence comprehension directly. Consequently, if sentence length and word difficulty are manipulated in an effort to ease text difficulty, text features such as relational coherence may suffer and actually make a story harder to comprehend.

Recently, investigators have been able to describe text features that influence comprehension more directly by taking into account what readers do in the process of reading. A key aspect of this approach is the consideration of how texts are organized and how readers represent text organization in memory.

Text organization can mean relationships between and among sentences or between and among larger segments of discourse. One focus of the research on text organization has been the creation of models of text. One type of model is the story grammar, which is a schematic representation of narrative text that readers are assumed to use to guide their comprehension and recall of stories (Mandler and Johnson 1977; Rumelhart 1975; Stein and Glenn 1979; Thorndyke 1977). Story grammars are based on a sequence of text events that make up a story episode, such as setting, initiating event, and conflict. Another direction of research in the creation of text models involves schemes for representing the relations of much smaller units of texts, called propositions. The organization of the propositions of a text is assumed to characterize the structure of a text that forms as a reader reads (Frederiksen 1975; Kintsch 1974; Meyer 1975).

Still another direction of research on text organization focuses on the actual statement of the relations among small units. That is, to what extent does the sequence of events make sense and to what extent does the surface structure of the text make the nature of these events and their relationships apparent? These issues are referred to under the rubric of text coherence. For a text to be coherent, it should include "statements of the events so that the events per se are readily understood and their causal relations are easily inferred from the surface order of events . . . and insure that causal sequences are not disrupted by introduction of new and irrelevant causal fields or chains or by descriptive detail that is unnecessary to the current chain" (Trabasso, Secco, and van den Broek 1984, p. 109).

There is a large body of research consistent with the notion that the coherence of texts affects their comprehensibility. This research has demonstrated that a number of aspects of text coherence affect comprehension. Among those aspects that have been shown to inhibit comprehension are the use of references that are ambiguous (Frederiksen 1981), distant (Cirilo 1981; Lesgold, Roth, and Curtis 1979), or indirect (Haviland and Clark 1974; Just and Carpenter 1978), inclusion of concepts for which the reader lacks requisite background (Chiesi et al. 1979; Pearson et al. 1979), lack of clear relationships between events (Black and Bern 1981; Kintsch, Mandel, and Kozminsky 1977; Stein and Nezworski 1978), and the inclusion of events or ideas that are irrelevant to the rest of the text (Schank 1975; Trabasso et al. 1984).

Creating More Comprehensible Texts

In working with basal reader stories we became aware, based on our experience working with children in reading classes, our familiarity with research on text features, and our own reactions as readers, that many of these stories lacked coherence. We then undertook the task of rewriting the two stories mentioned earlier, "The Raccoon and Mrs. McGinnis" and "The Donkey Egg." Our approach to creating more comprehensible texts was not based on a formal analysis or algorithmic process of revising every instance of certain problematic features, such as distant referents or missing events. Rather, we believed that our awareness of such text features would serve as a knowledge base that would alert us to problematic text situations and that our solutions to these problems would be guided by the question, "What is the best way to communicate a given idea?" (Pearson, 1974–75, p. 191).

This approach is in harmony with that of Davison and Kantor (1982), who believe that the best substitute for readability formulas for the creation of comprehensible text is the informed judgment of a writer or editor. According to Davison and Kantor, such an informed judge should possess knowledge of language, literary style, and how best to communicate the specific content and its relationships, and especially knowledge of what causes people problems in the course of processing text.

As we read the texts to be revised, we tried to monitor our comprehension processes in a conscious way in order to recognize text situations that seemed to cause us to have to do "extra work" toward constructing a representation, such as having to reprocess portions of text to understand a passage, or bring sophisticated levels of linguistic or world knowledge to bear. We engaged in this process for two reasons. One was to revise the texts to make them more comprehensible. The other was to produce a description of the text problems we dealt with that might be useful to others who were revising or writing texts for children.

The text problems we revised involved three levels of text—words, events, and relations—and fell into three categories. The first category consisted of problems with the surface form of the text, such as difficult referents or omitted grammatical categories. The second area was the knowledge assumed by the text, such as use of a word or event sequence that demanded knowledge likely to be unfamiliar to target-age children. The third problem category was the nature of the content, such as implied events, ambiguous words, or poorly drawn relationships between events.

We will illustrate the revisions we made and the rationale behind them by discussing the original and revised versions of an excerpt from "The Donkey Egg." We will then turn to evidence of the effects on comprehension of the problems we identified and their revisions. The evidence to be presented was drawn from protocols of the children in our experiment who read either the revised or original versions of the stories. Before reading the stories, the children were introduced to vocabulary identified in the teacher's manual from which the stories were taken; however, no lesson—that is, no story or SRU preparations pictures, or questions—accompanied the text. Let us remind the reader that the results of our experiment showed that we did succeed in making the stories more comprehensible (Beck et al. 1984).

We begin with a summary of the story. "The Donkey Egg" is an old Turkish tale involving the Hodja, a gullible character. At the beginning of the story, a sly friend gives the Hodja a pumpkin, telling him it is a donkey egg that will hatch a donkey. Weeks later, the "egg" softens and begins to smell, and the Hodja decides he must get rid of it. As he rolls the "egg" down a hillside, it hits a tree and bursts open, startling a rabbit. As the rabbit runs off, the Hodja mistakes it for a baby donkey and becomes distressed over his loss.

Let us now consider a passage from the original version of the story and describe how and why it was revised. The passage is the last paragraph of the story. It occurs just after the pumpkin has burst open at the bottom of the hill and startled a sleeping rabbit. Table 1 presents both versions of this passage.

The first changes made with the text segment (no. 1 in the table) involve reinstating the setting, "From the top of the hill," in order to mark a contributing cause for the Hodja's mistaking the rabbit for a donkey; that is, he was at a distance. Changing "It was" to "Hodja saw" was done to transform the author's description to the character's perception, thereby attempting to emphasize the point that Hodja sees the rabbit. The most important change in this segment is the addition "thought it was the baby donkey," thus making explicitly available the fact that Hodja mistook the rabbit for a donkey. Notice that this addition places in the foreground the reason for the Hodja's "Oh! The baby donkey at last!" at the beginning of text segment no. 2. This addition

TABLE 1

Original and Revised Texts of the End of the Donkey Egg Story

Original Text	Revised Text
1. It was a beautiful long-eared rabbit. The Hodja saw him.	From the top of the hill, Hodja saw the long-eared rabbit and thought it was the baby donkey.
2. "Oh," he groaned. "The baby donkey at last! The donkey egg was just ready to hatch. May heaven help us all," he shouted.	"Oh," he shouted. "There is the baby donkey. The donkey egg was just ready to hatch and I thought it was rotten. May heaven help us all."
3. "Now it has hatched and our baby donkey is lost forever!"	Then sadly he groaned, "The egg has hatched, but our baby donkey has run away. Now we will never have a second donkey."

also attempts to forestall the possibility that the line about Hodja's perception that the donkey has arrived will be taken literally—that is, that readers will think a baby donkey actually has appeared.

Text revision no. 2 involves the changing of some speech markers to what seems a little more logical, given the substantive changes we made. The sentence in the original—"The baby donkey at last!"—involved two changes. First, we identified the sentence as an ambiguous event and added "There is" to reduce the ambiguity. Second, we deleted "at last" because those words imply that the Hodja expected the hatching, which was not the case at this point in the story. The addition of "I thought it was rotten" reinstates what the Hodja had said in an earlier episode and is the motivation for Hodja taking the egg to the hill to dispose of it. Reinstating that the Hodja had thought it was rotten is an attempt to mark the notion that he no longer expected it to hatch and thus adds reason for his surprise.

In the third segment, changing "is lost forever" to "has run away" makes the loss of the "donkey" more immediate and concrete. It ties the loss to the rabbit's running away, rather than just to the general context of disposing of the "egg." Changing "it" to "the egg" avoids referent ambiguity. Thus it may help the reader reinstate the "rotten egg" theme and recall what brought Hodja to the hillside. Finally, the addition of "Now we will never have a second donkey" relates to the story premise; that is, the Hodja has one donkey and wants another.

76

Most of the changes we made in this part of the story were aimed at facilitating the children's construction of the appropriate end to the story, which is, as noted earlier, that Hodja *thinks* the pumpkin hatched a donkey because he *mistakes* the rabbit for a donkey—and because he is gullible enough to believe a donkey could hatch from an egg. The protocols of 14 of the 24 children who read the revised story contain statements that indicate they comprehended the ending. Some of the recalls about this part are quite explicit and include a cause for the mistaken identity—for example, "Well, there was a pumpkin that rolled down the hill, and it cracked. And there was a bunny rabbit sleeping by the tree, and [Hodja] saw the long ears of the bunny rabbit and thought it was a baby donkey."

Other children do not explicitly include a reason for the mistaken identity, but there is little question that they have a good representation of the ending: "And the rabbit ran, and Hodja looked down the hill and thought it was a donkey. And he said, 'A baby donkey!' And then he said—he groaned—and he said, 'The baby donkey ran down the hill.' And it was not a donkey."

It is interesting to note that, of the 14 protocols that we judged to have evidence that the ending was well represented, 13 use the word "thought" and state it as a reaction, such as "Hodja *thought* the rabbit . . ." and "He *thought* the donkey had arrived." The remaining child said, "But the baby donkey was really a rabbit." In addition to the 14 children whose protocols were judged to have evidence that the end of the story was well represented, there were two children who recalled the events of this last part of the story rather well, but did not relate one event to another—for example, "And there was a rabbit with long hair and brown ears. And then he ran away. Then [Hodja] said, 'Heaven will be on all of us,' and then the brown rabbit just ran away."

In contrast to the performance of the revised group, the *best* representation of the end of the story found in any of the protocols of the 24 children who read the original version of the story was, like the example just presented, a correct recitation of the events without the causal connections being drawn. But only five children who read the original story gave such a correct recitation, and there was not a single child who explicitly stated that the Hodja mistook the rabbit for a donkey.

Text Organization: Recommendations

The recommendations we offer for dealing with texts that lack coherence are directed at two audiences. The first is the producers of reading texts, and the second is teachers. Although their roles in solving the problems of less coherent texts are quite different, the primary issue for both text producers and teachers is to develop a deep understanding of characteristics of texts that present comprehension obstacles for young readers.

The focus of our revision work has been the statement of events and relations rather than the arrangement of story elements such as goals, plans, and actions, which is the domain of story grammar. However, several comments about story grammar are appropriate here. First, although we did not work directly with story grammar issues, many of our story revisions may have affected the comprehensibility of text structure at the story grammar level. For example, improving the coherence of an event or clarifying its relationship to other events could facilitate a correct interpretation of the role of that event within the story's grammar.

A second reason for discussing story grammar is that, within the domain of text organization, the concept of story grammar is very salient and useful. The concept is salient because well-formed stories do exhibit a consistent structure (Mandler and Johnson 1977; Rumelhart 1975; Stein and Glenn 1979; Thorndyke 1977). Story grammars are useful in that research evidence indicates that readers use the structure to guide their comprehension of narrative text (Mandler 1978; Rumelhart 1975; Stein and Glenn 1979; Stein and Nezworski 1978). Hence, familiarity with story grammar and the ability to detect how well stories conform, in a general way, to this structure are important tools for those who produce texts for children or interact with children and texts. This is not to suggest that one need be versed in formal methods of story grammar analysis but simply that one have a generalized understanding of the structure of narratives and be able to recognize when the plot of a story contains gaps.

We now turn our discussion to problematic aspects of text organization that were the focus of our text revision work. These characteristics of text, which bear on the coherent statements of text events and relations, have been described in various ways. The discussion by Trabasso et al. (1984) of coherent texts also reveals qualities of texts that lack coherence. These include poorly ordered statements that inhibit the comprehension of cause-effect sequences and the inclusion of irrelevant details or new unrelated sequences within the one being processed. Armbruster (1984) writes about the problem of text coherence under the label "inconsiderate texts." Texts may be inconsiderate because they lack "signaling," such as previews or summary statements, to emphasize certain ideas. Inconsiderate texts are also characterized by relationships that are not explicit, event sequences that are out of logical order, and the use of references that are unclear. In our text revision work, we have dealt with many of these same concerns in describing problems of surface structure, knowledge requirements, and nature of text content, which can occur at the word, event, or relational level within a text.

The importance of these various categories is not that their labels be learned, for, often, different writers discuss similar situations under different labels or certain text problems seem to fall into several potential categories. The categories need only be used as far as they help one to organize an understanding of problematic text features. The important notion is to develop an understanding of these problems so that one is able to recognize their occurrence in texts as one reads. Toward this end, we offer several examples of problematic text characteristics, which have been adapted from basal stories. In considering these examples it is important to remember that, although they may not present serious obstacles for the mature reader, the effect for a young reader may be different. Particularly when a number of such situations occur within a story, the cumulative effect can be quite devastating to comprehension.

First, consider an example of a difficult reference: " 'This coat is worn out,' Jane cried. She took the old rag and threw it into the trash basket." For this excerpt, it takes a somewhat sophisticated understanding of the use of references to realize that "old rag" refers to Jane's coat. Such problems can arise with the use of pronouns as well as with alternate labels, and they can be compounded in a text by distance from the referent or intervening nouns that may cause a reader to relate a reference to an incorrect referent.

Next, consider an example of a poorly drawn relationship between two text ideas: "Sally hoped her mother would bake a chocolate cake for her birthday. Her birthday would be no fun." The problem here is that the connection between these two ideas is missing; Sally's birthday will be no fun *if* her mother *does not* make a cake for her. Problems such as these are quite typical in the stories that appear in the earliest levels of the basal readers, where connectors may be avoided because beginning readers may not have been introduced to words like "because" or "unless," and efforts are made to keep sentences short. The result may be a text that is easy to decode but difficult to comprehend.

Now consider an example of an ambiguous text segment: "When everyone saw Bill in his new suit, they nodded and smiled at each other." It is not apparent from the sentence whether everyone is giving approval to Bill's suit or laughing at his odd taste in clothes. If the reader draws the wrong interpretation, or is left unsure of which interpretation to draw, comprehension is disrupted.

The final example is a text sequence that contains an irrelevant idea in its midst: "Donna ran into Ed in the airport. She was on her way to Florida for a week's vacation. It was good to see Ed again. She hadn't seen him in a long time." The sentence about going to Florida may lead the reader to believe that the trip is the focus of the sequence. The subsequent sentences about Ed, then, may cause a disruption to processing as the reader tries to sort out what is being communicated. Or the reader may not notice the conflicting possibilities and may end up with the incorrect interpretation that Ed went to Florida with Donna.

The knowledge that text producers and teachers gain from an awareness of text situations such as those we have discussed is used in different ways. Text producers can apply the knowledge in writing or revising texts. Teachers, on the other hand, work with the texts that are presented in the reading materials. Yet their knowledge of text characteristics can be used to guide their students' comprehension.

One way that teachers can compensate for a text that lacks coherence is by using components of the directed reading lesson to highlight aspects of the text that are suspected to contain problems. That is, discussion prior to reading or questions asked after reading can be used to guide children to think in ways that will promote comprehension despite the limitations of the text. For instance, imagine that the example about Bill's new suit was preceded in the text by a segment about Bill buying a suit from a slick salesman who convinced him to buy an outlandish outfit. The teacher could intervene to help children understand this concept and prepare them to realize that the upcoming text represents people snickering about Bill's appearance. Questions might be posed such as "What did Bill's new suit look like? How do you suppose Bill thought he looked? What might other people say or think about Bill's new suit?"

Another technique that a teacher might use is modeling the processing required to understand a difficult text passage. For instance, consider how a teacher might model the excerpt about Sally's birthday cake. The teacher might read aloud, "Sally hoped her mother would bake her a chocolate cake for her birthday. Her birthday would be no fun." Then the teacher could demonstrate that the excerpt caused her some comprehension trouble: "No fun? Why wouldn't her birthday be fun?" And then the teacher could go on to work out the problem, beginning with rereading the first sentence: " 'Sally hoped . . .' Oh, she wanted a chocolate cake, so if her mother *didn't* make the cake, then her birthday wouldn't be fun." In this way, a teacher illustrates that texts are sometimes problematic and demonstrates the kind of reader input that might be needed to solve problems that arise. Exposure to models of a skilled reader's processing can help children to anticipate problematic text situations and develop a basis for dealing with such situations.

Final Comment

In this paper we have illustrated how our understanding of two aspects of reading theory was applied to upgrading instructional practice. But the point of our discussion was not merely to show that our efforts have succeeded. Rather, we presented illustrations of the application of theory to practice to focus attention on the value of theoretical notions in a way that might help establish an appreciation of the consequences of these notions to the reading process.

For practical purposes, it is important that theory be understood at a rich level, but not necessarily at a formal level. To develop a rich understanding, it is not enough to read about and acknowledge the information that theory presents; the notions must be incorporated into one's approach to a problem, so that theory serves as a filter through which observations of children's interactions with text and consideration of instructional materials pass. Just as the extent and quality of prior knowledge affects comprehension, the extent and quality of understanding some theoretical issues affect the success of their application to practice.

References

Anderson, R. C., R. J. Spiro, and M. C. Anderson. "Schemata as Scaffolding for the Representation of Information in Connected Discourse." *American Educational Research Journal* 15 (1978): 433–40.

Armbruster, B. B. "The Problem of 'Inconsiderate Text'." In *Comprehension Instruction: Perspectives and Suggestions*, edited by G. G. Duffy, L. R. Roehler, and J. Mason. New York: Longman, Inc., 1984.

Beck, I. L., M. G. McKeown, E. S. McCaslin, and A. M. Burkes. *Instructional Dimensions That May Affect Reading Comprehension: Examples from Two Commercial Reading Programs* (LRDC Publication 1979/20). Pittsburgh: University of Pittsburgh, Learning Research and Development Center, 1979.

Beck, I. L., M. G. McKeown, R. C. Omanson, and M. T. Pople. "Improving the Comprehensibility of Stories: The Effects of Revisions that Improve Coherence." *Reading Research Quarterly* 19 (1984): 263–77.

Beck, I. L., R. C. Omanson, and M. G. McKeown. "An Instructional Redesign of Reading Lessons: Effects on Comprehension." *Reading Research Quarterly* 17 (1982): 462–81.

Black, J. B., and H. Burn. "Causal Coherence and Memory for Events in Narratives." *Journal of Verbal Learning and Verbal Behavior* 20 (1981): 267–75.

Chiesi, H. L., G. J. Spilich, and J. F. Voss. "Acquisitions of Domain-related Information in Relation to High and Low Domain Knowledge." *Journal of Verbal Learning and Verbal Behavior* 18 (1979): 257–73.

Cirilo, R. K. "Referential Coherence and Text Structure in Story Comprehension." *Journal of Verbal Learning and Verbal Behavior* 20 (1981): 358–67.

Clymer, T., et al. *Reading 720.* Lexington, Mass.: Ginn & Co., 1976.

Davison, A., and R. N. Kantor. "On the Failure of Readability Formulas to Define Readable Texts: A Case Study from Adaptations." *Reading Research Quarterly* 17 (1982): 187–209.

Frederiksen C. H. "Representing Logical and Semantic Structure of Knowledge Acquired from Discourse." *Cognitive Psychology* 7 (1975): 371–458.

Frederiksen, J. R. "Understanding Anaphora: Rules Used by Readers in Assigning Pronominal Referents." *Discourse Processes* 4 (1981): 323–48.

Haviland, S. C., and H. H. Clark. "What's New? Acquiring New Information as a Process in Comprehension." *Journal of Verbal Learning and Verbal Behavior* 13 (1974): 512–21.

Just, M. A., and P. A. Carpenter. "Inference Processes during Reading: Reflections from Eye Fixation." In *Eye Movements and Higher Psychological Functions,* edited by J. W. Senders, D. F. Fisher, and R. A. Monty. Hillsdale, N.J.: Lawrence Erlbaum Associates, 1978.

Kintsch, W. *The Representation of Meaning in Memory.* Hillsdale, N.J.: Lawrence Erlbaum Associates, 1974.

Kintsch, W. "Concerning the Marriage of Research and Practice in Beginning Reading Instruction." In *Theory and Practice of Early Reading,* vol. 1, edited by L. B. Resnick and P. A. Weaver. Hillsdale, N.J.: Lawrence Erlbaum Associates, 1979.

Kintsch, W., T. S. Mandel, and E. Kozminsky. "Summarizing Scrambled Stories." *Memory and Cognition* 5 (1977): 547–52.

Lesgold, A. M., S. F. Roth, and M. E. Curtis. "Foregrounding Effects in Discourse Comprehension." *Journal of Verbal Learning and Verbal Behavior* 18 (1979): 291–308.

Mandler, J. M. "A Code in the Node: The Use of a Story Schema in Retrieval." *Discourse Processes* 1 (1978): 14–35.

Mandler, J. M., and N. S. Johnson. "Remembrance of Things Parsed: Story Structure and Recall." *Cognitive Psychology* 9 (1977): 111–51.

Meyer, B. J. F. *The Organization of Prose and Its Effect on Memory.* Amsterdam: North Holland Publishing, 1975.

Pearson, P. D. "The Effects of Grammatical Complexity on Children's Comprehension, Recall, and Conception of Certain Semantic Relations." *Reading Research Quarterly* 10 (1974–75): 155–92.

Pearson, P. D., J. Hansen, and C. Gordon. "The Effect of Background Knowledge on Young Children's Comprehension of Explicit and Implicit Information." *Journal of Reading Behavior* 11 (1979): 201–9.

Resnick, L. B. *The Science and Art of Curriculum Design* (LRDC Publication 1975/9). Pittsburgh: University of Pittsburgh, Learning Research and Development Center, 1975.

Rumelhart, D. E. "Notes on a Schema for Stories." In *Representations and Understanding: Studies in Cognitive Science,* edited by D. G. Bobrow and A. Collins. New York: Academic Press, 1975.

Rumelhart, D. E. "Schemata: The Building Blocks of Cognition." In *Theoretical Issues in Reading Comprehension,* edited by R. J. Spiro, B. C. Bruce, and W. F. Brewer. Hillsdale, N.J.: Lawrence Erlbaum Associates, 1980.

Schank, R. C. "The Structure of Episodes in Memory." In *Representation and Understanding: Studies in Cognitive Science,* edited by D. Bobrow and A. Collin. New York: Academic Press, 1975.

Smith, N. B. *Reading Instruction for Today's Children.* Englewood Cliffs, N.J.: Prentice-Hall, 1963.

Spilich, G. J., G. T. Vesonder, H. L. Chiesi, and J. F. Voss. "Text Processing of Domain-related Information for Individuals with High and Low Domain Knowledge." *Journal of Verbal Learning and Verbal Behavior* 18 (1979): 275–90.

Stein, N. L., and C. G. Glenn. "An Analysis of Story Comprehension in Elementary School Children." In *Advances in Discourse Processing,* vol. 2, *New Directions in Discourse Processing,* edited by R. O. Freedle. Norwood, N.J.: Ablex, Inc., 1979.

Stein, N. L., and T. Nezworski. "The Effects of Organization and Instructional Set on Story Memory." *Discourse Processes* 1 (1978): 177–93.

Stein, N. L., and T. Trabasso. "What's in a Story: An Approach to Comprehension and Instruction." In *Advances in the Psychology of Instruction,* vol. 2, edited by R. Glaser. Hillsdale, N.J.: Lawrence Erlbaum Associates, 1982.

Thorndyke, P. W. "Cognitive Structures in Comprehension and Memory of Narrative Discourse." *Cognitive Psychology* 9 (1977): 77–110.

Thorndyke, P. W., and F. R. Yekovitch. "A Critique of Schemata as a Theory of Human Story Memory." *Poetics* 9 (1980): 454–69.

Trabasso, T., T. Secco, and P. van den Broek. "Causal Cohesion and Story Coherence." In *Learning and Comprehension of Text,* edited by H. Mandl, N. L. Stein, and T. Trabasso. Hillsdale, N.J.: Lawrence Erlbaum Associates, 1984.

Weaver, P. A., and L. B. Resnick. "The Theory and Practice of Early Reading: An Introduction." In *Theory and Practice of Early Reading,* edited by L. B. Resnick and P. A. Weaver. Hillsdale, N.J.: Lawrence Erlbaum Associates, 1979.

The Potential and Real Achievement of U.S. Students in School Reading

ALAN C. PURVES
University of Illinois at Urbana-Champaign

"I write; let others learn to read."—Joseph Conrad

If one reads the popular writers on reading achievement and literacy in the United States, one quickly becomes aware of a series of paradoxes. Some writers will claim that there is a high degree of illiteracy among the student and adult population; others will claim almost universal literacy (Harste and Mickulecky 1984). The U.S. population as a whole is one of the highest consumers of print in the world, and book, magazine, and newspaper circulations are high (Guthrie 1981). On the other hand, the National Assessment of Educational Progress (1981*a*, 1981*b*) and some other surveys of literacy (e.g., Hunter and Harman 1979) cite appalling statistics. One of the reasons for this confusion lies in the definitions of literacy currently in use. Literacy has been variously defined as being able to read one's name, being able to read the Constitution aloud, being able to answer quite complex questions about an installment loan policy, and being able to read a philosophical novel.

Another source of confusion is the apparent failure to distinguish between reading as an activity that takes place in the home or the work site and reading as a school activity (see Shultz, Florio, and Erickson 1982). In this paper, I shall focus my attention on the latter. To make clear the distinction, an individual outside of school may purchase or borrow a novel, read it, and put it down or perhaps recommend it to a friend, saying something like, "You ought to read this; it is good." In school that statement would not be accepted as proof that the individual had read and understood the novel. Reading the novel in school involves a series of complex activities before, during, and after the reading to demonstrate something called comprehension or appreciation or understanding. The individual must be prepared to answer oral or written questions about the content, structure, or implications of the text, must be prepared to produce oral, dramatic, or cinematic reenactment of the text. In school, the student must also be prepared to read different types of text on demand, shift subject matter and style every 45 minutes or so, have the reading interrupted, and particularly read texts that deal with subjects of little interest written in styles that may be opaque or downright incomprehensible. I remember observing a class of high-school sophomores and being told that two girls "couldn't read." The class was dealing with contemporary poetry; the two girls sat in the back reading a magazine about film stars and discussing an article intelligently. They could read, but they could not or would not do school reading.

Like many other activities that occur in school, school reading has come to be a complex domain more or less related to the broader domain. The reason for this situation lies in part in schools having a special life of their own. Why and whether this should be so remains outside the scope of this paper. I shall, however, seek to define the domain of school reading and then say something about what we know of the achievement of U.S. students in relation to this domain.

The Domain of School Reading

School reading, like many other school subjects, is an activity. As Leont'ev (1973), citing Galperin, has explained, an "activity" has an independent goal of which the subject is consciously aware. Leont'ev goes on to claim that an activity comprises "acts," which usually begin as separate activities. Acts comprise "operations" about which the subject is not necessarily conscious. To take a simple example from reading instruction, for the young child decoding is an activity. Later, it becomes an act and then an operation. Even for the expert, interpreting a poem probably remains an activity. Leont'ev describes a "skill" as the ability to perform an act optimally and a "habit" the ability to perform

---

ALAN C. PURVES is a professor of English education at the University of Illinois at Urbana-Champaign. He is chairman of the International Project Council of the International Association for the Evaluation of Educational Achievement Study of Achievement in Written Composition and is the author of *Achievement in Reading and Literature: The United States in International Perspective* (National Council of Teachers of English, 1981).

an operation optimally. To these categories, I would add the term "preference" or "style" as referring to those acts or activities that the subject selects from a range of possible acts or activities.

The domain of school reading may be defined as an activity involving a number of discrete acts and preferences (see fig. 1). One may see that the figure is divided first into what is often referred to as "reading competence" and "reading preference" (or occasionally "reading performance"). The distinction is made primarily on the basis of the criteria used. Competence is usually associated with a set of standards of performance to which a number of observers can agree. There may indeed be a national consensus, although as I have indicated earlier, such consensus has not been reached in the United States. Preferences, on the other hand, appear to be desired behaviors, but the standards are either vague or idiosyncratic. They usually refer to what the student "will do" as opposed to what the student "will be able to do." Often, too, they remain unmeasured except at a descriptive level; they are hardly used to determine the academic success or failure of the student, although they may have diagnostic value. Nonetheless they are often seen as constituents of the "good reader" and are cited as curricular goals (Purves 1971). A good school reader, for example, will choose to read writing of quality and will avoid "trash."

As one moves to the next level of specificity, one sees that reading competence comprises three distinct acts: the acquisition of knowledge, the application of certain processing skills, and the use of certain analytic techniques. Each of these may be connected to a major approach to verbal comprehension: the "knowledge-based," the "bottom-up," and the "top-down" (Sternberg, Powell, and Kaye 1982). Although these approaches have had their partisans, Sternberg et al. argue that they are complementary, and common sense would tend to support that argument. It is apparent that to read any text, particularly literary texts, a reader needs to bring to bear background knowledge, reading skills, and comprehension strategies (Purves 1971).

Preference also is composed of two complementary activities, what one might call habits while reading and preferred styles in discourse about reading. The first group includes such operations as developing and adjusting rate to suit the text and the task. A good reader does not read a poem in the same fashion or with the same speed as might be used with a novel. Similarly a good reader will adjust rate for a mathematics text and a history text. In addition to rate, the good reader may also automatically change the method of marking a text; a history text might call for the use of a highlighter, a mathematics text the use of paper and pencil. Reading interests might be said to belong to this group of behaviors as well, for school reading demands

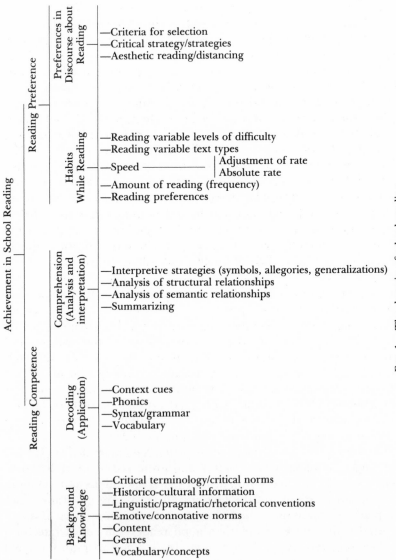

FIG. 1.—The domain of school reading

a shared taste, what might be called a middle-brow culture as expressed in the kinds of reading students should habitually select when given the opportunity.

Preferred styles in discourse refers to the kinds of talk or writing about a text that students are called upon to perform and that they later choose to perform voluntarily (Purves 1971). By the end of secondary school, a student is expected to be able to read a literary text aesthetically (Rosenblatt 1978)—that is, to enter into a "transaction" with the text under the terms of which contemplation rather than subsequent action reigns supreme. At the same time, readers are not to become so involved personally with the text that they cannot view it as an object; readers are to develop the role of the "spectator" rather than the "participant" (Applebee 1978). Furthermore, readers are expected to talk or write about the text in certain specified ways—to talk about meaning or theme and about how theme and meaning are presented, for example, or to talk about the historical background of the text (Purves, Foshay, and Hansson 1972). If such is true of language classes, I suspect similar results would be obtained in talking about science reading or history reading. Those texts are not to be read aesthetically. These sets of preferences constitute what Stanley Fish (1980) has called being a member of "an interpretive community." Communities also have shared perceptions, predilections, and language. By sharing these preferences, readers may discuss texts with one another; interpretive communities may be as small as a single class, or they may be broader, encompassing a type of classroom or an entire society.

I have said earlier that competence and preference are intertwined. Evidence for this assertion comes from the finding of survey research in achievement in literature that students at the end of secondary school who share the approach to a text that is favored by teachers are also the students who perform best on a measure of the comprehension of texts. The good reader, it would appear, simultaneously learns the "approved" questions to ask when discussing or writing about a text (Purves, Harnisch, Quirk, and Bauer 1981). Again, I would argue that the style of discourse would mark the good reader in history or science.

The Role of Knowledge

Having moved from the general activity of school reading to its constituent acts, one can begin to break these acts down further to the specific acts and operations that underlie the broader activities. Perhaps one can illustrate these activities best by examining the various acts and operations that would constitute a good reader's reading of a particular text. I shall illustrate by using as examples a poem that has frequently appeared in the secondary school curriculum, the sonnet by John Keats, "On First Looking into Chapman's Homer," and an excerpt from *The National Geographic* (Grove 1976, p. 175).

> Much have I travell'd in the realms of gold,
> And many goodly states and kingdoms seen;
> Round many western islands have I been
> Which bards in fealty to Apollo hold.
> Oft of one wide expanse had I been told
> That deep-brow'd Homer rules as his demesne;
> Yet did I never breathe its pure serene
> Till I heard Chapman speak out loud and bold:
> Then felt I like some watcher of the skies
> When a new planet swims into his ken;
> Or like stout Cortez when with eagle eyes
> He star'd at the Pacific—and all his men
> Look'd at each other with a wild surmise—
> Silent, upon a peak in Darien.

Astride a gleaming motorcycle, Felipe Brillembourg roared into a dawn filled with the hum and smog of Caracas traffic. Ahead lay a busy day: four hours of teaching engineering at Simon Bolivar University; a planning session for a graduate program; a meeting with an industrial group to form a new chemical company; consultation with his stockbroker.

At 25, the sixth-generation descendant of Dutch immigrants to Venezuela finds it easy to become involved in matters of national development, for his is a nation thirsting for technical skills. "There is terrific challenge for young people here," he had told me.

At the same time that Felipe was weaving his way through the bumper-to-bumper snarl of the *autopista,* a Yanomamo Indian was padding along a forest path near the headwaters of the Orinoco River. A tapir had been sighted near the village of Hasubowateri, and its 300-pound bulk would feed many families.

The Indian's hand gripped a palm-wood bow and three seven-foot arrows made of cane, and his eyes scanned the dense foliage as he ran along the path. Raiders from another village were expected, and ambush is the accepted method of warfare among these forest people. The Yanomamo tongue has no words for "national development."

It has long been known that, in order to read a text, a person must know the words in the text. Various research studies have indicated that a person needs to know about 75 percent of the words in order to get a general idea of a passage and 90 percent of the words in order to answer more specific questions. In both passages there are words that appear a bit more incidental to the reading than others; "Darien" need simply be recognized as a place name, and a "tapir" as an animal. "Apollo" is probably more crucial to construing the meaning, although one could figure out that he must be the god of poets, but to figure that out the reader must know the meaning of both "bards" and "fealty." In addition to the words, however, a good reader would appear to have to know something about genres, at least that Keats's poem is a poem; if the reader knew that it was a Petrarchan sonnet, the reader would also know that the division of thought will occur after the eighth line. Similarly, if a reader knew that paragraphs represented units of meaning in prose, the reader might be better able to see that the paragraphs in the Grove passage establish a structural relationship of ideas.

Whether one needs to know something of the content of a passage before reading the passage has been discussed extensively, but it appears clear from recent research that some prior knowledge is indeed helpful. To know something about South America, if not Venezuela, helps a reader deal with the prose piece, just as knowing that Chapman was a translator of Homer helps with the sonnet. In neither case does the text provide that information; it assumes it. As Updike remarked in an interview, "I trust the reader's head to have something in it."

In addition to specific content in the text, the reader of literature often needs to have some historico-cultural information. It is not enough to know that Homer was a poet; a reader needs to know that Homer was considered the first great poet and that his epics have influenced virtually all European poets. Similarly, one needs to know something of the history of exploration in the New World. It is less important to know that Keats's poem was written shortly after the discovery of the planet Uranus. It is probably also less important to know something of Keats's life and his lack of education, particularly his lack of Greek, which set him apart from most of his contemporary poets.

In addition to knowing the denotation of words, a reader needs to know the connotative value of words. "Astride a gleaming motorcyle" suggests opulence and power, and Brillembourg is to be seen as someone quite different from a Hell's Angel. "Hum and smog" and "bumper-to-bumper snarl" also help to help create an image of the city that contrasts with the single Indian with his three arrows. Knowledge of connotation also aids the reader of the sonnet, particularly when dealing with the dead metaphor "eagle eyes." Most connotations are a matter of norm or convention that a writer is relatively sure a reader shares.

As important as these conventions are, even more so, perhaps, are the grammatical and syntactic conventions that writers also assume readers know. Both passages use inverted structures, for example, which might be confusing to a reader who did not know that the subject may follow the verb in a declarative sentence.

School reading also assumes a shared knowledge of certain meta-linguistic terminology. Included in this category relevant to these two passages might be terms like "noun," "verb," "sentence," "paragraph," "comparison," "cause-effect," "foot," "line," "metaphor," "image," "symbol," and "sonnet." Some have also argued that, to read a poem, a person also needs a fairly good knowledge of phonetic, grammatical, and syntactic linguistics (Laff 1984). These terms and the concepts behind them occur frequently in tests, even tests of reading comprehension given in junior high schools. The possession of these terms and concepts aids the reader in discourse about the text, if not in actually comprehending the text.

It would appear then that a fair burden of knowledge rests on the shoulders of a good school reader. Many times that knowledge is presumed by teachers and evaluators. As we shall see later, it is the lack of this knowledge that lies beneath the relatively poor performance of students in the United States. Although people read to acquire knowledge, it seems appropriate to venture that much more knowledge goes into reading a text in school than emerges from it.

Skills and Abilities

Much of the knowledge that has been acquired is transformed into a skill that is applied to a text, such as decoding the text. One applies one's knowledge of vocabulary, morphology, and grammatical and syntactic conventions to the text at hand. It is the use of this knowledge that underlies the act of using context to determine meaning. For example, a reader uses phonetic knowledge to sound out "autopista," morphological knowledge to determine that it is a compound word, vocabulary knowledge to recognize "auto," grammatical knowledge to determine that it is a noun, syntactic knowledge to determine that it is connected to "bumper-to-bumper snarl." All of this can be used to derive an approximate meaning of the word without ever having seen the word before.

This set of skills forms the focus of reading instruction in the first two or three years of school, wherein each of the acts becomes an activity. In the later years another set of skills becomes the focus, those directed at what has been called comprehension or the derivation of meaning from a text. "Meaning" itself is a multivalent term and has occasioned a great deal of scholarly debate (Purves 1979). It is used to describe the paraphrasable content of a text, the author's intention in writing the text, the consensual interpretation derived by experts, and the average interpretation of a large number of readers and any consensual reading by a designated group (Fish 1980; Wellek and Warren 1956). E. D. Hirsch (1976) distinguishes between meaning and significance, which is what an individual reader "takes away" from the text (or brings to it), and asserts that meaning and significance include not only ideational but emotive and aesthetic aspects.

When a reader derives or makes meaning, the reader both follows certain strategies and applies various schemata to the text. These schemata, also referred to as conventions and frameworks, concern both the content and form of the text, so that a reader will relate the text to previous knowledge of people in Latin America or in developing countries generally or to previous knowledge of sailing, geography, and poets. But the reader will also relate the text to previous knowledge of such structures as comparison-contrast or sonnets and metaphorical relationships. In school reading, such application of schemata becomes an activity, and there is practice in the application of these schemata— what is often referred to as analysis or critical reading. In class, for example, students reading the Grove passage might be asked to discuss the relationship between the first two and second two paragraphs, to note the points of similarity and contrast. In a literature class, students might be asked to look at the rhyme scheme of Keats's sonnet and at the relationship between octave and sestet, as well as to determine what words in the octave indicate that the poet is talking about reading rather than sailing. In an advanced class, they might be expected to note that the word "silent" contains all the major phonemes in the rest of the poem and thus epitomizes the meaning and tone of the poem (Hymes 1958). In either class, students will probably be asked for a summary or paraphrase of the text, to present what is usually referred to as the main idea.

In literature classes, students will also be asked for the underlying theme of the text. When they respond, they will be called on to apply a different set of schemata and a set of strategies that ask them consciously to look at certain phenomena—such as the point of view of the writing, the use of repetition or contrast, the prominence of certain words or phrases, the relation of text to title—and to determine their allegorical or symbolic import. In so doing, they relate the concrete data of the text to an abstraction or to a set of conventions. A student reading a beast fable would be expected to relate the figure of the wolf, for example, to a conventional set of attributes about wolves (greed, viciousness, treachery) and to conclude that the wolf is not an animal but a "shorthand" representation of these characteristics. A reader interpreting the *National Geographic* passage would not have these conventions, but might be expected to see that the two people are both hunters and individual entrepreneurs. A reader interpreting the sonnet, might be expected to talk about the aesthetic experience, which is the theme of the poem, and about the thrill of discovery that can occur when one reads a masterwork.

As one can see, in school, reading a text—either a literary or a nonliterary text—involves a large number of acts and operations, many of which are treated as activities at various points of the curriculum. It is expected that students will become skilled in these various acts so that reading texts and then either talking or writing about them become skills. But there is more to school reading than skill.

Habits and Preferences

Students have to read a great deal in school. Reading is part of every subject area from mathematics to physical education, and students must read thousands of pages during a school year. They are also expected to read voluntarily—to use the library, join book clubs, read books rather than watch television. In short, they not only must read as a part of the job of being a student but they have to like it and become "lifelong readers" or "recreational readers," two terms often used in school objectives. More than that, they must develop the capacity both to increase the absolute rate of their reading so that they can read a 300-page novel in a day and to vary the rate of their reading according to the type of text. At the secondary school level, a long assignment in history might be 60 pages; a long assignment in mathematics might be one page. Both are to take equal amounts of time; what distinguishes them are the propositional structure of the text material, the operations and length of time the reader is to remember the content, and the amount of specific information to be remembered.

Not only must students acquire these variations in rate, but also be able to shift from one text type to another on demand. Students must shift subjects every 45 minutes or so and in switching must also adjust their reading rates and the types of comprehension skills required. In moving from a poetry class to a social studies class, for example, they might have to move from an atmosphere where reading a text with metaphors is seen as one of the virtues of the text to an atmosphere where reading such a text is to awaken a sense that metaphors are signs of propaganda.

Yet another kind of habit that students are to develop is "the reading habit" and more particularly the habit of reading more difficult texts and texts that bespeak a middle-brow if not high-brow culture. We know that students' reading interests and preferences change as they pass through school from fiction to nonfiction, from childish characters to adult characters (Purves and Beach 1972; Purves et al. 1972). We do not know, however, the causes of such changes, whether they result from maturation or instruction. One suspects a bit of both, for "good" readers, those who score well on reading tests, have different preferences than their age mates. Such differences probably result from increased performance, which enables readers to seek out more mature texts.

I have said that good students read more difficult texts, but this simplification hides the fact that we really know little of what constitutes the difficulty of a text. Difficulty at times appears to be lexical, syntactic, cohesive, propositional, structural, tonal, symbolic, or a combination of these. Keats uses more complex syntax than does Grove, but he does signal the propositional relationships and Grove does not. Keats uses metaphor and simile; Grove uses symbol. Keats uses rhyme and meter; Grove uses phrasal repetition. I emerge with a vague sense that the sonnet is more "difficult" for a secondary school student than the prose passage, but probably because it is a less familiar genre and it builds on allusion. Nonetheless, I cannot derive nor have others derived an adequate calculus of text difficulty, although Baten (1981) has come closer than most. Still, school readers are expected to read and to discourse about texts that are arranged in some order of difficulty.

The mention of discourse leads to the area of preferred styles that a school reader is expected to develop. Because so much of what is done with school reading involves simultaneous or subsequent discourse, a student inevitably learns some preferred modes and topics of discourse (Purves et al. 1972, 1981). These include what are referred to as response preferences and as explicit criteria for judging or selecting a text, although the two are somewhat intertwined. Based on a content analysis of student writing about literary texts, Purves and Rippere (1968) were able to derive a set of measures to determine what approaches to a writing about a text students preferred. The results of the investigation showed that, although the text determined to a certain extent what questions a school reader raised, by the end of secondary school, students in the United States and other countries had developed a "style of response" that was independent of the text. The style of response was clearly related to the country in which the student lived and to the style of response preferred by the teacher. This finding clearly supports the claim that readers become members of interpretive communities (Fish 1980), which may be as small as a single classroom, but tend to have certain common elements across classrooms that suggest a consensus of communities within a country.

As an aspect of style of response, students tend to learn that certain criteria for selecting texts are preferred. These criteria are not necessarily what they apply in selecting their reading material, but they are aware of the standards of the community that calls one kind of literature trash and another kind classical. They also become able to say something of why trash is called trash and what characteristics might pertain to a classic.

The final sort of preferred styles that is acquired in school might also perhaps be classified as a habit. It is the capacity to enter into what Louise Rosenblatt (1978) has called an "aesthetic transaction" with a text. Rosenblatt distinguishes between "aesthetic" and "efferent" reading, the latter implying that the reader will take something away from the text and that the text is instrumental, whereas the former implies that the reader and that the text is an end. Efferent reading is demanded in most science and social science classes, but not in literature class. The reader in this case is involved with the text and aware of its form as well as its content and seeks to bear away little save the memory of the experience. At the same time, school literature reading demands that the reader also act as critic, that the reader must create a distance from the next so as to talk about the text apart from the experience of reading it. Applebee (1978) refers to this as the "spectator role," following terminology used by Harding (1962). In literature class, the reader is expected not only to experience the text but to perform certain intellectual operations with respect to the text and the experience (Purves 1980). The reader, then, becomes a conscious critic. And in becoming a critic, the reader must bring to a level of conscious activity many of the acts and operations that had become skills and habits. School reading, particularly the reading of literature, then, is a cycle of operations, acts, and activities that form an almost Gordian knot.

The Relation of Growth and Instruction to Achievement in School Reading

Having seen that reading in school is a complex activity, before one can comment about achievement, one needs to examine those acts and operations in the activity that form a part of instruction. It may be that some aspects of reading achievement will ineluctably occur whether a person is specifically instructed in their use or not. Others appear to result from explicit training, and still others may appear to follow from the acculturation that is schooling, what Broudy (1973) calls the interpretive and associative uses of learning. They are acquired as the result of an individual's participating in the workplace that is school. As we examine these issues, we see achievement in reading has been portrayed by people having different psychopedagogical approaches. I would argue that each of the three approaches is a partial view of the situation.

Reading Achievement as Growth

From our earlier survey of the acts of reading, we can deduce that individuals will change in some of these acts simply as a result of growing up and being in the world. Much of the knowledge of the content of reading texts is acquired outside of the classroom, through exposure to realia, television, and other media. Some, of course, may be explicitly taught in various classes, but much is not. I would suspect that only a small portion of the content of the Grove passage would have been learned in school, yet the author and the editors of *National Geographic* can assume much of that knowledge by their readership (which, of course, is restricted to people who one might expect to have the knowledge).

Because much is learned outside of school, writers can prepare materials for children of different ages; they know that their school-age readers will have some knowledge of schools and vacations, that junior high school readers will be aware of sexual maturity and parent-child conflicts, that senior high-school readers will be aware of automobiles, sex, and drugs. Little of the material of "graded' texts is graded because of the curriculum of the schools, most because of the age of the readers.

Research such as that of Chomsky (1969), Loban (1963), and Strickland (1962) has shown that as children mature so does their working knowledge of certain grammatical and syntactic structures. Again, school appears to play a minor part in the acquisition of such knowledge. Although none of the studies looked at unschooled children, most imply that what was learned was not consciously taught. School also plays a relatively small role in the acquisition of a speaking vocabulary, and possibly a small role in the development of a reading vocabulary after a person begins to read voluntarily, although there is little research evidence to support or deny this assertion. It would also seem probable that a knowledge of the connotations of words is also gradually acquired through experience.

97

What appears to result most clearly from growing up is reading preference, followed by the ability to assume the spectator role. The various reading interest studies clearly indicate changes in preference as students become older and an increased differentiation of the preferences of boys and girls (Purves and Beach 1972). That this is not the result of schooling would seem to follow from the universality of the changes across language and cultures (Purves et al. 1972). School probably has some influence on preferences, but it tends to be localized (VanNord 1980). Similarly, children seem to grow into the spectator role without the benefit of instruction (Applebee 1978). Applebee attributes this shift to the general loss of egocentrism as suggested by Piaget (1926/1962).

It would seem, then, that some aspects of reading achievement and some of the differences observed between younger and older readers are simply a function of growing up. As one grows up, one loses some of the naiveté of the very young reader; despite the attempts of some educational reformers of the late 1960s to hold on to that one aspect of naiveté—the participant role—it too simply dwindles away. Only by a great effort on the part of certain writers of fiction and the acquiescence of readers can it be regained (Cott 1983).

Reading Achievement as the Development of Skills

Most commonly, people in reading education see achievement in reading as the development of skills, from the decoding skills to the skills of comprehending and interpreting texts of varying difficulty. One of the strongest adherents of this view is Jeanne S. Chall, who, in a recent article (Chall 1983, p. 5), attributes most of the changes in performance to instructional practices—"an earlier start, more and earlier phonics, harder basal readers grade for grade, more home instruction, more help to those who needed it, and the like." It would seem clear that most children do receive phonics instruction in school and are taught a sight vocabulary, how to use context clues, and about syntactical and structural complexity—or at least presented with increasingly complex materials. Students are also presented with a variety of content and a lesser variety of text types, particularly after they leave elementary school and are asked to decode those texts and to say something about what they mean.

All of these we can think of as skills that are consciously taught or sequenced so that students will become more proficient in using them. At the same time, these skills have been and are adapted to the level of maturity of the student—or to an assumed level of maturity based on readability formulas—so that students become increasingly adept at dealing with texts presumed to be at their level or a little bit above or below it. The curriculum offers "graded" materials and asks the students to practice the same set of operations over and over again, with the change being only in the level of material, not in the nature of the mental acts and operations assigned. Then in the secondary school there tends to be a shift to a different—or at least a modified—set of acts and activities. At this point "critical reading," interpretation, and analysis of text materials, particularly in literature becomes a staple of instruction in literature classes and less so in social studies.

Achievement as the Development of Discourse and Interpretative Strategies

In secondary school the focus of reading instruction changes, and so too does the notion of achievement that reading becomes almost co-terminous with literature. Achievement in reading becomes less a matter of skill balanced by maturity than it does the matter of placing into operation of set of taught strategies of discourse about what has been read. The strategies involved in the derivation of meaning and the analysis of texts included instruction in certain metalinguistic terms, such as the names of genres and structures as well as terms like "plot," "character," "act," "scene," or "personification." The students are asked to recognize these terms and to apply them to a variety of literary texts. But more than label texts or parts of texts, students are asked to use these analytic tools in order to say something about the theme or "hidden meaning" of the text. In some cases, they may even be taught a set of strategies for determining the qualities of a character, defining the point of view, or determining the symbolic import of a text. More often than not, however, the instruction tends to be by example or trial and error (Purves 1980).

At the same time that students are learning these strategies with literary texts, they are learning to use different or at least modified strategies with other school texts. They are also taught—or at least they learn—to modify their habits of reading according to the subject of the text, the course, and the desired outcomes from having read the text. Most important, however, students are being taught what the appropriate forms of oral or written discourse about a text might be for different subjects. In secondary schools in the United States, for example, students in literature learn that it is most appropriate to talk about the content of the text rather than its form, to talk about the text's meaning and moral rather than its aesthetic effect (Purves et al. 1981). This situation extends to other subjects, where the rhetoric of a text is virtually ignored except in the occasional lesson or propaganda. As we shall see in the next section, they appear to learn what is expected of them when they discourse about a text, although they might not do it very well.

Achievement in school reading, then, is again a complex of acts and operations, habits, and preferences, some of which accompany maturation, but many of which are taught. There is also a shift in the instructional emphasis that occurs sometime in junior high school and that appears to cause some disjunction as to both the definition of achievement and the degree to which U.S. students fulfill those definitions.

To talk about the potential achievement in school reading by U.S. students is to raise a set of issues that have gone relatively unnoticed in educational measurement. In seeking to specify the domain more precisely, we have seen that the range of skills, habits, and preferences is large. We have seen that there is a lack of certainty as to what might constitute a difficult text. And we have seen that we are dealing with skills, habits, and preferences that might result from instruction as well as maturation. It would appear that the potential achievement of students would comprise something like the following: the capacity to decode, comprehend, and talk or write in preferred modes about a variety of texts, dealing with a variety of subjects, in a variety of genres and styles, having greater or lesser degrees of allusion to a larger body of literature, and having a variety of connotative or tonal qualities; the capacity to perform these acts and operations on demand; the willingness to perform these acts and operations both in and out of school; and the readiness to see that these acts and operations have value and that there are degrees of quality in texts that have been determined by custom. If this definition seems daunting, let me add one further thought: reading is essentially an internal act that is solitary and private; achievement in school reading demands a variety of forms of utterance and exposition concerning this internal act, so that when we measure the potential achievement of students, we are never entirely sure that we are measuring reading skill; we may be measuring expository skills.

What Is Known about the Achievement of U.S. Students in Reading

Although there have been many surveys of reading achievement in the United States, it is clear from the preceding discussion that many of these surveys have limited themselves in their definition of the domain or have not bothered to be comprehensive. Very few assessments of reading in this or other countries have paid attention to the issue of prior knowledge in the construction of measures; even fewer have sought to look at habits and preferences. Most have limited themselves to the use of a single type of measure—either the passage followed by a set of multiple-choice questions or a cloze-type exercise with a passage that has missing words or phrases that must be filled in. Both types of test tend to focus on the skills of literal reading, with very little attention given to more complex issues of comprehension. One of the reasons for this limitation is the limitation of the multiple-choice or cloze format and their inability to handle any sort of ambiguity (Purves 1971, 1981). It is quite clear from the discussion of the domain of school reading that a program of measuring achievement would be a highly complex undertaking indeed.

Only two surveys have attempted to look at the broad spectrum of achievement of students in reading and literature: the National Assessment of Educational Progress (NAEP) and the International Association for the Study of Educational Achievement (IEA) studies of reading and literature. The former has been carried out periodically since the late 1960s; the latter was carried out in 1970 and will probably not be repeated until 1990. In some ways the studies can be compared, but in other ways they cannot, primarily because of the multiple matrix sampling used in the NAEP, which has prohibited intertask correlations.

In 1981, the National Assessment of Educational Progress produced two reports on the changes in achievement in reading over the preceding decade. One report (NAEP, 1981*b*, p. iii) gave the following picture:

> Results of three reading assessments indicate that significant gains by 9-year-olds, first observed between the 1971 and 1975 assessments, continued into the third reading assessment. Performance of 13- and 17-year-olds remained relatively stable from the first to the third assessment, with 13-year-olds gaining slightly in literal comprehension while 17-year-olds declined slightly in inferential comprehension.
>
> Nationally, 9-year-olds' overall reading performance level rose 3.9 percent. They made significant gains in reference skills (4.8 percent), literal comprehension (3.9 percent) and inferential comprehension (3.5 percent).
>
> The largest gains among 9-year-olds' reporting groups occurred for black students (9.9 percent), students who reside in the Southeast (7.5 percent), those who attend schools in rural communities (6.0 percent) and those who attend schools in disadvantaged urban communities (5.2 percent).

Nationally, 13-year-olds registered a significant increase in performance in literal comprehension from the first to the third assessment.

The only significant overall gain among the 13-year-olds' reporting groups occurred for black students (4.2 percent).

Nationally, the performance level of 17-year-olds declined significantly (2.1 percent) in inferential comprehension.

Three groups at each age—students in the Southeast, blacks, and males—narrowed the gap between them and the nation, although they continue to perform below the national level.

The other report (NAEP, 1981a, pp. 1–2) presented the following summary:

What Students Can Do
1. Almost all students recognized the value and utility of reading.
2. By age 17, most read a range of materials appropriate for their age level.
3. Older students displayed stronger comprehension skills and were more versatile in writing about what they read than were younger students.
4. . By age 17, most students expressed their *initial* ideas and judgments about what they read, particularly when these involved personal reactions.
5. Older students provided more evidence to support their assertions than younger students.

Countervailing Tendencies
1. Teenagers read little for their own enjoyment, spent more time watching television than they spent reading, did not read for long periods of time and preferred movies to books.
2. About 10 percent remained unable to read even simple materials.
3. Older students displayed less commitment to reading than did younger students.
4. Very few students at any age *explained* their initial ideas and judgments through reference either to the text or to their own feelings and opinions.
5. The evidence cited by older students does not reflect effective strategies for approaching a text; explanations remained superficial and limited. The overwhelming majority of students lacked strategies for analyzing or evaluating in the interest of deepening their understanding of what they read.

The most significant finding from this assessment is that while students learn to read a wide range of material, they develop very few skills for examining the nature of the ideas that they take away from their reading. Though most have learned to make simple inferences about such things as a character's behavior and motivation, for example, and could express their own judgments of a work as "good" or "bad," they generally did not return to the passage to explain the interpretations they made.

These results from NAEP show most clearly the problem that was referred to at the end of the last section. It would appear that by age 17 a large proportion of U.S. students have the skills of reading; they tend to lack the expository writing ability that is demanded by school reading. We do not know whether this is a failure in reading or in writing. There is some evidence from a Swedish study that this difference has not been fully appreciated (Hansson 1964). In that study, using the semantic differential and an open-ended response, Hansson found no difference on the first measure between three groups of people: adults who had finished comprehensive school, university students, and university professors. The first group, however, was unable to write more than a sentence or two about their understanding of the text. The semantic differential showed these adults could read; they could not perform the activity demanded of school readers. Such seems to be the case of U.S. students at the end of secondary school. This is not a startling finding; it differs little from what I. A. Richards (1929) found among Cambridge graduates.

If we turn to the IEA studies, we find some confirming evidence for the NAEP findings (figs. 2 and 3). The comprehension scores on nonliterary and literary texts by 14-year-olds are slightly above an international mean, those of 17-year-olds below that mean. U.S. students perform about as well as the mean on measures of reading speed, but 17-year-olds rank very poorly on measures of vocabulary and interest. They do tend to evidence a great deal of personal involvement in what they read. Making international comparisons, however, is risky for means tend to hide that a range exists among national school systems of the proportion of 17-year-olds in school or retentivity. If one adjusts these mean literature scores of 17-year-olds for retentivity, one finds that U.S. students perform better than the students of most other countries in the study (fig. 4). Again, these findings corroborate the NAEP findings that our very "good" students are very good indeed.

The IEA study also examined the "response preferences" of students and found that U.S. students tended to concern themselves with symbolic meanings, themes, and moral interpretations and to a lesser extent with structure and literary devices. Their choice correlated quite highly (.50) with that of their teachers. The students in secondary school appear to be well on their way to being members of an American

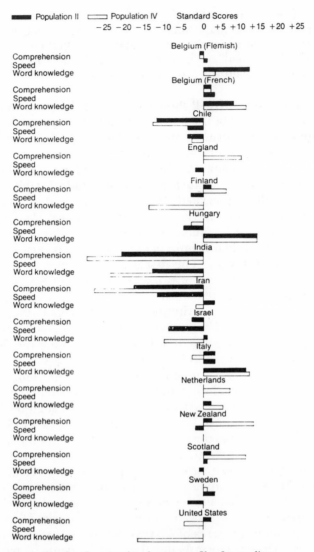

Fig. 2.—Cross-national score profiles for reading

interpretive community. Unfortunately, the IEA studies did not include an open-ended response (except for a very small subsample); therefore the issue of expository abililty cannot be determined. However, the study did look at the correlates of achievement and found that the best readers by the end of secondary school tended to be girls (particularly in literature) from high socioeconomic groups and that these students

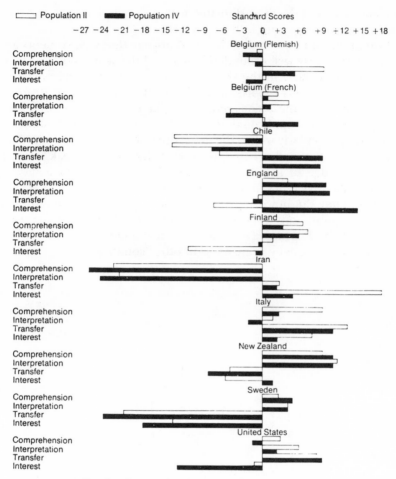

FIG. 3.—Cross-national score profiles for literature

also most closely conformed to the interpretive norms of the school, most frequently read on their own, and most frequently expressed interest in reading and literature. They also tended to watch more television than the poor readers; they seem to do more of everything.

One aspect of the IEA test that was further studied (Purves et al. 1981) was the performance of students on different item and text types. That analysis revealed that, with both nonliterary and literary texts, the most difficult items for 14-year-olds were those that required the students to use metalinguistic terms of which they had little knowledge, such as "metaphor," "cause-effect," or "comparison-contrast." These students also had the most difficulty with passages that were not narratives, again suggesting little exposure.

From both of these studies, it would appear that U.S. students are by and large fairly well grounded in many of the skills associated with reading, particularly in the skills related to understanding narrative texts. As the various reports of the Center for the Study of Reading have pointed out, these skills represent what is present in most school reading programs up through the fourth or fifth grade. U.S. students do not do particularly well in the many other aspects of school reading that we have outlined. Their word knowledge appears weak, as does their knowledge of literary terms and allusions and their ability to read diverse text types and handle the expository aspects of school reading. They do, however, seem to join the symbolic-moralistic interpretive community that has characterized U.S. readers since the landing of the Pilgrims. Nonetheless, a few quite successful readers remain, proportionally as many as in other countries.

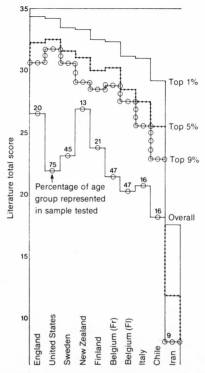

FIG. 4.—Degrees of excellence in population IV (secondary school seniors) for literature, giving the mean scores of top 1 percent, 5 percent, 9 percent, and overall group.

Conclusion

Student achievement in reading has to be seen in the context of school because that is where reading is taught, and school reading is a complex activity made up of skills, habits, and preferences, both in the activity of reading and in the various kinds of exposition about what has been read. A reader in school becomes part of a community of readers who share certain values and habits of discourse as well as habits of reading. Achievement in reading appears to result from a combination of maturation, exposure, and instruction. At the same time the real effects of school reading must be seen in what is read and what is said about what is read by the adult population.

In the United States, schools appear to do a fairly good job with some of the aspects of reading, but they seem to fail to do well with the expository aspects of school reading—at least for a majority of students. One might say that this result represents a failure on the part of the U.S. school system, but a cross-national comparison suggests that the failure is shared by most other countries. We keep our less able students in school longer than do many other countries. They do appear to learn something while they are in school, and perhaps many of them are at least awakened to the potential of school reading. It may well be too much to hope that a larger proportion of the population will become good school readers. At the same time, I believe that we should try with all of our students. Perhaps if we try harder and are more explicit about what we mean by school reading and more explicit in our teaching, we can increase the proportion.

References

Applebee, A. N. *The Child's Concept of Story: Ages Two to Seventeen.* Chicago: University of Chicago Press, 1978.

Baten, L. "Text Comprehension: The Parameters of Difficulty in Narrative and Expository Prose Texts: A Redefinition of Readability." Unpublished Ph.D. dissertation, University of Illinois at Urbana-Champaign, 1981.

Broudy, H. "Research into Image Association and Cognitive Interpretation." *Research in the Teaching of English* 7 (1973): 240–59.

Chall, J. S. "Literacy Trends and Explanations." *Educational Researcher* 12 (November 1983): 3–8.

Chomsky, C. *The Acquisition of Syntax in Children from 5 to 10.* Cambridge, Mass.: MIT Press, 1969.

Cott, J. *Pipers at the Gates of Dawn: The Wisdom of Children's Literature.* New York: Random House, 1983.

Fish, S. *Is There a Text in This Class?: The Authority of Interpretive Communities.* Cambridge, Mass.: Harvard University Press, 1980.

Grove, N. "Venezuela's Crisis of Wealth." *National Geographic* 150 (August 1976): 175–200.

Guthrie, J. Reading in New Zealand: Achievement and Volume. *Reading Research Quarterly* 17 (1981): 6–27.

Hansson, G. *Dikt i Profil*. Göteborg: Akademi-förlaget-Gumperts, 1964.

Harding, D. W. "Psychological Processes in the Reading of Fiction." *British Journal of Aesthetics* 2 (1962): 133–47.

Harste, J., and L. Mickulecky. "The Context of Literacy in Our Society." In *Becoming Readers in a Complex Society*, Eighty-third yearbook of the National Society for the Study of Education, part 1, edited by A. C. Purves and O. Niles. Chicago: National Society for the Study of Education, 1984.

Hirsch, E. D., Jr. *The Aims of Interpretation*. Chicago: University of Chicago Press, 1976.

Hunter, C. S. J., and D. Harman. *Adult Illiteracy in the United States*. New York: McGraw-Hill Book Co., 1979.

Hymes, D. "Phonological Aspects of Style: Some English Sonnets." In *Style in Language*, edited by T. Sebeok. Bloomington: Indiana University Press, 1958.

Laff, N. S. "Aesthetic Use of Language and Literary Experience: An Introductory Pedagogical Stylistics." Unpublished Ph.D. dissertation, University of Illinois at Urbana-Champaign, 1984.

Leont'ev, A. A. "Some Problems in Learning Russian as a Foreign Language." *Soviet Psychology* 11 (1973): 1–117.

Loban, W. *The Language of Elementary School Children* (Research Report No. 1). Champaign, Ill.: National Council of Teachers of English, 1963.

National Assessment of Educational Progress. *Reading, Thinking and Writing: Results from the 1979–80 National Assessment of Reading and Literature* (Report No. 11-L-01). Denver, Colo.: Educational Commission of the States, 1981. (*a*)

National Assessment of Education Progress. *Three National Assessments of Reading: Changes in Performance, 1970–1980* (Report No. 11-R-01). Denver, Colo.: Education Commission of the States, 1981. (*b*)

Piaget, J. *The Language and Thought of the Child*. London: Routledge & Kegan Paul, 1962. (Originally published, 1926.)

Purves, A. "Evaluation of Learning in Literature." In *Handbook on Formative and Summative Evaluation of Student Learning*, edited by B. S. Bloom, J. T. Hastings, and G. Madaus. New York: McGraw-Hill Book Co., 1971.

Purves, A. "That Sunny Dome: Those Caves of Ice: A Model for Research in Reader Response." *College English* 40 (1979): 802–12.

Purves, A. "Putting Readers in their Places: Some Alternatives to Cloning Stanley Fish." *College English* 42 (1980): 228–36.

Purves, A. "Competence in Reading." In *The Nature and Measurement of Competency in English*, edited by C. Cooper. Urbana, Ill.: National Council of Teachers of English, 1981.

Purves, A., and R. Beach. *Literature and the Reader*. Urbana, Ill.: National Council of Teachers of English, 1972.

Purves, A., A. W. Foshay, and G. Hansson. *Literature Education in Ten Countries*. Stockholm: Almquist and Wiksell, 1972.

Purves, A., D. Harnisch, D. Quirk, and B. Bauer. *Reading and Literature: American Achievement in International Perspective*. Urbana, Ill.: National Council of Teachers of English, 1981.

Purves, A., and V. Rippere. *Elements of Writing about a Literary Work* (Research Report 9). Champaign, Ill.: National Council of Teachers of English, 1968.

Richards, I. A. *Practical Criticism: A Study of Literary Judgment.* New York: Harcourt Brace, 1929.

Rosenblatt, L. *The Reader, the Text, the Poem: The Transactional Theory of the Literary Work.* Carbondale: Southern Illinois University Press, 1978.

Shultz, J., S. Florio, and F. Erickson. "Where's the Floor? Aspects of the Cultural Organization of Social Relationships in Communication at Home and in School." In *Children In and Out of School,* Language and Ethnography, series 2, edited by P. Gilmore and A. A. Glatthorn. Washington, D.C.: Center for Applied Linguistics, 1982.

Sternberg, R., J. S. Powell, and D. Kaye. "Comprehending Verbal Comprehension." Unpublished manuscript, 1982.

Strickland, R. "The Language of Elementary School Children: Its Relationship to the Language of Reading Textbooks and the Quality of Reading of Selected Children." *Bulletin of the School of Education, Indiana University* 38, no. 4 (Entire issue) (1962).

VanNord, J. *The Reading Interests of Gifted Students and Curriculum Adaptations in the Secondary School: A Comparison over Time* (Curriculum Laboratory Development Report No. 5). Urbana: University of Illinois, 1980.

Wellek, R., and A. Warren. *Theory of Literature,* 3d ed. New York: Harcourt, Brace, and World, 1956.

Literacy Instruction in American Schools: Problems and Perspectives

JUDITH A. LANGER
Stanford University

This examination of literacy instruction in American schools reviews studies conducted during the past 10 years in the fields of reading and writing and identifies some major themes that extend across them. These studies of instructional practice will be examined in terms of the notions of instruction that guide current practice, as well as in terms of recent notions of literacy. Recent research efforts will be reviewed in light of these views. Finally, the beginnings of an alternative view of instruction will be presented.

Notions of Literacy

While notions of literacy and what it means to be a literate individual have taken on different meanings at many points in history (Resnick and Resnick 1977), it is argued here that throughout the twentieth century the underlying views of literacy instruction seem to have remained relatively stable, as have the underlying beliefs about teaching and learning. During the first half of this century, issues in reading and writing instruction were essentially issues of curriculum: what should be taught and how to evaluate the success of that teaching. Early analyses (Davis 1944; Gates 1921; Gray 1919; Pressey and Pressey 1921; Richards 1929; Thorndike 1917) were concerned with describing the skills students lacked in order to define the skills that should be included in the curriculum. Implicit in this model was an orientation that treated the purposes guiding the reading or writing activity as essentially irrelevant. That is, the activities themselves and the work that resulted received the focus, while the functional aspects of that activity were largely ignored. Although the purposes may have remained unstated because of their perceived inherent relation to the activity, the practice activities themselves tended to become separate from the more complete and purposeful activities to which they initially belonged. At times the skills were thought to be best taught out of context, and at times within the context of larger, meaningful units of text. At times the focus was on diagnostic testing to individualize each student's program of subskill learning, and at times all students were thought to benefit from exposure to the entire developmental sequence of skill training.

Although differing in their implementation, these approaches all viewed the teacher as a provider of information. They also relied heavily on testing to determine what the students needed to know. The teacher's craft was one of knowing the range of skills, diagnosing what the students still needed to learn, providing instruction directed at the missing skills, and testing to see if the instruction had been effective.

This version of curriculum is based on an industrial metaphor (Callahan 1962) and is often accompanied by a fairly complex management plan that controls the sequence of diagnostic testing, provision of appropriate instruction, evaluation, and reteaching. The materials and activities developed to accompany such a program are structured to provide students with myriad opportunities to practice what they cannot already do. With some shifts in emphasis across the years, this version of curriculum dominated instruction throughout the first half of the twentieth century and formed the basis of the curriculum reform movement in the 1960s.

By mid-century, however, an alternative model of the nature of learning in general, and of literacy learning in particular, was beginning to emerge in studies of cognitive and linguistic development. In particular, Piaget (e.g., Inhelder & Piaget 1958) and Bruner (e.g., Bruner 1973; Bruner, Goodnow, and Austin 1956), in their studies of children's

---

JUDITH A. LANGER is an associate professor in the School of Education, Stanford University. Her research focuses on aspects of reading and writing processes and the relationships among knowledge, language, and performance in reading and writing and how these intersect with learning and instruction. She is co-author of *Reader Meets Author: Bridging the Gap*. Her second and third books, *Understanding Reading and Writing Research* and *Children's Reading and Writing: Structures and Strategies*, will be published in 1985. Langer is editor of *Research in the Teaching of English*.

conceptual development, were beginning to argue that conceptual development is characterized by gradually more sophisticated, rule-governed systems of hypotheses or representations of the world, rather than by the gradual acquisition of separately identifiable skills that do not necessarily go together when the process occurs. In the field of literacy learning, this shift toward treating the child as an active problem solver led to a shift away from the identification of isolated skills that needed to be tested and taught and toward a focus on higher order goals. This shift permitted consideration of ways in which a student's topical, structural, and pragmatic knowledge affects the processes of reading and writing. This concern with process—the interpretations made, as well as the understandings that ensue—has dominated research in both reading and writing over the past two decades, though, unlike the earlier studies of literacy, it has not yet had much effect on the world of instructional practice.

In part the detachment of this body of work from the instructional context is a function of its lack of focus on school-related tasks and problems. While the earlier work on learning grew out of instructional issues, the mid-century research focused on issues of human learning and cognition in general. Perhaps because it lacked a direct link with issues of schooling, the impact of this work on literacy instruction in schools has remained slight. The theoretical constructs do not provide models either of curriculum or of instruction; they focus on the learner, not on the teacher, and do not specify how or what to teach. "Process approaches" to both reading and writing instruction have been extrapolated from these studies and have been a major theme in the pedagogical journals, but their status as research-based constructs is at best ambiguous and, given the nature of the research base, to some extent misleading.

It has only been quite recently, with the incorporation of sociological and anthropological notions of literacy events and literacy environments into studies of learning (e.g., Cook-Gumperz, Gumperz, and Simon 1982; Heath 1983), that educational theorists and researchers have begun to reintroduce notions of context into studies of literacy learning, and thus to begin to provide a coherent framework for considering issues of literacy instruction—of teaching as well as learning. While cognitive models of literacy learning have carried us quite far from our early views of curriculum, the tension in the translation of these views into instructional models is forcing the reconceptualization of new and more encompassing models of instruction—models that can be incorporated into educational settings and make a difference.

This essay is concerned with the state of literacy instruction, broadly defined, in American schools and classrooms. It focuses on students'

113

ability to read and write for the many differing pragmatic and aesthetic purposes that reading and writing serve within our culture. Thus the concern here will be less on mastery of particular reading or writing subskills and more on the differing contexts in which students are asked to read and write as part of their school experience, as part of the subjects they study as well as in their reading or language arts classes. Some of the major studies of the current state of instruction in reading and writing will be reviewed and a description of what research has to say about classrooms, textbooks, and testing will be given as each relates to literacy instruction. Limitations inherent in current practice will be explored, and an alternative view of instruction will be suggested.

What Students Learn

Since 1969, the National Assessment of Educational Progress (NAEP) has collected information about the educational achievement of more than 1 million 9-, 13-, and 17-year-olds in reading and writing as well as other subject areas. The results of the assessments of reading and writing suggest that literacy instruction in American schools has been relatively successful, at least to the extent that success is defined in terms of the traditional basic skills (NAEP 1975, 1976, 1978, 1981*a*, 1981*b*, 1981*c*). In reading, students can respond adequately to literal and inferential questions about what they have read, and in writing they show adequate control of the mechanics of written language— grammar, spelling, punctuation, and usage. These skills are directly related to the curriculum subskills found in the early views of instruction described above; the relative success in these areas implies that students do indeed learn what we set out to teach them.

Yet if the National Assessment results suggest success with the basics, there are some disturbing undercurrents in the remainder of the results. Tasks requiring higher-level critical thinking skills remain troublesome across the age groups studied, and students' commitment to reading and writing erodes as they pass through the educational system.

These trends are highlighted in a 1981 report, *Reading, Thinking, and Writing.* (NAEP 1981*c*). This report compared student performance on a range of tasks, all based on the same reading passages. Some tasks assessed initial interpretations and lower-level understanding, usually through multiple-choice questions. Other tasks asked students to explain or defend these initial interpretations, usually in brief paragraphs. Still others assessed attitudes toward written language, either in general or in the context of specific reading selections. In a series

114

of items, students were asked to read a poem or literary passage and then to answer one multiple-choice question relating to an evaluation of that passage (whether they like it or not), their judgments of character, plot, or mood, or the emotions or feelings the text provoked. The students were then required to write a paper defending or explaining why they responded to the multiple-choice question as they had; they were told to refer to their own personal experiences as well as information in the piece they had just read to explain their responses.

The results indicated that students at all three ages assessed (9, 13, and 17) were able to comprehend a wide range of passages and form their own judgments about the work they had read. At the same time, however, they had difficulty, across all ages, examining, elaborating, or explaining their ideas. Although more than 70 percent of the students tested could answer a multiple-choice question requiring them to draw an inference about what they had read, even at age 17 only 10–15 percent could successfully write an explanation or defense of why they answered as they did. As the report (NAEP 1981c, p. 2) described the results, "Students seem satisified with their initial interpretations of what they have read and seem genuinely puzzled at requests to explain or defend their point of view. As a result, responses to assessment items requiring explanations of criteria, analysis of text or defense of a judgment or point of view were in general disappointing. Few students could provide more than superficial responses to such tasks, and even the 'better' responses showed little evidence of well-developed problem-solving strategies or critical-thinking skills."

Results concerning student attitudes were equally mixed. On the one hand, almost all students were willing, in the abstract, to attest to the general value and utility of reading and writing activities. On the other hand, the older students read little for their own enjoyment, spent more time watching television than they spent reading, and preferred movies to books. Responses on an item that asked directly about enjoyment of reading were typical of many items in the assessment. At age 9, 81 percent claimed to enjoy it "very much"; by age 17, only 42 percent still claimed to do so.

These patterns of results are consistent across a variety of assessments. As items require more critical thinking, performance tends to decline, even among the groups that usually are considered to be advantaged (Barrow, Mullis, and Phillips 1982). At the same time, students seem to grow increasingly disenchanted with the activities they are learning to master.

We can begin to understand these findings by examining some recent studies of reading and writing instruction. In general, the studies reviewed in the following section suggest that seatwork and paperwork abound, but that there is relatively little thoughtful interaction between teachers and students, between students and students, or between students and the ideas they are reading or writing about.

The Characteristics of Instruction

In a 1978 report to the Ford Foundation, Graves noted that American students are seldom asked to write. What writing there is consists of workbook exercises and drills emphasizing traditional subskills, such as penmanship, vocabulary, capitalization, punctuation, and grammar. There is similarly little emphasis on writing instruction. What passes for writing instruction is talk *about* writing—teachers do not guide students in how to *do* actual writing, nor do they encourage students to write on their own. Graves mustered a variety of sources of evidence to substantiate his claims. In a survey of 17-year-olds, for example, he found that three-quarters of them did not write anything at all in a two-week period, while in another survey of school systems reputed to stress writing, second graders averaged only three pieces of writing over a three-month period, and secondary school students wrote even less frequently.

Applebee (1981), in the most comprehensive recent study of writing instruction in secondary schools, examined the students' writing activities in each of the major academic subject areas in a national sample of schools. He reported that, although 44 percent of the observed lesson time was devoted to writing, those activities tended to require mechancial slot-filling or multiple-choice responses. Only 3 percent of class time was devoted to activities in which students were asked to write a paragraph or more, and almost all of that writing was done for purposes of examination. Patterns of emphasis in homework assignments were essentially identical. In general, extended activities with writing used as a vehicle for thoughtful explorations of the content being studied were almost never observed to occur.

In a follow-up study, Applebee (1984) and his colleagues studied teachers who had incorporated process-oriented literacy activities into their instruction in order to foster students' critical thinking about new concepts and deemphasize rote learning and recitation. Studying individual teachers over extended periods of time, the researcher found that a continuing emphasis on teaching specific content and testing to evaluate the success of that teaching undermined the usefulness of the process activities. When grades were based on the accuracy of performance, students' attention focused from the start on providing

116

a polished performance rather than on using process activities to extend their understanding of the concepts they were studying. Even in classrooms where the teachers believed in the power of writing as a tool for extending students' understanding, the students distributed their attention and interest in response to the grading system rather than in response to the teachers' stated goals. From the students' perspective, process-oriented explorations of new material were simply tasks to be completed in isolation from one another, with little perceived relationship to their final written products.

More recently, Applebee and Langer (1984) have extended this work to document the effects of using specific writing tasks to further student understanding of new concepts as part of the regular classroom curriculum. Teacher planning, classroom activity, curriculum "coverage," and patterns of student learning are being studied in high school science, social studies, home economic, and English classes, as they occur over time. Analyses of the first year's data have highlighted the complexity of instructional change. Even teachers who are deeply committed to giving students a role in their own learning, who have sought new instructional approaches, and who are committed to the notion that writing can help foster learning are guided in their teaching by what Barnes (1976) calls a "transmission" view of teaching. In this view, the role of the teacher is to be the purveyor and evaluator of ideas, and the role of the student is to be the recipient of them, with little room for the students to take an active role in interpreting or synthesizing what they are learning. The dominance of the transmission view of teaching is not surprising, since these beliefs govern educational interactions in America even at the university level; however, they leave little room for the thoughtful cogitations that lead toward reasoned learning.

While students can be active learners in many different situations, the more restricted roles, which leave the student little room for active involvement in new learning, are equally evident in the teaching of reading. Durkin (1978–79), after studying reading instruction in 24 fourth-grade classrooms, reported that almost no comprehension instruction took place; the teachers were assignment givers and checkers. Much of their teaching was in fact assessment, testing what students had understood by examining their responses to questions about the reading. Instructional time was spent giving, completing, and reviewing assignments. Durkin also examined patterns of instruction during social studies lessons, but found that none of the teachers conceived of the social studies reading as a time to focus on students' comprehension skills. Instead, the concern was for covering the content and mastering the facts.

Durkin's findings are disturbing, even if one accepts the traditional instructional model in which curriculum is based on instruction in needed skills, followed by testing. What seems to be happening in the classrooms she studied is that the *instructional* phase of that model has virtually disappeared, being replaced by an incessant cycle of practice and testing. A study by Duffy and McIntyre (1980) can be interpreted similarly. After observing six primary-grade teachers, they concluded that the teachers consistently monitored their students' reading development through the use of commercial materials and that the major "instructional" activity was to check the accuracy of pupil responses. Duffy and Roehler (1982) reach similar conclusions in a later report.

Collectively, these studies of literacy instruction suggest that teachers perceive themselves as evaluators of student learning, using brief answers to brief questions as indicators of learning. The pattern in written activities is similar to that in oral discussion, which usually proceeds through cycles in which the teacher asks a question, a pupil responds, and the teacher provides an evaluation (Duncan and Biddle 1974; Mehan 1979). Furthermore, the focus is on "coverage" of content as opposed to student learning (Barr 1973–74, 1975; Clark and Yinger 1980; Peterson, Marx, and Clark 1978), and decisions in both instruction and evaluation are dominated by an implicit belief that coverage itself in some way *constitutes* (rather than correlates with) learning.

While there have been no experimental studies to examine directly the relation between coverage and learning, the work of a number of ethnographers (e.g., Collins 1982; Cook-Gumperz, Gumperz, and Simon 1982; Erickson, 1977; Erickson and Shultz 1981; Green and Wallat 1981; McDermott 1977a, 1977b) has indicated that the classroom is in itself a sociocultural context where communication is deeply intertwined with learning. Their work suggests that coverage needs to be considered in terms of *how* the student engages in the activity as well as its scope and frequency. Furthermore, their work indicates that literacy instruction is differentially determined by *who* the students are. The restricted teacher and student roles described above by definition limit personal interaction and instructional dialogue; classroom routines proceed on the basis of brief and inherently predetermined responses (Collins 1982; Mehan 1979). The growing body of ethnographic studies suggests the need for literacy instruction to account for the differing language and world views that students and teachers bring to school and the particular language they use to convey their ideas to others; the communicative aspects of the learning environment play an important role in the instructional enterprise.

Instructional Models in Textbooks

Textbooks and their accompanying exercise materials play a prominent role in the traditional model of literacy instruction; they are one of the major sources of instructional and practice exercises and often provide series of unit mastery tests for the assessment phase of the instructional cycle. Recent studies of textbook material make clear the limited nature of the roles they envision for teacher and student alike.

After completing the classroom study discussed earlier, Durkin (1981) examined the suggestions for comprehension instruction in the teachers' manuals that accompanied five major basal reading series. Findings were similar to those from her classroom observation study; the manuals gave more attention to assessment and practice of comprehension skills than to direct and explicit instruction. Although they briefly alluded to procedures for teaching comprehension, they provided the teacher with little to help students learn how to go about it. Based on these analyses, Durkin attributed the dismal findings of her classroom study to the absence of more overt instructional models in the teachers' manuals. The model of instruction used by the basal readers, she suggested, is based on the belief that children learn by practice rather than by receiving effective explanations and instruction.

Beck, Omanson, and McKeown (1982), after analyzing a number of basal reading texts and suggested lesson structures (Beck, McKeown, McCaslin, and Burkes 1979), redesigned a number of third-grade reading lessons to include more content-oriented prereading preparation, accompanying pictures, and questions interspersed after each silent reading section. Their revisions were based on their views that prior topic knowledge aids comprehension, as does the highlighting of central content. They identified the key concepts and designed activities to activate or present these concepts before the students were asked to read the passages. Structured reading units were separated by activities designed to focus on key or upcoming events. Questions asked after each structured reading unit were designed to help the readers develop their own story maps. Both the revised and control lessons were given to 24 third graders each. Their findings suggest that comprehension benefited most from activities that helped students focus on their own knowledge and that required their active involvement in the information-building process, in contrast to the types of activities suggested in the teachers' manuals.

Similarly, Langer (1981, 1982, 1984a) developed a prereading activity at the request of teachers who found teachers' manuals inadequate in helping them bridge the gap between their students' knowledge and the material being presented in their textbooks. Langer's activity integrates instructional assessment with prereading instruction and sets the teacher's role as one of listening carefully to what students say and creating conditions under which their text-related knowledge is brought to awareness and applied. Teachers are told how to select key concepts contained in a text, how to elicit knowledge about those concepts, and how to evaluate the extent of student understanding based on the responses given. Furthermore, information about how to structure class dialogue to help students access or gain topic knowledge is also provided. This activity, involving active dialogue between teacher and student (Langer 1984*a*), was found to raise available background knowledge significantly and, in turn, to improve comprehension of moderately difficult material.

The writing assignments found in student texts call for no more student involvement than do the suggested reading activities. Applebee (1984) examined high school textbooks to learn about the kinds of writing tasks students are asked to do after they have read an assignment. Ten trained raters rated the activities in the three most popular ninth- and eleventh-grade textbooks in seven separate subject areas. Across a variety of analyses, Applebee found that the majority of activities required only word- and sentence-level skills and could be answered by rote repetition from material presented in the textbook. Activities requiring the text-level language skills necessary for connecting ideas or developing extended arguments were minimal. Restricted writing activities (fill-in-the-blank and multiple-choice) abounded, and, even when extended writing was solicited, it was generally optional rather than required. While a variety of restricted writing activities were used, Applebee found that across subject areas the short-answer exercise requiring anywhere from a phrase to a two-sentence response was the most frequent. Simple copying exercises played an important part in business education texts, while the emphasis in foreign-language texts was divided among manipulation of syntactic constructions, responding to comprehension questions, and comprehension drill requiring responses of two sentences or less. The range of extended writing tasks was limited, with few suggestions for personal or imaginative writing. As in his study of classroom writing assignments, Applebee found that the predominant audience in textbook assignments was the teacher in the role of examiner; no more than 1 percent of the exercises provided a wider audience for student writing. In general, Applebee suggests that the writing experiences provided in high school textbooks are even more narrow and limiting than the assignments observed in his studies of actual classroom practice.

Beyond the limited range of activities that textbooks provide, a number of studies have suggested that textbook passages are poor models of writing (Gilliland 1972; Kintsch and Vipond 1979; Redish 1979); the texts do not comply with either micro- or macrostructural conventions typical of their genre and are therefore poor models for either writing or reading. In particular, Anderson, Armbruster, and Kantor (1980) suggest that subject-area textbooks are "written by committee"; they are not written by someone who wishes to share a body of known information with the reader. This feature, in addition to the desire to include certain critical points of "curriculum" information and to comply with certain readability formulas, leads to a text that is difficult to read. Information tends to be presented in dense lists, without benefit of the elaboration necessary to make a point or provide a context. Armbruster and Anderson (1982) developed generic text structures that are appropriate for historical discourse on topics generally included in social studies texts. Their historical structure follows the story grammar form of goal, plan, action, and outcome. It is their assumption that a textbook explanation of a historical event consists of a response to questions associated with each of the slots. For example, one instantiation of the structure they describe looks like this:

> During the 1670's, several English colonies were founded along the coast of North America. The first permanent settlement was Jamestown, established in 1607 in what now is Virgina. The second Plymouth, was set up in 1620 in what now is Massachusetts.
> These settlements were primarily commercial ventures, undertaken in the hope that the settlers might raise the products England had to import from the East and thus make the mother country more self sufficient. Commercially the North American colonies were disappointing; few of the original investors got their money back, to say nothing of making profits. [Armbruster and Anderson 1982, p. 8]

The goal, Armbruster and Anderson state, is in the fourth sentence: to become self-sufficient. That same sentence also contains the plan, signaled by "in the hope that." The action is stated in the first sentence, the third and fourth sentences are elaborations of the action, and the outcome is in the fifth sentence. In evaluating three textbook segments using this analysis, they found that two of the three did not meet their criteria for instantiation. In all three cases the events were described in detail, but the main ideas and explanations were largely missing.

Bruce, Rubin, and Starr (1981) suggest that readability formulas are at best unhelpful, and at worst detrimental, to both teaching and learning; they cause writers to distort the texts they write and cause

121

teachers to make inaccurate decisions about student/text matches. Furthermore, tailoring apparently difficult texts to fit readability formulas may increase text difficulty by multiplying the number of inferences the reader must make (Davison, Kantor, Hannah, Hermon, Lutz, and Salzillo 1980). Instead of these text-based notions of readability, Rubin (1981) argues for the notion of conceptual readability; this focuses less on text characteristics such as sentence length and word length and more on how the concepts are presented. While syntax, word length, and vocabulary have been shown to affect text difficulty, more recent views of reading comprehension suggest that ease of comprehension is also a function of the reader's knowledge and experiences, the topic, the construction of the text, and the contextual variables that affect and are affected by the purpose for reading and the environment surrounding the reading experience. These factors call for a more complex, multivariate model for assessing text difficulty.

The Limitations of Tests

As we have seen, testing plays an integral part in the model of curriculum that dominates in most classrooms. Test construction is generally guided by what the test writers think *should* be taught; tests are used to diagnose the knowledge already attained and to identify what to teach next, as well as to evaluate the success of the teaching (and the need for re-teaching). Evaluation of student learning is deeply embedded in the exercises and activities that accompany textbooks, examined in the previous section. In addition, schools and districts tend to rely on formal testing programs to monitor educational progress and evaluate the effectiveness of educational programs. In a national study of testing in the schools, Dor-Bremme and Herman (1983) found that in elementary schools, 5 percent of available instructional time was devoted to testing as compared with 19 percent of the time in secondary schools. Principals were most influenced by standardized norm-referenced tests (as opposed to teacher-made tests) for use in communicating with parents and monitoring achievement in their schools. In secondary schools, standardized tests were also used for class placement, though teachers reported they had more confidence in their own judgments than in the results of the testing program. Both teachers and principals regarded mandated standardized tests as less useful than teacher-made tests and classroom observation data as a basis for making judgments about student achievement. While these findings could be interpreted as reason to consider discontinuation of standardized test use, it is more helpful to interpret them as a call for major reform of the content and goals of standardized tests, as a mandate to develop tests that more closely reflect the curriculum goals of today, based on the complex understandings of reading comprehension supplied by the past 10 years work in discourse theory (see Langer [1984*b*] for elaboration of this issue).

Other investigators have begun to question the validity of standardized tests as measures of achievement. Royer and Cunningham (1978) suggested a notion of "minimal comprehension" that views reading as a constructive process that necessarily involves an interaction between the reader's knowledge and the ideas presented in the text. With this notion in mind, they concluded that most reading comprehension tests do not distinguish between lack of background knowledge and lack of skill; therefore these tests are unable to meet the purposes the tests set for themselves. While there no doubt is a correspondence between lack of knowledge and lack of skills, the tests, as they are presently constructed, cannot tease apart these critical components.

Also focusing on reader knowledge, Applebee (1971) and Tuinman (1974) independently showed that successful performance on reading comprehension tests is not necessarily attributable to having understood the test passages; many of the items on standardized tests of reading comprehension can be answered simply on the basis of the reader's knowledge. It is possible to receive acceptable scores on some reading tests without reading the test passages at all.

Even when students do read the passages, it is unclear that the skills required are those drawn on in other reading situations. Langer (1984*b*; in press), in a text semantic analysis of multiple-choice standardized reading comprehension tests, has shown that the language and structure of reading test items create a host of unusual cognitive demands on readers who are attempting to understand a passage and select appropriate responses to test items. She concluded that test items tend to be a genre unto themselves and make performance demands that are not generalizable to other reading situations. Her analyses reaffirm that test results cannot be used to understand the comprehension abilities of individual students; although there is a correlation between standardized test scores and the ability to process text successfully, the tests neither measure the processes involved in the development of meaning from text nor do they evaluate a reader's ability to manage those processes.

Furthermore, the theoretical constructs used in the development of test items are heavily text based and do not reflect ways in which readers' text understanding develops or how this understanding is used when readers answer questions about what they have read. One curious consequence is that, although readers will usually try to answer a question by reasoning from their integrated understanding of a passage they have read, test questions meant to be easier often force them to resort to lower-level problem-solving skills that do not reflect their general comprehension at all. Take the following test passage from the Gates-MacGinitie Primary C, Form 1, reading test as an example.

> If a bronco buster wants to win a rodeo contest, he must obey the contest rules. One of these rules is that the rider must keep one hand in the air. A rider who does not do this will be disqualified.
> 1. A bronco buster who ignores the rules is
>   1) skillful 2) disqualified 3) chosen 4) winner

In the study, the students were asked to read the question stem, to anticipate a response without seeing any of the four choices, and then to choose among them. This was meant to be a literal question, presumably easy for students to answer because it is based on information directly stated in the text. However, Langer found that 67 percent of the students answered from their final understanding of the passage, the text world they had developed throughout the reading of the passage. All of the students in Langer's study (third graders) ended the passage with an envisionment of someone riding something, with one hand in the air and holding onto something; this was apparent when they were asked to "act out" what was happening in the passage. They used this knowledge as the basis for their response to the test question, whether or not they got the question right. Thus they explained, "He's disqualified 'cause he just ignores the rules," and "That's what happens; you get kicked out if you don't obey the rules." Similarly, another explained in justifying "winner," "If you don't follow the rules, you'll cheat and have a better chance to win." The remaining students (33 percent) explained their answers by a simple visual match, pointing to the "disqualified" in the text, even though they did not know what the word meant.

Those students who returned to the text to answer the question relied simply on the visual match rather than remembering or rereading for literal meaning. Langer (1984*b*) describes a number of similar results, raising questions about ways used to describe comprehension complexity. Her findings suggest that readers do not necessarily act upon the same assumptions upon which test items are based and that specific test-taking skills that focus on word- or sentence-level matching sometimes play an unintentional role in successful performance and may in turn receive an undue emphasis in instruction.

These criticisms of standardized tests do not challenge their role as predictors of subsequent achievement; in fact, current psychometric technology is quite effective in generating tests that function well in this role. What these analyses do challenge is the role of tests in the instructional cycle, as valid measures of skills that have been developed in a preceding instructional session, or of skills that may need to be developed in a subsequent session.

To recapitulate, literacy instruction in the United States is structured around a relatively consistent notion of instruction, one that defines relatively clear roles for teacher and student. In this view, knowledge is conceptualized as a body of information to be transmitted from teacher to student; the role of the teacher is one of organizing that knowledge in as logical and efficient a manner as possible; and the role of the student is one of remembering what has been imparted. This view carries with it its own technology, to organize the knowledge to be transmitted (textbooks and accompanying exercise material), and to monitor the success of the enterprise (through unit tests and the apparatus of standardized testing).

While this view itself may leave little room for criticism, the assumptions underlying it and its operation within the classroom may well be responsible for the instructional problems identified in the studies cited above. Findings suggest that in practice, the current view of instruction is easily distorted, incorporating (1) measures of achievement that do not reflect students' mastery of the process of understanding, (2) reading materials (primarily textbooks) that are ill-structured and divorced from any real communicative intent, and (3) exercises in subskill learning that remain divorced from the broader ends the subskills were originally to have furthered. A number of characteristics of student learning can also be traced to these distortions: (4) although lower-level literacy skills seem to be well-learned, higher-level skills remain underdeveloped; and (5) students tend to be disengaged from the subject matter and from reading and writing in general.

Rather than simply a scenario of ineffective implementation of instruction, these characteristics seem to be logical outcomes of a view of instruction in which knowledge is conceptualized as separate from the meaning-laden whole and in which the relation between teacher and student is seen as one of conveying knowledge rather than mutually exploring their interpretations. This in turn leads to a search for an alternative view that is more consistent with current understanding of the process of language learning, as well as with the goals of fostering language and reasoning skills.

Toward an Alternative View of Effective Instruction

In response to findings such as those described above, Applebee and Langer (1983) and Langer and Applebee (1984) have begun to develop an alternative view of effective instruction. Their concerns are not so much with psychological models of learning as with the context of the classroom; their criticism of what they have been finding in schools (Applebee 1984) is based on the implicit models from which teachers seem to be working. These models have complex roots, some of which may be representative of major psychological models, such as Bloom's (1971) work on mastery learning, Gagne's (1977) work on the conditions of learning, or Goodwin and Klausmeier's (1975) work on facilitating student learning. However, Langer and Applebee's studies of classrooms suggest that the teachers' use of these models is erratic and may at times misrepresent the behaviors the authors intended. Rather than questioning the existing psychological models, the emerging view of effective instruction presented here is being developed for different purposes, as a "model-in-context." It posits a view of instruction that is contextually imbedded and articulates with day-to-day practice as well as with the psychological and linguistic literatures. It offers a bridge between the worlds of theory and practice. This view of instruction grows out of language learning research (cited below) sharpened by work in instructional settings; it now needs to be tested in a series of more controlled series.

The model views literacy learning as an extension of earlier child language processes and places the concomitant instructional issues within the frameworks of language learning. Studies that have analyzed the principles underlying successful instructional dialogue are the most relevant here. The notion that dialogue can function as a "scaffold" to support early language learning was developed by Bruner and his colleagues (Bruner 1978; Ninio and Bruner 1978; Ratner and Bruner 1978), who used it to examine adult/child dialogue. They described how the child learns more sophisticated language functions through supportive dialogue in which the mother extends the child's new language skills and prevents the child from sliding back to earlier forms. Wertsch, McNamee, McLane, and Budwig (1980), elaborating on the work of Vygotsky (1962, 1978), similarly focuses on the role of social interaction in the development of language and thought. Wertsch et al.'s work suggests there is a gradual internalization of the assistance provided by the adult, with the child not only responding correctly to the adult's directives but actually taking over the responsibilities of the adult in "talking through" the steps of the task. Studies such as

126

these suggest that, in language learning, the presence of a supportive dialogue allows the child to accomplish tasks that could not have been accomplished alone and, at the same time, allows the child to internalize procedures that lead toward later independent performance.

Similar to these patterns in child language development, the most successful literacy instruction observed by the Langer and Applebee project team occurred when the students and the teacher had shared understandings of the specific goals of an instructional activity, as well as a shared sense that the activity required a collaborative interaction if it was to be completed successfully (see Palinscar and Brown [in press] for a similar argument).

Applebee and Langer (1983) and Langer and Applebee (1984) have used the concept of instructional "scaffolding" as a way to examine the nature of instructional interaction. This concept can be applied to the range of instructional settings that occur in schools—from the dialogue that takes place between teacher and students to the practice activities in students' texts and workbooks. The scaffolding provided in any given situation can be more or less structured and more or less effective. The notion of scaffolding provides a framework for recognizing significant dimensions of instruction-dimensions that Langer and Applebee have described in the context of particular classrooms, and the direct effects of which can be manipulated and tested in controlled studies. This view of instruction makes it possible to separate, and separately assess, the information provided from the manner in which it is delivered in instructional settings.

The notion of instructional scaffolding builds on analyses of the characteristics of parent/child interaction that contribute to the rapid pace of early language development, adapted to the somewhat different tasks inherent in formal schooling. Applebee and Langer (1983) and Langer and Applebee (1984) have described five characteristics of instructional interaction that were critical to the success of activities in the classrooms they studied, but that were often lacking in the activities the teachers planned:

1. *Student ownership of the learning event.*—The instructional task must permit students to make their own contribution to the activity as it evolves, thus allowing them to have a sense of ownership for their work. They must develop their own reasons for participating in the activity rather than simply completing the task because it has been assigned by the teacher. The notion of ownership does not preclude the teacher's introducing an activity. The activities introduced, however, must leave the student room to make a contribution beyond simply repetition of information or ideas drawn from the teacher. For example, the assignment can provide room for the student's value judgments

or for reorganization of the content being studied: "Write a newspaper article giving critical information that you feel will be helpful for people who are deciding for whom to vote." This contrasts with an assignment that restricts the student to information previously presented by the teacher or textbook, such as, "Write an election article telling who the candidates are, the parties they represent, and their major platforms."

2. *Appropriateness of the instructional task.*—The instructional task must grow out of knowledge and skills the students already have, but must pose problems that cannot be solved without further help. The task, then, needs to be sufficiently difficult to permit new learning to occur, but not so difficult as to preclude new learning.

3. *Supportive instruction.*—Once the student and teacher understand that help is necessary, direct instruction in the form of questioning, modeling, or constructive dialogue is offered to help the student develop a successful approach to the task. The student learns new skills in the process of doing the task in a context where instruction provides the scaffolding or support necessary to make the task possible.

4. *Shared responsibility.*—The teacher's role in the instructional event needs to be more collaborative than evaluative. It is one of helping students toward new learning, rather than of testing the adequacy of previous learning. The teacher's responses to student work help the students rethink efforts and rework ideas as they move toward more effective solutions to the problem at hand.

5. *Internalization.*—Over time, instruction should change in response to the student's internalization of the patterns and approaches practiced with the teacher's assistance. (Too often, "effective" lesson patterns become an unchanging part of the instructional routine, for sequences of textbook lessons as well as for individual teachers. In these cases, students are "helped" to do things they can already do on their own.) Instruction must be sensitive to the fact that, as students gain new knowledge and skills, the instructional interaction should change as well. The student's contribution to similar tasks will increase while the teacher's concerns will shift toward more sophisticated issues or approaches. The amount of dialogue may actually increase as the student becomes more competent, with the interaction shifting from simple questions or directives toward a more expert exploration of options and alternatives.

This view of instruction permits a fusion of the need for direct instruction in new skills with the recent concern with reading and writing processes. The critical feature is that the instruction take place in a context where student as well as teacher has an active role to play in the literacy event. There must be room for a shared exchange of ideas between teacher and student and an underlying understanding about their roles and goals—who needs the help, who gives the help, what help is needed, and why.

Once engaged in this model of instructional scaffolding, student and teacher roles necessarily change, and along with them the nature of lessons and learning change; instruction takes on a different face that requires new uses of materials and new ways to assess whether learning has taken place. In this model of instruction, the teacher retains the role of planner and initiator of classroom activities. However, the activities need to be planned to provide scope for the students to develop their own purposes rather than simply providing responses to fit into the teacher's predetermined framework.

The notion of instructional scaffolding is useful in examining the teaching of Jane Martin, a high school social studies teacher who has been participating in the Applebee and Langer (1984) study. During the first year of work with one of Ms. Martin's classes, a research assistant observed 28 lessons, held 12 planning sessions with her, and conducted 55 interviews with her students. Jane Martin was an experienced teacher with a reputation as one of the most successful teachers in her district. The mood of her class was always positive; she and her students shared a mutual liking for one another. As teacher, Ms. Martin saw her role as provider of information, while protecting her students from failure. To do this, she established a highly controlled learning environment where the students were expected to display their new learnings in a predetermined structure.

As an example of Ms. Martin's teaching, consider an assignment on China that required two weeks to complete and that resulted in papers that were unusually long for her class. Martin's assignment sheet was labeled "The Big Paper," and it opened with this statement: "WE, and I do mean WE, are going to write a paper." There followed a two-week calendar with due dates:

Tuesday: Instructions given.
Wednesday: Turn in thesis statement with three good supporting arguments by the end of class.
Thursday: Flesh out your thesis and try for a rough draft.
Friday: Rough drafts due at the start of class.
Tuesday: Group work on corrected drafts.
Thursday: Polishing of rough drafts.
Friday: Final papers due at the start of class.

Ms. Martin monitored each stage of the writing process, with corrections and suggestions made along the way. Jenny's outline (her thesis and three supporting arguments) looked like this:

Looking ahead in China's future, some important things are starting to develop:
A. Health
    1) women and men are doctors
    2) more research
    3) trained doctors
B. Equality between men and women
    1) jobs
    2) divorce
    3) living arrangements when married
C. Education
    1) required to have an education
    2) military training is required
    3) college is open to all people

Jenny was late submitting her outline to Ms. Martin, and Ms. Martin was late getting it back to Jenny. Interviewed midway in the second week, Jenny reported that she could not go forward with her work because "[Ms. Martin] still hasn't checked my outline. I started doing my rough draft and then Mike [another student] said I really shouldn't because she hasn't checked my paper, and I don't know if I'm doing it right."

The next day, Jenny received approval for her outline—an OK written on the top of the page with "this needs to be reworked" next to the first sentence and "good proofs" near the bottom of the page.

Jenny's final paper, with her arguments given advance approval, was quite predictable in content. The last paragraph read, "In conclusion, China's future is definitely looking better. There is more equality between the sexes, more medical research, and a better educational system."

Tom, on the other hand, had a different kind of problem. At first he was excited about his topic. He said, "I knew I wanted to write something toward China the promised land or getting better, 'cause that's the way [Ms. Martin] made it look—you know, the way she set it up like a little formula with a main topic and supporting details. So it was just a matter of getting the facts together."

However, at the rewriting stage, he needed some help. "The hard part was rewriting it after [Ms. Martin] made corrections . . . 'cause I had to restate some things that I really didn't understand how to restate. I didn't know how she wanted me to do it."

Eventually, he had a conference with the teacher, and she told him what to include. Tom wrote in the restatements as Ms. Martin suggested them and copied the entire piece over as a final draft.

While both papers were long and coherent, the students spent surprisingly little time actually thinking about what they were going to write, points they wished to make, or ways to organize or present their information. Their roles were rather passive, they were required to know what was expected, to keep track of the information presented in class and in the textbook, and to transcribe it rather than use it to extend or develop new meanings. Both students received good grades, both felt they had done what had been asked of them, and Ms. Martin felt her students had learned the China section of the curriculum.

Somehow, though, the students knew, and Jane Martin came to realize, that, although they had gotten through this assignment and likely could get through many other assignments like it, there was something missing.

If we consider this instructional sequence in terms of the criteria of effective scaffolding, two problems are immediately apparent. First, and in this case most important, the sequence subverts the students' attempt to take ownership for what they are doing. Even Tom, who began with considerable excitement, soon found himself tracing out the argument Ms. Martin wanted rather than developing his own. At its most extreme, though relatively typical in this class, this even involved accepting the teacher's rewordings without understanding what they meant. Tom could have taken ownership for his writing by selecting a topic or form in which to present his own responses to Ms. Martin's assignment. Instead, he wrote about the ideas he thought she expected, in ways she expected them to be presented. Her reasons for keeping such total control were benevolent ones, stemming from her concern with protecting the students from any kind of failure. At the same time, unfortunately, she also protected them from something quite basic to literacy learning—learning to manipulate and control their own ideas in ways they could not have done before.

The second problem stems directly from the first: the sequence Ms. Martin planned provided too much support, helping the students accomplish what they should have been learning to accomplish without help. Again, in her concern with protecting them from failure, she failed to remove the scaffolding after it was no longer needed. While students in her class needed considerable help in organizing their writing, they also needed room to change ideas, add new ones, and reorganize the piece as the writing developed. The structure she provided left no room for that to occur.

Both these problems derive directly from the instructional model from which Ms. Martin was operating. As teacher, she had information that must be provided to the students; as students, they had to demonstrate they had learned, and could recite, the information she had

131

provided. That the level of engagement in the task, as well as the level of intellectual activity, remained low seems a relatively direct consequence of her assumptions about instruction.

This lesson is not unlike those observed in other classrooms in the study taught by other teachers (see, e.g., Marshall 1984). The teacher's role and the student's role are not unlike those reported in the many status studies we reviewed at the beginning of this article. It is another example of higher-level thinking and reasoning having no place in the instructional models on which literacy instruction is currently based. They are not purposely being overlooked; they simply are not what counts. They are not where instruction starts, nor are they what is evaluated as a measure of success. To change this requires more than simply ringing variations on current models of instruction; it requires a reconceptualization of the role of teacher and student in instructional interaction. The notion of instructional scaffolding is one beginning, where the teacher is directly involved in providing instructional support, but where thinking and learning belong to the student.

Summary

The studies reviewed here suggest that literacy instruction in the United States limits students' opportunities for thoughtful engagement in reading and writing tasks. Reading and writing activities require "right" answers more often than an elaboration of ideas, and instruction focuses more on checking the correctness of responses than on helping students extend their learning. An alternative view of effective instruction, grounded in part in studies of instruction and in part in the child language literature, has been suggested as a way to begin to move beyond the limitations apparent in current practice. The notion of instructional scaffolding provides both a framework for analyzing ongoing instruction and a metaphor that teachers may find helpful in reformulating their practice. Unlike the notions of curriculum that underlie current practice, instructional scaffolding leaves room for encouraging higher-order reasoning as well as the basic skills. It may also offer a way to integrate recent scholarly attention to reading and writing processes with the practical and pressing concerns of the classroom.

References

Anderson, T. H., Armbruster, B. B., and Kantor, R. N. *How Clearly Written Are Children's Textbooks? Or, Of Bladderworts and Alfa* (Reading Education

Report No. 16). Urbana: University of Illinois at Urbana-Champaign, Center for the Study of Reading, 1980. (ERIC Document Reproduction Service No. ED 192 275)

Applebee, A. N. "Silent Reading Tests: What Do They Measure?" *School Review* 80 (1971): 86–93.

Applebee, A. N. *Writing in the Secondary School: English and the Content Areas* (Research Report No. 21). Urbana, Ill.: National Council of Teachers of English, 1981.

Applebee, A. N. *Contexts for Learning to Write: Studies of Secondary School Instruction.* Norwood, N.J.: Ablex, 1984.

Applebee, A. N., and J. A. Langer. "Instructional Scaffolding: Reading and Writing as Natural Language Activities." *Language Arts* 60 (1983): 168–75.

Applebee, A. N., and J. A. Langer. *Moving towards Excellence: Writing and Learning in the Secondary School Curriculum* (Report to National Institute of Education, Grant No. NIE-G-82-0027). Manuscript in preparation, 1984.

Armbruster, B. B., and T. H. Anderson. *Structures for Explanations in History Textbooks, or So What If Governor Stanford Missed the Spike and Hit the Rail?* (Technical Report No. 252). Urbana: University of Illinois at Urbana-Champaign, Center for the Study of Reading, 1982. (ERIC Document Reproduction Service No. ED 218 595)

Barnes, D. *From Communication to Curriculum.* Harmondsworth: Penguin Books, 1976.

Barr, R. C. "Instructional Pace Differences and Their Effect on Reading Acquisition." *Reading Research Quarterly* 4 (1973–74): 526–54.

Barr, R. C. "How Children Are Taught to Read: Grouping and Pacing." *School Review* 83 (1975): 479–98.

Barrow, K., I. V. S. Mullis, and D. L. Phillips. "Achievement and the Three R's: A Synopsis of National Assessment Findings in Reading, Writing and Mathematics." Paper presented at the annual meeting of the American Educational Research Association, New York, March 1982.

Beck, I. L., M. G. McKeown, E. S. McCaslin, and A. M. Burkes. *Instructional Dimensions that May Affect Reading Comprehension: Examples from Two Commercial Reading Programs.* Pittsburgh: University of Pittsburgh, Language Research and Development Center, 1979. (ERIC Document Reproduction Service No. ED 197 322)

Beck, I. L., R. C. Omanson, and M. G. McKeown. "An Instructional Redesign of Reading Lessons: Effects on Comprehension." *Reading Research Quarterly* 17 (1982): 462–82.

Bloom, B. S. "Mastery Learning and Its Implications for Curriculum Development." In *Confronting Curriculum Reform,* edited by E. W. Eisner. Boston: Little, Brown, 1971.

Bruce, B., A. Rubin, and K. Starr. *Why Readability Formulas Fail* (Reading Education Report No. 28). Urbana: University of Illinois at Urbana-Champaign, Center for the Study of Reading, 1981.

Bruner, J. *Beyond the Information Given.* New York: W. W. Norton, Inc., 1973.

Bruner, J. "The Role of Dialogue in Language Acquisition." In *The Child's Conception of Language,* edited by A. Sinclair et al. New York: Springer-Verlag, 1978.

Bruner, J. S., J. J. Goodnow, and G. A. Austin. *A Study of Thinking.* New York: John Wiley & Sons, 1956.

Callahan, R. E. *Education and the Cult of Efficiency*. Chicago: University of Chicago Press, 1962.

Clark, C., and R. Yinger. *The Hidden World of Teaching: Implications of Research On Teacher Planning* (Research Report No. 77). East Lansing: Michigan State University, Institute for Research on Teaching, 1980.

Collins, J. "Discourse Style, Classroom Interaction, and Differential Treatment." *Journal of Reading Behavior* 14 (1982): 429–37.

Cook-Gumperz J., J. J. Gumperz, and H. D. Simons. *Final Report on School/ Home Ethnography Project* (Report to National Institute of Education, Grant No. NIE-G-78-0082). Unpublished manuscript, University of California, Berkeley, 1982.

Davis, F. B. "Fundamental Factors of Comprehension in Reading." *Psychometrics* 9 (1944): 185–97.

Davison, A., R. N. Kantor, J. Hannah, G. Hermon, R. Lutz, and R. Salzillo. *Limitations of Readability Formulas in Guiding Adaptations of Texts* (Technical Report No. 162). Urbana: University of Illinois at Urbana-Champaign, Center for the Study of Reading, 1980. (ERIC Document Reproduction Service No. ED 184 090)

Dor-Bremme, D., and J. L. Herman. *Testing in the Schools: A National Profile*. Los Angeles: University of California at Los Angeles, Center for the Study of Evaluation, 1983.

Duffy, G., and L. McIntyre. *A Qualitative Analysis of How Various Primary Grade Teachers Employ the Structured Learning Components of the Direct Instruction Model when Teaching Reading* (Report No. 80). East Lansing: Michigan State University, Institute for Research on Teaching, 1980.

Duffy, G., and L. R. Roehler. "The Illusion of Instruction." *Reading Research Quarterly* 17 (1982): 438–45.

Duncan, M. J., and B. J. Biddle. *The Study of Teaching*. New York: Holt, Rinehart & Winston, 1974.

Durkin, D. "What Classroom Observations Reveal about Reading Comprehension." *Reading Research Quarterly* 14 (1978–79): 491–533.

Durkin, D. "Reading Comprehension Instruction in Five Basal Reader Series." *Reading Research Quarterly* 16 (1981): 515–44.

Erickson, F. "Some Approaches to Inquiry in School-Community Ethnography." *Anthropology and Education Quarterly* 8 (1977): 58–69.

Erickson, F. R., and J. Shultz. "When Is a Context? Some Issues and Methods in the Analysis of Social Competence." In *Ethnography and Language in Educational Settings*, edited by J. Green and C. Wallet. Norwood, N.J.: Ablex, 1981.

Gagne, R. M. *The Conditions of Learning*. New York: Holt, Rinehart & Winston, 1977.

Gates, A. I. "An Experimental and Statistical Study of Reading Tests." *Journal of Educational Psychology* 12 (1921): 303–7.

Gilliland, J. *Readability*. London: University of London Press, 1972.

Goodwin, W. L., and H. J. Klausmeier. *Facilitating Student Learning*. New York: Harper and Row, 1975.

Graves, D. *Balance the Basics: Let Them Write*. New York: Ford Foundation, 1978. (ERIC Document Reproduction Service No. ED 192 364)

Gray, W. S. "Principles of Method of Teaching Reading as Derived from Scientific Investigation." *National Society for the Study of Education Yearbook 18, Part II*. Bloomington, Ill.: Public School Book Company, 1919.

Green, J. L., and C. Wallat. "Mapping Instructional Conversations: A Sociolinguistic Ethnography." In *Ethnography and Language in Educational Settings,* edited by J. Green and C. Wallat. Norwood, N.J.: Ablex, 1981.

Heath, S. B. *Ways with Words: Language, Life and Work in Communities and Classrooms.* New York: Cambridge University Press, 1983.

Inhelder, B., and J. Piaget. *The Growth of Logical Thinking from Childhood to Adolescence.* London: Routledge & Kegan Paul, 1958.

Kintsch, W., and D. Vipond. "Reading Comprehension and Readability in Educational Practice and Psychological Theory." In *Perspectives on Memory Research,* edited by L. Nilsson. Hillsdale, N.J.: Lawrence Erlbaum Associates, 1979.

Langer, J. A. "From Theory to Practice: A Pre-reading Plan." *Journal of Reading* 25 (1981): 152–56.

Langer, J. A. "Facilitating Text Processing: The Elaboration of Prior Knowledge." In *Reader Meets Author/Bridging the Gap,* edited by J. A. Langer and M. T. Smith-Burke. Newark, Del.: International Reading Association, 1982.

Langer, J. A. "Examining Background Knowledge and Text Comprehension." *Reading Research Quarterly* 19 (1984): 468–81. (*a*)

Langer, J. A. *Levels of Questioning: An Alternative View.* Manuscript in preparation, University of California, Berkeley, School of Education, 1984. (*b*)

Langer, J. A. "How Readers Construct Meaning: An Analysis of Reader Performance on Standardized Test Items." In *Cognitive and Linguistic Analyses of Standardized Test Performance,* edited by R. Freedle. Norwood, N.J.: Ablex, in press.

Langer, J. A., and A. N. Applebee. "Language, Learning, and Interaction: A Framework for Improving the Teaching of Writing." In *Contexts for Learning to Write: Studies of Secondary School Instruction,* edited by A. N. Applebee. Norwood, N.J.: Ablex, 1984.

Marshall, J. D. "Process and Product: Case Studies of Writing in Two Content Areas." In *Contexts for Learning to Write: Studies of Secondary School Instruction,* edited by A. N. Applebee. Norwood, N.J.: Ablex, 1984.

McDermott, R. P. "The Cultural Context of Learning to Read." In *Issues in the Evaluation of Reading* (Linguistics and Reading Series No. 1), edited by S. Wanat. Arlington, Va.: Center for Applied Linguistics, 1977. (*a*)

McDermott, R. P. "Social Relations as Contexts for Learning in School." *Harvard Educational Review* 47 (1977): 198–213. (*b*)

Mehan, J. *Learning Lessons: Social Organization in the Classroom.* Cambridge, Mass.: Harvard University Press, 1979.

National Assessment of Educational Progress. *Writing Mechanics, 1969–1974: A Capsule Description of Changes* (Report No. 05-W-01). Denver, Colo.: Educational Commission of the States, 1975.

National Assessment of Educational Progress. *Reading in America: A Perspective on Two Assessments* (Report No. 06-R-01). Denver, Colo.: Education Commission of the States, 1976.

National Assessment of Educational Progress. *Reading Change, 1970–1975: Summary Volume* (Report No. 06-R-21). Denver, Colo.: Education Commission of the States, 1978.

National Assessment of Educational Progress. *Writing Achievement, 1969–79: Results from the Third National Writing Assessment,* vol. 1, 2, and 3 (Report No. 10-W-01, 02, 03). Denver, Colo.: Education Commission of the States, 1981. (*a*)

National Assessment of Educational Progress. *Three National Assessments of Reading: Changes in Performance, 1970–1980* (Report No. 11-R-01). Denver, Colo.: Education Commission of the States, 1981. (*b*)

National Assessment of Educational Progress. *Reading, Thinking, and Writing: Results from the 1979–80 National Assessment of Reading and Literature* (Report No. 11-L-01). Denver, Colo.: Education Commission of the States, 1981. (*c*)

Ninio, A., and J. Bruner. "The Achievement and Antecedents of Labelling." *Journal of Child Language* 5 (1978): 1–15.

Palinscar, A. S., and A. L. Brown. "Reciprocal Teaching of Comprehension-Fostering and Monitoring Activities." *Cognition and Instruction,* in press.

Peterson, P. L., R. W. Marx, and C. M. Clark. "Teacher Planning, Teacher Behavior, and Student Achievement." *American Educational Research Journal* 15 (1978): 417–32.

Pressey, L., and S. L. Pressey. "A Critical Study of the Concept of Silent Reading." *Journal of Educational Psychology* 12 (1921): 25–31.

Ratner, N., and J. Bruner. "Games, Social Exchange and the Acquisition of Language." *Journal of Child Language* 5 (1978): 391–401.

Redish, J. "Readability." In *Drafting Documents in Plain Language,* edited by D. A. McDonald. New York: Practicing Law Institute, 1979.

Resnick, D. P., and L. B. Resnick. "The Nature of Literacy: An Historical Exploration." *Harvard Educational Review* 47 (1977): 370–85.

Richards, I. A. *Practical Criticism: A Study of Literary Judgment.* London: Kegan Paul, Trench, Trubner & Company, 1929.

Rubin, A. *Conceptual Readability: New Ways to Look at Text* (Reading Education Report No. 31). Cambridge, Mass.: Bolt Beranek and Newman Center for the Study of Reading, 1981.

Royer, J. M., and D. J. Cunningham. *On the Theory and Measurement of Reading Comprehension* (Technical Report No. 91). Urbana: University of Illinois at Urbana-Champaign, Center for the Study of Reading, 1978. (ERIC Document Reproduction Service No. ED 157 040)

Thorndike, E. L. "Reading as Reasoning: A Study of Mistakes in Paragraph Meaning." *Journal of Educational Psychology* 8 (1917): 323–32.

Tuinman, J. J. "Determining the Passage-Dependency of Comprehension Questions in Five Major Tests." *Reading Research Quarterly* 10 (1974): 207–23.

Vygotsky, L. S. *Thought and Language.* Cambridge, Mass.: MIT Press, 1962.

Vygotsky, L. S. *Mind in Society.* Cambridge, Mass.: Harvard University Press, 1978.

Wertsch, J. V., G. W. McNamee, J. B. McLane, and N. A. Budwig. "The Adult-Child Dyad as a Problem-Solving System." *Child Development* 51 (1980): 1215–21.

What Works in Teaching Composition: A Meta-analysis of Experimental Treatment Studies

GEORGE HILLOCKS, JR.
University of Chicago

As one part of a comprehensive review of research related to the teaching of composition, I have conducted an integrative review or meta-analysis of experimental treatment studies completed from 1963 through 1982. Among many researchers in the field of composition, such studies are currently in disrepute. Cooper and Odell (1978, p. xiii) claim that the authors included in their *Research on Composing* share "one audacious aim—that of redirecting and revitalizing research in written composition." Their aim was to redirect research away from the kind of experimental studies summarized by Braddock, Lloyd-Jones, and Schoer in 1963. They argue that the Braddock et al. review was based on the assumption that "We already had a thorough understanding of written products and processes" (p. xiv), an assumption that Cooper, Odell, and their co-authors see as unwarranted. They believe that "ultimately, comparison-group research may enable us to improve instruction in writing" (p. xiv), but not before such research is "informed by carefully tested theory and by descriptions of written discourse and the processes by which that discourse comes into being" (p. xiv). Emig (1982) sees much less promise for "comparison group" studies. Her attack is launched against the whole "positivist" research "paradigm," by which she apparently means testing hypotheses in experimental designs in or out of laboratories.

The most vituperative attack against experimental studies was launched by Graves (1980). He claims that such research in writing is "an exercise for students to apply courses in statistics to their dissertations" (p. 914). Referring to experimental studies conducted between 1955 and 1972, Graves claims that most of this research "wasn't readable and was of limited value. It couldn't help teachers in the classroom"

(p. 914). Experimental research, he charges, "is written for other researchers, promotions, or dusty archives in a language guaranteed for self-extinction. . . . The data cannot be exported from room to room . . . [Teachers] have been unable to transfer faceless data to the alive, inquiring faces of the children they teach the next morning" (p. 918). What Graves presumably means by this curious metaphor is that the findings of experiments cannot be applied with comparable results in other than the experimental classrooms. If Graves in particular is right, we should find that results of experiments on similar instructional variables have little in common, that their results are highly heterogeneous.

Despite the current disdain for experimental studies, it seemed wise to examine them for a number of reasons. First, the total number of experimental studies completed in the past 20 years exceeds the total number of studies included in the Braddock bibliography. Second, even a cursory review of the published studies indicates that many of them have heeded the advice of Braddock and his colleagues, who had rightly bemoaned the lack of carefully designed experiments. Third, new techniques have been available for integrating the results of experimental studies since 1978.

Selection of Studies

This review attempts to examine every experimental study produced between 1963 and 1982. These include over 500 published studies, dissertations, studies in the Education Resources Information Center (ERIC) catalog, and studies in mimeographed form. Three researchers, including the author, worked independently to screen all of the studies. They read all studies except dissertations in their entirety. In the case of dissertations, they examined abstracts first. If the abstract clearly indicated that the dissertation did not meet the criteria listed below, they rejected it. All other dissertations, with the exception of four located in late 1982, were ordered and read.

While it is possible to include all available studies in a meta-analysis, coding them for variations in design, it seemed reasonable to include only those studies that met the following minimal criteria.

GEORGE HILLOCKS, JR., is an associate professor in the Departments of Education and English at the University of Chicago.

First, by definition, the study had to involve a treatment—some combination of conditions, instruction, practice and/or feedback over some period of time leading to a posttest. Studies that examine the effects of certain conditions on a single piece of writing were not included in the meta-analysis but will be reviewed elsewhere. Thus, Bridwell's (1980) carefully designed study of revision was not included in the meta-analysis because it does not represent a sustained treatment but, rather, examines the effects of a set of conditions on a single piece of writing.

Second, a study had to make use of a scale of writing quality applied to samples of writing. Studies that use only standardized test results were excluded, as were studies that involve writing samples but only counted errors or various syntactic features. This condition permits asking the following question in the meta-analysis, Which treatments appear to produce the greatest gains in writing quality? A few studies were excluded because rating procedures did not score compositions along a scaled continuum. Rather, they used a method in which judges were presented with compositions written by matched pairs of students and asked to choose the better piece of writing. The researcher then assigns a score to each piece of writing based on the number of judges selecting it as the better of its pair. Such scores, while reasonable, appear to have a meaning substantially different from that of a scale score. For example, if two compositions lie at the upper end of the scale, say at 6 and 7, on a seven-point scale, and if seven judges consistently pick the latter paper as superior, it would receive a score of 7, while the paper scored 6 on the scale would receive a score of 0. The difference between the 6 and 7 scores and the 0 and 7 scores would have a powerful, and misleading, impact on effect sizes.

Third, to be included in the meta-analysis, a study had to exercise minimal control for teacher bias. Specifically, if only two teachers were involved, each must have taught one class for each treatment. If teachers did not teach all treatments, then at least two different teachers must have taught each, so that total teachers were at least twice the number of treatments.

Fourth, to be included, a study had to control for differences among groups of students. In a few cases students were randomly assigned to treatment groups. In one study, the students were carefully matched (Sbaratta 1975). When students were not randomly assigned to treatments or not matched, studies must have used direct pre and post measures of composition ability for both experimental and control groups. Standardized tests did not suffice. Reviewers also looked for evidence that treatments were assigned randomly. However, because such information was frequently absent, this criterion could not be applied systematically.

Fifth, compositions must have been scored under conditions that help to assure validity and reliability. The compositions must have been coded for scoring and precautions taken so that raters could not infer the treatment, the teacher, the time of writing, or the identity of students. Two or more raters must have rated each composition and their scores summed or averaged, *or* procedures for training raters and the subsequent reliabilities must have been reported. Nearly every study reporting reliabilities indicated them to be .70 or higher. Most were over .80. All studies included used some version of holistic, analytic, or primary trait scoring.

A few studies that met the stipulated criteria were regrettably eliminated because the data presented did not allow for the extraction of means and standard deviations for pretests and posttest, which was necessary for calculating effect sizes.

Meta-analysis

The techniques used in the analysis are based on the work of Glass (1978) and particularly on the statistical model developed by Hedges (1981, 1982*a*). A meta-analysis computes standard scores for various treatments' gains or losses by dividing the difference between posttest scores, adjusted for the difference between pretest scores, by the pooled standard deviation of posttest scores for all groups in the study. The resulting score, commonly called effect size, reports a given treatment gain (or loss) in terms of standard score units. Thus, a given treatment might be said to have an experimental/control effect size of .5 standard deviations, meaning that the gain for the average student in the experimental group is .5 standard deviations greater than for the average student in the control group.

Effect sizes can be accumulated across studies. Using the techniques developed by Hedges (1981), this meta-analysis weights each effect size by the reciprocal of its variance so that the accumulation is not simply an average of raw effect sizes, but a mean effect size dependent on the variance of its constituents.

The major goal of the meta-analysis is to explain the variability among the characteristics of the treatments in relation to the variability of their effect sizes. That involves categorizing the treatments along various dimensions (e.g., instructional mode, focus of instruction, duration), comparing mean effect sizes of treatments grouped together, and testing the studies grouped together for homogeneity (Hedges

1982*b*). The simple comparison of mean effect sizes provides useful information about the effectiveness of treatments. In this regard, Graves's criticism of experimental studies is important. Graves claims that "the data" (by which we must assume he means findings) cannot be transferred from any particular study to another classroom. If he is correct, then we should expect the studies of similar instructional variables to produce widely different results. If he is not correct, if experimentally tested treatments can be transferred from one set of classes to another, then the results for treatments with similar variables should be similar. Some test is useful to determine the extent to which similarity among results exists, or put another way, to determine the extent to which a given mean effect is representative of its constituents.

The homogeneity test asks "whether the variability in effect size estimates is greater than would be expected if all the studies shared a common underlying effect size" (Giaconia and Hedges 1982, p. 584). It yields a chi square statistic that indicates the statistical significance of differences among treatments grouped together. The higher the statistic, the more significant the variability among treatments. To be labeled homogeneous in this study, a grouping must have a homogeneity statistic (H) that is not significant at $p < .01$. If a set of treatments has common, identifiable characteristics and is homogeneous, then we can assume that their mean effect size is representative of all studies in the grouping—not simply an average—and that the effects are the result of their shared characteristics. When that is the case, the explanatory power of the category is greater. Similarly, if the summed homogeneity statistics for categories of treatments along a given dimension is not significant, then we can assume that the dimension or set of categories fits the data well and has a high level of explanatory power.

Each experimental and control treatment was examined in detail and coded for the presence or absence of certain variables. Two advanced graduate students in measurement, evaluation, and statistical analysis coded the studies independently, agreeing on 87 percent of their decisions. They conferred to resolve disagreements. The author coded all studies and agreed with 98 percent of the graduate students' resolved codings. The remaining 2 percent were resolved in consultation.

Variables will be examined in terms of experimental/control effect sizes — the difference between posttest scores, adjusted for differences between pretest scores, and divided by the pooled standard deviation of posttest scores for all groups in the study. When useful, the variables will also be examined in terms of the pre/post effect size — the difference between the pretest and posttest scores for a given treatment, divided by the pooled standard deviation of pretest scores for all groups in the particular study.

These data, given the complex coding, can be examined along several dimensions. This paper examines three of the dimensions: duration of the treatment, mode of instruction, and focus of prewriting instruction. A future report will examine other dimensions, including teacher comment and revision. For each category in a dimension, the treatments must be independent of other categories in the same dimension. That is, a treatment included in the analysis of a given dimension, such as mode of instruction, may occur in only one category. The dimensions, however, are not independent. Duration, for example, includes all 73 experimental/control effect sizes. Mode of instruction includes 29 experimental/control effects for which a particular mode (e.g., individualized) was coded in the experimental but not in the control groups. The 39 experimental/control treatments appearing in focus of instruction also appear in the duration dimension. The dimensions of mode and focus examine 48 experimental/control treatments of which 19 appear in both dimensions. Table 1 presents a cross tabulation of the treatments by the dimensions of mode and focus.

Given the requirements of homogeneity for the explanation of effect sizes and the experience of researchers in the social and physical sciences, it will be unreasonable to expect the analysis to explain 100 percent of the data categorized in any given dimension. The question is how much of the data can be eliminated without invalidating any claim to explanatory power. Previous research indicates that the best estimators of effect size may involve elimination of 20 to 30 percent of the data (Huber 1977). Ground rules for this study are somewhat more restrictive, permitting the elimination of fewer studies to achieve homogeneity. After establishing overall mean effect sizes and homogeneity statistics, four studies that contributed most heavily to the heterogeneity—two with high positive and two with high negative effect sizes—were removed. These four studies represent about 5 percent of the 75 controlled treatments. Thereafter, for the analysis of a given dimension, no more than 15 percent of the experimental/control treatments in the categories of that dimension will be eliminated to achieve homogeneity, including those dropped for substantive reasons. If homogeneity is not possible, after eliminating 15 percent, we must conclude that the dimension and the categories included in it lack a high level of explanatory power. The data available do not fit the explanatory model well. On the other hand, if the effect sizes for similar experimental variables are homogeneous, within the limits prescribed, then we must admit that the variable categories have explanatory power and that treatments are indeed transferable.

142

TABLE 1

Numbers of Treatments Appearing Both in the Dimension of Instructional Mode and the Dimension of Instructional Focus

Focus (N = 39)	Mode (N = 29)			
	Presentational (N = 4)	Natural Process (N = 9)	Individualized (N = 6)	Environmental (N = 10)
Grammar (N = 5)	⋯	⋯	2	⋯
Sentence combining (N = 5)	⋯	⋯	⋯	⋯
Models (N = 7)	3	⋯	⋯	1
Using criteria (scales, etc.) (N = 6)	⋯	⋯	⋯	2
Inquiry (N = 6)	⋯	⋯	⋯	2
Free writing (N = 10)	⋯	9	⋯	⋯

All Treatments

The 60 studies remaining after the application of the criteria outlined above include 75 experimental/control treatments and involve 11,705 students, 6,313 in experimental treatments and 5,392 in control treatments. Of these treatments, 10 are at the elementary level (eight at sixth grade), 32 are secondary level, 31 are at the college freshman level, and two are mixed elementary and secondary. They permit calculation of 73 experimental/control effect sizes (not possible in two studies), 65 experimental pre/post effect sizes, and 56 control pre/post effect sizes. The experimental/control mean effect size is .28 with a homogeneity statistic of 411.08, highly significant at $p < .01$. All experimental/control treatments taken together are anything but homogeneous. Four treatments contribute heavily to the heterogeneity. Of the two positive treatments, one involves simulation gaming among college freshmen in need of remedial work. A second involves a tutorial treatment with high school students. Of the two negative treatments, one involves a "self-paced" instructional treatment for college students who were required to attend classes only when they felt they needed to. The second involves the use of heuristics with elementary school students. These four experimental/control treatments were removed for subsequent analysis but will be examined briefly later. Their removal reduces H to about 200, still indicating highly significant heterogeneity among the treatments. This high level of heterogeneity indicates the need for further analysis to determine which variables explain it.

Duration

Composition researchers frequently comment that the brevity of a treatment results in no significant differences between the treatment groups. Burton (1973, p. 117) comments that experimental treatments "over a period of only a few weeks or months have been predestined to conclusions of 'no significant differences,' since one thing that is known, at least, is that improvement in general aspects of writing ability is a slow, gradual process." Wesdorp (1982, p. 37) believes that a "main reason for findings of non-significant differences" is that experimental treatments "are of very short duration."

If duration of treatments is a significant factor, one might expect longer treatments to display greater effect sizes than shorter treatments, and one might expect the duration of treatments to be positively correlated with their effect sizes. All experimental/control effect sizes in this study can be grouped by their duration. A glance at table 2 indicates clearly that there are no significant differences among groups of treatments less than 13 weeks, more than 12, less than 17, or more than 16. Nor are they homogeneous. Furthermore, the correlation between duration of treatment and raw effect size is $-.02$, suggesting no relationship between duration of treatment and change in the quality of writing. These results do not support the contention that duration is an important factor in the appearance of significant or nonsignificant differences. Other variables must account for the differences among treatments.

Mode of Instruction

"Mode of instruction" refers to the configuration of variables characteristic of certain teacher/classroom relationships and activities, particularly the role played by the teacher and the kinds of activities in which students engage. The classification of modes used here derives from a study conducted among college freshman composition classes at a large midwestern state university (Hillocks 1981). Through extensive classroom observation, Hillocks identified four modes of instruction, classified instructors, and compared attitudes of the students on several attitude factors that differed by the modes of instruction identified. The present study uses three of those modes (presentational, natural process, and environmental, which are defined below) and adds a fourth, individualized. The fourth mode in the 1981 study was a mixed mode, which could not be used here.

Although the 60 studies included in this analysis tend to avoid dealing with mode of instruction explicitly, in favor of focus of instruction, a perusal of the studies indicates that they are often not only concerned with different focuses of instruction but with different modes of instruction. For example, a given study may contrast a treatment that focuses on practice in developing ideas for writing with one that focuses on the analysis of rhetorical techniques in a set of essays. In addition to this clear difference in the focus of instruction, however, the treatments may contrast in another way. The first may be conducted in large part through peer interaction in small groups while the analysis of models takes place under the direction of the instructor with little or no peer interaction. Unfortunately, many studies did not provide adequate information to classify the mode of instruction. Some provided no information at all about control treatments except to say they were traditional or standard.

145

TABLE 2

Duration: Summary of Experimental/Control Effect Size Statistics

| Duration | Mean Effect | SD | 95% Confidence Interval | | H | df | Maximum H for Nonsignificance at $p < .01$ |
			Lower	Upper			
Under 13 weeks ($N = 39$)	.28	.028	.23	.33	153.48	38	61.14
Over 12 weeks ($N = 34$)	.28	.024	.23	.33	277.61	33	54.72
Under 17 weeks ($N = 58$)	.27	.021	.23	.31	395.74	57	84.70
Over 16 weeks ($N = 15$)	.31	.038	.24	.39	34.48	14	29.13

Presentational Mode

The presentational mode is characterized by (1) relatively clear and specific objectives, such as to use particular rhetorical techniques; (2) lecture and teacher-led discussion dealing with concepts to be learned and applied; (3) the study of models and other materials that explain and illustrate the concept; (4) specific assignments or exercises that generally involve imitating a pattern or following rules that have been previously discussed; and (5) feedback coming primarily from teachers. The presentational mode is undoubtedly the most common mode of instruction in composition. Certainly it has more in common with what Applebee (1981) found in the schools than has any other mode. Presentational treatments in this study are three times more frequent than any other. At the same time the presentational treatments included in this study are undobutedly more carefully thought out than is the common school approach found by Applebee.

Natural Process Mode

The natural process mode is characterized by (1) generalized objectives, such as to increase fluency and skill in writing; (2) free writing about whatever interests the students in a journal or as a way of "exploring a subject"; (3) writing for audiences of peers; (4) generally positive feedback from peers; (5) opportunities to revise and rework writing; and (6) high levels of interaction among students. Treatments in this mode often refer to the teacher as a "facilitator" whose role is to free the student's imagination and promote growth by sustaining a positive classroom atmosphere. They avoid the study of model pieces of writing, the presentation of criteria, structuring the treatment around sets of skills or concepts, rhetorical or other, and using the teacher as the primary source of feedback. Treatments in this mode provide a low level of structure and are nondirectional about the qualities of good writing. In fact, proponents of this nondirectional mode of instruction believe that students are only stultified by exposure to what they see as arbitrary criteria, models, problems, or assignments. In the words of Parker (1979, p. 36), "Writing demands usually to be preceded by a period of exploratory talk about what the students have chosen to write on, a time in which ideas and the language to express them can be generated. It demands also the freedom for students to choose the forms suitable to their material and their purposes. . . . Writing is learned by doing it and sharing it with real audiences, not by studying

147

and applying abstract rhetorical principles in exercises which the teacher alone will read and judge." Parker's dicta help clarify both the natural process mode and the presentational mode with which he contrasts it.

Environmental Mode

The environmental mode is characterized by (1) clear and specific objectives, such as to increase the use of specific detail and figurative language; (2) materials and problems selected to engage students with each other in specifiable processes important to some particular aspect of writing; and (3) activities, such as small group problem-centered discussions, conducive to high levels of peer interaction concerning specific tasks. Teachers in this mode, in contrast to the presentational, are likely to minimize lecture and teacher-led discussion, structuring activities so that, while teachers may provide brief introductory lectures, students work on particular tasks in small groups before proceeding to similar tasks independently. Although principles are taught, they are not simply announced and illustrated as in the presentational mode. Rather, they are approached through concrete material and problems, the working through of which not only illustrates the principle but engages students in its use. For example, writing about one of 30 seashells so that another student will be able to read the composition and choose the seashell described, from among the 30, illustrates both the necessity of thinking about possible audience responses and the necessity for using precise detail. While the teacher may urge students to think about the audience and to write specifically, as in the presentational mode, the immediate, concrete activity has the potential for engaging students in the use of the principles and provides feedback from peers.

In contrast to the natural process mode, the concrete tasks of the environmental mode make objectives operationally clear by engaging students in their pursuit through structured tasks. Thus, while a natural process treatment requires students to respond to each other's writing, the criteria for doing so come from the student. In contrast, in one environmental treatment, the teacher leads a brief discussion of a sample of student writing, helping students apply a set of criteria to it. Following that discussion, the sixth graders apply the same criteria to other pieces of writing, not only judging the piece but generating ideas in response to several questions about it in order to improve it. Use of the criteria or scale involves concrete revisions (Sager 1973). While the environmental mode shares the ideas of emphasizing processes

148

(other than listening to a teacher) and student interaction with the natural process mode, it differs sharply from the latter in the structure of the materials and activities.

The presentational mode, which is probably the most common mode of composition instruction in secondary schools and colleges, emphasizes the role of the teacher as presenter of knowledge about writing. The natural process mode, currently promulgated by the National Writing Project and by many of its numerous subsidiaries around the country emphasizes the student as the generator of ideas, criteria, and forms. The environmental mode appears to place teacher and student more nearly in balance, with the teacher planning activities and selecting materials through which students interact with each other to generate ideas and learn identifiable writing skills. The balance among all elements of the instructional situation suggests the name "environmental mode."

A concrete example will help to clarify the distinctions among these three modes of instruction. Suppose a curricular goal is to write effectively about personal experience. A presentational instructor would be likely to explain the characteristics of "good" personal experience writing, lead students in reading and discussing samples of such writing, ask students to write such compositions on their own, and finally correct and grade them.

A natural process "facilitator" would be likely to ask students to write in journals several times a week and select those entries they would like to write about in extended compositions. They might be asked to write about this entry, or some other idea, "simply filling a page in order to learn how writing helps them discover what they know, what they do not know, and, in fact, what they want to write about" (Myers 1983, p. 28). Students might be asked to discuss what they have written with peers, in an effort to generate additional ideas or questions to write about. Or they may, according to Buckley and Boyle (1983, p. 62), "map" their stories by placing "a controlling idea in the center of their map and use brainstorming techniques until they have many childhood memories for their paper. They select the 'best incidents' for the map, with the central idea in the middle and supporting incidents or ideas on the extensions." After completing their "maps," students "tell their stories to a group or a partner." Meanwhile, the "listeners are mapping to give information to the speakers, who can then reevaluate their organization." Although Buckley and Boyle speak of evaluation here, they provide no criteria for evaluation of organization. The key feature, whether students use "mapping" or not, is that they receive feedback from peers concerning very early ideas and after each draft, one or more of which is eventually turned in to the teacher. Feedback from peers and the teacher is usually designated as being positive. In

149

short, students are given opportunities to explore ideas before writing, to develop a draft, to receive feedback, and so on. In this way the teacher simply facilitates the development of ideas and forms that the students have within themselves.

In contrast, the environmental teacher is likely to break the task of personal experience writing into components—for example, writing about setting and people, developing and resolving conflict, and using dialogue effectively. Students might be asked to write as specifically as possible about faces in photographs, attempting to capture unique expressions and facial qualities. They might then meet in small groups, sharing the pictures and what they have written and applying a set of teacher-supplied questions or criteria before revising. The revisions might then receive positive feedback from the teacher on the strongest details. In a different activity, students might pantomime a character in a situation: waiting in the principal's or dentist's anteroom, sitting on the bench waiting to go into an important game, or walking down a dark street fearful of being followed. The audience writes several sentences trying to capture the details of bodily movements, facial expressions, and so forth of the pantomimers. Students might read what they have written aloud, with the teacher or peers reinforcing the strongest details. In a more complex activity, students might be given a set of kernel situations involving conflicts between two people and asked to choose one or invent their own. They would then be asked to develop and act out a dialogue between the two characters. Their audience might supply feedback, using questions supplied by the teacher to guide their evaluations. This activity would be followed by writing out a dialogue, perhaps with details about the appearance of the characters and setting. Feedback would come from peers, the teacher, or both. Such activities would lead to the writing of an extended paper about a personal experience, and this writing might very well include brainstorming for ideas, the production of more than one draft, and feedback at various points.

Individualized Mode

In the individualized mode of instruction, students receive instruction through tutorials, programmed materials of some kind, or a combination. The focus of instruction may vary widely, from mechanics to researching, planning, and writing papers. The chief distinction is that this mode of instruction seeks to help students on an individualized basis.

The descriptions of treatments did not always present adequate information for identifying the mode of instruction. Nearly all ambiguities involved making a choice between environmental and pre-sentational. For example, a description might present the kinds of problems and materials appropriate to environmental instruction, but say nothing to indicate the presence of student interaction. In such cases the instructional mode was coded as unclear. In the case of several control treatments, no description was provided. These were coded 0. In what follows, experimental/control effects were analyzed for the presence of a treatment in the experimental condition but *not* in the control.

Results for Mode of Instruction

Table 3 summarizes the results for mode of instruction. Clearly, the environmental mode is responsible for higher gains than the other modes. The difference between the environmental mode and natural process is significant at $p < .0001$ ($z = 4.15$); between environmental and individualized, it is significant at $p < .0005$ ($z = 3.66$). Three of the modes (presentational, environmental, and individualized) have homogeneous effects. Three problems remain. First, the natural process mode has significant variability. Second, the homogeneity statistic for all groups ($H = 51.58$) is significant at $p < .01$, with 25 degrees of freedom. Third, the presentational mode includes only two studies with four treatments, one of the studies including three presentational treatments in experimental condition and a nondescript treatment in the control, conditions that permit very little confidence in the results for the presentational mode.

The heterogeneity of natural process treatments can be reduced without affecting the mean effect size appreciably by removing the studies with the largest positive and negative effect sizes. In Adams (1977), the study with the largest positive effect size of .56, the ex-perimental treatment made no gain. The entire effect size is due to a loss of $-.56$ for the control groups. The loss for the control group is easy to speculate about. Every mechanical or structural error in every composition written by students in the control group was marked. Final comments were brief and directed to errors in organization. Apparently, no positive comments were included. The students were expected to correct their errors and turn in the revised compositions. Such a treatment ought to be negative enough to result in a substantial loss. It did.

A second study contributing greatly to the heterogeneity of the natural process group (Walker 1974) had losses in both experimental and control groups. However, the experimental treatment based on

TABLE 3

Mode of Instruction: Summary of Experimental/Control Effect Size Statistics

	Mean Effect	SD	95% Confidence Interval		H	df	Maximum H for Nonsignificance at $p < .01$
			Lower	Upper			
All meta-analysis treatments (N = 73)	.28	.018	.24	.32	411.08	72	102.60
Treatments (four outliers removed) (N = 69)	.24	.019	.20	.27	169.28	68	98.00
Treatments included in mode of instruction analysis (N = 29)	.24	.025	.19	.29	73.83	28	48.27
Natural process (N = 9)	.19	.037	.11	.26	23.15	8	20.08
Environmental (N = 10)	.44	.050	.34	.53	12.83	9	21.66
Presentational (N = 4)	.02	.114	-.20	.24	.92	3	11.33
Individualized (N = 6)	.17	.064	.06	.28	14.68	5	15.08
Treatments categorized by mode of instruction (N = 29)	...	...	...	...	51.58	25	44.3

Macrorie's *Telling Writing* had a substantially greater loss than did the control, resulting in an experimental/control effect size of − .27. But the reasons for that loss are not so apparent as they are in the Adams (1977) study. At any rate, removal of these two studies reduces the mean effect size to only .18 from .186, but reduces *H* to 14.44 from 23.15.

In the individualized group, one study contributes heavily to both the mean and the heterogeneity (A. E. Thibodeau 1973). Its removal reduces the mean effect size to .09 from .167 and *H* to 7.20 from 14.68. Speculation about its relatively high experimental/control effect size of .45 is not possible without more detailed information about the treatments than the dissertation provides.

As table 4 indicates, the removal of these three studies reduces the heterogeneity in the dimension of mode and its categories to homogeneity ($H = 35.39$, *df* = 22, not significant at $p < .01$). The dimension explains 89.6 percent of the 29 treatments categorized as having an identifiable instructional mode in the experimental group and some other in the control.

Since the characteristics of each treatment group were coded, inspection of mean pretest-to-posttest effect sizes regardless of experimental or control status is possible. The mean pretest-to-posttest effect for 33 presentational treatments is .18, considerably higher than might be expected from the original analysis; for nine natural process treatments, .26; for nine environmental treatments, .75; and for seven individualized treatments, .24. Examining the treatments in this way indicates that their relative positions have changed only slightly, with the presentational and environmental treatments being somewhat stronger in relation to the others. While the differences among the presentational, natural process, and individualized modes are not significant, the environmental gain is three times the gain for the others

TABLE 4

Mode of Instruction with Outliers Removed

	Effect Size	*H*	*df*
Presentational	.02	.92	3
Natural process	.18	14.44	6
Environmental	.44	12.83	9
Individualized	.09	7.20	4
Total modes		35.39	22

NOTE.—All *p*'s were not significant.

and is significantly different from them at $p < .0001$ (between environmental and natural process, $z = 7.74$; between environmental and individualized, $z = 6.35$). In short, these pretest-to-posttest results, which are summarized in table 5, confirm and clarify the results of the analysis of the experimental/control effect size.

Focus of Instruction

The third dimension for analysis involves particular focuses of instruction—that is, types of content or activities that teachers of composition expect to have a salutary effect on writing. These include the study of traditional grammar, work with mechanics, the study of model compositions to identify features of good writing, sentence combining, inquiry, and free writing. These share the supposition that they precede writing and prepare for it or occur early in the writing process (e.g., free writing). For that reason, they are examined separately from instructional treatments that follow writing, such as feedback and revision.

For inclusion in the analysis of this dimension, the focus of instruction had to appear in the experimental treatment but not in the control. To insure independent sets of treatments, studies had to be grouped by their primary focus, if more than one focus were included in an experimental treatment. In two instances, for example, studies included a modicum of practice in sentence combining. In one case, free writing received greater emphasis and more instructional time. In the second, inquiry received the emphasis and time. Accordingly, the first was grouped with free writing and the second with inquiry. In most cases, such decisions were not necessary.

Grammar and Mechanics

Despite the conclusion of Braddock et al. in 1963, grammar, defined as the study of parts of speech and sentences, remains a common treatment in composition instruction in schools and colleges. Only one study included in this meta-analysis, however, used grammar as an experimental treatment not present in the control (Elley, Barham, Lamb, and Wylie 1975). A treatment was coded as including mechanics if it attended to matters of usage and punctuation through use of set classroom exercises or a particular text. Only two studies attended to mechanics in the experimental treatment and not in the control. However, certain treatments used grammar, mechanics, or a combination

TABLE 5

Mode of Instruction: Summary of Mean Pretest-to-Posttest Effect Size Statistics

Mode	Mean Effect	SD	95% Confidence Interval		H	df	Maximum H for Nonsignificance at $p < .01$
			Lower	Upper			
Presentational ($N = 32$)	.18	.026	.13	.23	95.65	31	52.16
Natural process ($N = 9$)	.26	.035	.19	.33	29.24	8	21.66
Environmental ($N = 9$)	.75	.053	.64	.85	101.75	8	21.66
Individualized ($N = 9$)	.24	.060	.12	.36	8.32	6	16.80

in the control but not in the experimental. Furthermore, their experimental treatments did not overlap with other focuses listed below. For purposes of comparison, these treatments were reversed so that the grammar/mechanics treatments were considered experimental while their opposite treatments were taken as controls. This provided a total of five experimental/control treatments focusing on grammar or mechanics in one treatment but not in the other.

Models

The study of model pieces of writing or discourse is one of the oldest tools in the writing teacher's repertoire, dating back to ancient Greek academies, which required that their students memorize orations. In today's composition curricula, use of models of excellence is still common. Usually, students are required to read and analyze these pieces of writing in order to recognize and then imitate their features. Six studies (with seven treatments) make use of models in the experimental treatment and not in the control.

Sentence Combining

The sentence combining treatment is one pioneered by Mellon (1969) and O'Hare (1973), who showed that practice in combining simple sentences into more complex ones resulted in greater t-unit length, a t-unit being a traditionally defined main clause and all of its appended modifiers. Very simply, students are asked to consider sentences such as no. 1 and no. 2 and then, by following specific cues or their own imaginations, to produce something like no. 3: (1) The pirates were whistling "Lili Bolero"; (2) The pirates rowed from the ship to the island; (3) Whistling "Lili Bolero," the pirates rowed from the ship to the island.

That this treatment results in students' writing longer t-units is hardly open to question. But a number of critics question that it produces writing of higher quality. Four studies of sentence combining met the criteria for inclusion in this meta-analysis. A fifth study, by Faigley (1979), was included with these four because, although it traces its ancestry to a different source (Christensen 1967), it focuses on the manipulation of syntax not so much by combining sentences but by adding free modifiers to main clauses. Thus, five studies are included in this set, each with one experimental/control treatment.

Scales

Seven studies, each with one experimental/control treatment, were categorized as involving students in the use of scales, defined as a set of criteria embodied in an actual scale or set of questions for application to pieces of writing. Depending on the study, students apply the criteria to their own writing, to that of their peers, to writings supplied by the teacher, or to some combination of these. The scale must be manifest in some concrete form, not simply existing in the mind of the teacher and used as part of class discussion. Generally, the instructional use of scales engages students in applying the criteria *and* formulating possible revisions or ideas for revisions.

For example, in a study by Clifford (1981), college freshmen worked with four sets of criteria that served as guides to revision. The first, rather general set of questions was used after initial writing in response to the "oral brainstorming" of an assignment. Its purpose was to help students, who worked in small groups, respond "to their ideas and feelings about the content, but also offer suggestions about what details to leave out or stress, what to put first or last" (pp. 42–43). For the following class, students wrote a first draft and made five copies for use in small groups. In their small groups, the freshmen discussed and wrote comments on five compositions other than their own using separate "feedback sheets" on sentence structure, organization, and support. Each feedback sheet presented questions that imply criteria. For example, the feedback sheet for support includes such questions as, "Is there a central idea, an abstraction, a generalization reducible to a sentence? Where is it? Is the writer trying to prove or disprove this idea? Illuminate it? Are reasons, examples or explanations given to support the idea? Where? What do you think of the writer's support? Evaluate it" (Clifford 1977, p. 254).

The groups then exchanged their writing with another group for evaluation. "Each student carefully read one essay and filled out an evaluation sheet indicating the strongest and weakest parts while also making concrete suggestions for revisions" (Clifford 1981, p. 43). The students then proceeded to final drafts, having received six evaluations of their own work and having evaluated six others. According to Clifford's precise account, the application of the criteria on the various feedback and evaluation sheets and making suggestions for revision consumed 80 percent of the class time during the semester.

Other treatments of this type share the consistent use of criteria, their application to pieces of writing by others, and the emphasis on making suggestions for revisions. Students ordinarily are taught the

157

criteria before they set out to apply them independently. However, the treatments differ in certain details. For example, the Sager (1973) study provides sixth graders with compositions selected for the absence or presence of certain features, depending on the specific set of criteria students are learning. Thus, students see examples of well-elaborated compositions as well as poorly elaborated ones. With the latter, they are given sets of prompts to help them develop appropriate elaborations. All treatments in this set do not provide for systematic variation of the compositions to which students are to apply criteria—a feature that may be very useful in teaching them.

Inquiry

A treatment was coded as focusing on inquiry when it presented students with sets of data (or occasionally required students to find them) *and* initiated activities designed to help students develop skills or strategies for dealing with the data in order to say or write something about it. Ordinarily, activities are designed to enhance particular skills or strategies such as formulating and testing explanatory generalizations, observing and reporting significant details to achieve an effect, or generating criteria for contrasting similar phenomena. In this sense, instruction in inquiry is different from instruction that presents models illustrating already formed generalizations, significant details, or criteria and that may demand that students produce such features in their own writing. It is also different from instruction that provides stimuli for writing (e.g., films, music, cartoons, charts, or graphs) but that does not focus on strategies for analyzing the data at some level.

Studies coded as using inquiry must present students with data or have them collect it, *and* they must teach one or more strategies for dealing with the data. The strategies range from describing in detail to hypothesizing and testing hypotheses. A study by Hillocks (1979) presents students in experimental groups with various sets of data and asks them to think of words, phrases, sentences, and whole compositions to describe them. Tape-recorded sounds, for example, are played for students who are asked to suggest words and phrases that describe the sound. (Indicating the source is not enough.) The teacher pushes for more and more detail and precision. After describing several sounds orally, students are asked to write sentences about the last one they talked about, incorporating whatever oral suggestions they think best convey the character of the sound. Students may read their sentences aloud for feedback from the class or teacher. The teacher continues such activities with variations until judging that the students are capturing the unique features of the sounds in words. Then students move to writing a short composition that features the sounds of some place. This study features a series of activities that move from observation of various phenomena to the precise recording of details, with the phenomena ranging from individual sounds and tactile sensations to places and experiences that present complex sets of data for observation and interpretation, culminating in writing about personal experience.

The experimental treatment in a study by Troyka (1973) aims at teaching argumentative writing to remedial college freshmen writers. It attempts to teach a series of skills from formulating and supporting generalizations to predicting, evaluating, and countering arguments from other points of view. The teachers of experimental groups present students with sets of data about various controversial fictional situations. One of these concerns a pollution problem in a small coastal community. In addition to presenting details about the pollution and how it affects the tourist trade in the town, it also presents information about several townspeople and their relationship to the problem: a conservationist concerned about the balance of nature in the area, an executive of the chemical plant responsible for the pollution, an unemployed male hoping to be hired at the chemical plant, a member of the Department of Environmental Conservation responsible for working out a compromise, and so forth.

Groups of students playing these various roles examine the available data, develop an argument from the point of view suggested in the statement of their role, and present their arguments at a simulated public hearing. In developing their arguments, students must consider not only the data about mounting levels of pollution and the effects on wildlife, beaches, and tourism but the probable economic effects of forcing the chemical plant to reduce its output of wastes and the positions likely to be taken by other role players. The pedagogical emphasis, then, is on learning strategies basic to developing an effective argument that will contribute to a solution. Limiting the available data, as Troyka's "simulation games" do, allows students to concentrate on the strategies of formulating and supporting generalizations, predicting and countering other arguments, and so forth without being overwhelmed by data as they might be in a real situation.

Free Writing

Free writing is a treatment commonly prescribed in the professional literature, particularly since the early seventies. Generally, it involves asking students to write about whatever they are interested in, in journals, which may be considered inviolate, or in preparation for sharing ideas, experiences, and images with other students or with the teacher. Such writing is free in two senses: topics are not prescribed, and the writing is ordinarily not graded. The idea underlying this treatment is simply that allowing students to write without restrictions will help them discover both what they have to say and their own voices in saying it. Ten studies with 10 experimental/control treatments meet the requirements for this group.

Results for Focuses of Instruction

Table 6 reveals the experimental/control effect sizes for each focus of instruction. Students in the grammar/mechanics treatments score .29 of one standard deviation *less* than their peers in no grammar or mechanics treatments. The mean effect size of $-.29$ is homogeneous ($H = 8.85$ with 4 degrees of freedom). These results are supported by the pretest-to-posttest mean effect for all treatments using grammar in experimental or control conditions. The pretest-to-posttest mean effect sizes for those 14 studies is .06. In contrast, the mean pretest-to-posttest effect size for the 75 treatments that do not mention grammar of any kind have a mean effect size of .44. (Grammar was coded as traditional, transformational, purposely excluded, irrelevant [when the description of the treatment made no mention of grammar], or zero [when no description of the treatment was available]. The effect size here is based on treatments coded with grammar as irrelevant.) This difference is quite large ($z = 9.27, p < .0001$).

Furthermore, 27 treatments (experimental or control) incorporate mechanics, yielding a pretest-to-posttest mean effect size of .268, $H = 207.35$. A single treatment is responsible for much of the heterogeneity. Its removal lowers H to below 81.00 and the pretest-to-posttest mean effect size to about .18. The 74 treatments that do not mention mechanics have an effect size of .40, $H = 1016.19$. The difference between treatments with mechanics and those without is significant ($z = 3.88, p < .0001$). Clearly, as with grammar, treatments including mechanics predict significantly lower qualitative change in writing than those that regard mechanics as irrelevant.

The mean experimental/control effect size for studies focusing on models in the experimental groups but not in the control is .22, significantly higher than the grammar experimental/control effect size. The seven treatments in six studies are homogeneous ($H = 5.31$, $df = 6$).

TABLE 6

Focus of Instruction: Summary of Experimental/Control Effect Size Statistics

Focus	Mean Effect	SD	95% Confidence Interval		H	df	Maximum H for Nonsignificance at $p < .01$
			Lower	Upper			
Treatments included in focus of instruction analysis (N = 39)	.26	.023	.21	.30	84.48	38	62.4
Grammar (N = 5)	−.29	.059	−.40	−.17	8.85	4	13.27
Sentence combining (N = 5)	.35	.083	.19	.51	1.89	4	13.27
Models (N = 7)	.22	.057	.11	.33	5.31	6	16.80
Scales (N = 6)	.36	.078	.21	.51	6.89	5	15.08
Free writing (N = 10)	.16	.035	.09	.23	27.25	9	21.66
Inquiry (N = 6)	.56	.076	.41	.71	8.73	5	15.08
Treatments categorized by focus of instruction (N = 39)	...	...	...	...	58.92	33	54.70
With two outliers removed (N = 37)	...	...	...	...	49.90	31	52.15

The mean experimental/control effect size for the five studies focusing on sentence combining activities is .35 and is also homogeneous ($H = 1.89, df = 4$). Although the effect size is not significantly different from that for the study of models, it is significantly greater than that for the grammar treatments.

The mean experimental/control effect size for the use of scales is .36 and is homogeneous ($H = 6.89, df = 5$). While the treatment is not significantly different from sentence combining, it is significantly different from three of the six focuses examined: grammar, models, and free writing.

The mean experimental/control effect size for the six treatments focusing on inquiry is .56, the highest mean effect size for any instructional focus. It, too, is homogeneous with $H = 8.73$ and $df = 5$. It is significantly higher than grammar, models ($z = 3.75, p < .0002$), scales ($z = 1.96, p < .05$), sentence combining ($1.98, p < .05$), and free writing ($z = 4.99, p < .0001$).

Finally, the mean effect size for the 10 treatments using free writing as a major instructional tool is .16. However, it is not homogeneous ($H = 29.25, df = 9$). Although free writing has a significantly stronger effect than grammar and mechanics, it is significantly lower than sentence combining ($z = 2.12, p < .05$), scales ($z = 2.35, p < .02$), and inquiry ($z = 4.99, p < .0001$).

With all studies included, the dimension of instructional focus comes close to homogeneity ($H = 58.92, df = 33$, with 54.70 required for nonsignificance at $p < .01$). The main source of this heterogeneity is the free-writing category ($H = 27.25$). The Adams (1971) study displays a high positive standardized residual, as it did in the natural process category, and should be removed for substantive reasons, its gain being entirely dependent on losses in the control groups. The removal of a second treatment, Witte and Faigley (1981), this one with a high negative standardized residual, along with Adams, increases the mean for free writing to .17 from .16 but reduces H to 18.23, which is not significant at $p < .01$, $df = 7$. The removal of these two studies reduces H for the dimension to 48.58, not significant at $p < .01$, $df = 31$.

To achieve homogeneity for each focus and in the dimension as a whole, only two of 39 treatments were removed. The dimension of instructional focus, then, has a high level of explanatory power, accounting for nearly 95 percent of the 39 treatments included in it.

Removal of Outliers

While the results reported above are clear, the critical reader may ask about the extent to which removal of outliers distorts the results. Four treatments were removed initially because of their contribution to heterogeneity, reducing the number of treatments from 73 to 69. Subsequently, three treatments were removed from the dimension of instructional mode and two from instructional focus to achieve homogeneity. As we have seen, the removal of the latter did not appreciably change the mean effect sizes. However, a question remains about the four studies removed initially. Did their removal change the results significantly?

Two of those studies (Troyka 1973; Smith 1974) were classified as using inquiry. Their inclusion in the results for inquiry increases the mean effect size from .56 to .97 but also increases H from a nonsignificant 8.85 to a highly significant 87.37. The Troyka (1973) experimental treatment was also classified as environmental. Its inclusion with other environmental treatments raises the mean effect size from .44 to .65. Both changes are clearly quite large. The Loritsch (1976) and Smith (1974) treatments were both classified as individualized treatments. Their inclusion increases the mean effect size slightly from .17 to .24. The Loritsch study could not be classified for instructional focus. It provided programmed materials and individual conferences that were not described but that college freshmen could utilize as they felt the need. The treatment with the greatest negative effect size (Ebbert 1980) provided instruction in heuristics and remained a one-of-a-kind treatment. It could not be classified for instructional mode. Clearly, the removal of these studies did not distort the direction of the findings. On the contrary, those that can be explained tend to reinforce the findings in that they increase effect sizes in the expected direction.

Summary and Discussion

These findings have important ramifications for instructional practice, policymaking, and research. First, they indicate that the dimensions of effective instruction are quite different from what is commonly practiced in schools and colleges on the one hand (the presentational mode) and what has been recommended by some adherents of the National Writing Project on the other (the natural process mode). In the most common and widespread mode (presentational), the instructor dominates all activity, with students acting as the passive recipients of rules, advice, and examples of good writing. This is the least effective mode examined, only about half as effective as the average experimental treatment.

In the natural process mode, the instructor encourages students to write for other students, to receive comments from them, and to revise their drafts in light of comments from both students and the instructor. But the instructor does not plan activities to help develop specific strategies of composing. This instructional mode is about 25 percent less effective than the average experimental treatment, but about 50 percent more effective than the presentational mode. In treatments that examine the effects of individualized work with students, the results are essentially the same.

I have labeled the most effective mode of instruction "environmental" because it brings teacher, student, and materials more nearly into balance and, in effect, takes advantage of all resources of the classroom. In this mode, the instructor plans and uses activities that result in high levels of student interaction concerning particular problems parallel to those they encounter in certain kinds of writing, such as generating criteria and examples to develop extended definitions of concepts or generating arguable assertions from appropriate data and predicting and countering opposing arguments. In contrast to the presentational mode, this mode places priority on high levels of student involvement. In contrast to the natural process mode, the environmental mode places priority on structured problem-solving activities, with clear objectives, planned to enable students to deal with similar problems in composing. On pretest-to-posttest measures, the environmental mode is over four times more effective than the traditional presentational mode and three times more effective than that natural process mode.

Like modes of instruction, the focuses of instruction examined have important ramifications for instructional practice.

Grammar.—The study of traditional school grammer (i.e., the definition of parts of speech, the parsing of sentences, etc.) has no effect on raising the quality of student writing. Every other focus of instruction examined in this review is stronger. Taught in certain ways, grammar and mechanics instruction has a deleterious effect on student writing. In some studies a heavy emphasis on mechanics and usage (e.g., marking every error) results in significant losses in overall quality. School boards, administrators, and teachers who impose the systematic study of traditional school grammar on their students over lengthy periods of time in the name of teaching writing do them a gross disservice that should not be tolerated by anyone concerned with the effective teaching of good writing. Teachers concerned with teaching standard usage and typographical conventions should teach them in the context of real writing problems.

Models.—What I have referred to as teaching from models undoubtedly has a place in the English program. This research indicates that emphasis on the presentation of good pieces of writing as models is significantly more useful than the study of grammar. At the same time, treatments that use the study of models almost exclusively are less effective than other available techniques.

Free writing.—This focus asks students to write freely about whatever interests or concerns them. As a major instructional technique, free writing is more effective than teaching grammar in raising the quality of student writing. However, it is less effective than any other focus of instruction examined. Even when examined in conjunction with other features of the "process" model of teaching writing (writing for peers, feedback from peers, revision, and so forth), these treatments are only about two-thirds as effective as the average experimental treatment and less than half as effective as environmental treatments.

Sentence combining.—The practice of building more complex sentences from simpler ones has been shown to be effective in a large number of experimental studies. This research shows sentence combining, on the average, to be more than twice as effective as free writing as a means of enhancing the quality of student writing.

Scales.—Scales, criteria, and specific questions that students apply to their own or others' writing also have a powerful effect on enhancing quality. Through using the criteria systematically, students appear to internalize them and bring them to bear in generating new material even when they do not have the criteria in front of them. These treatments are two times more effective than free-writing techniques.

Inquiry.—Inquiry focuses the attention of students on strategies for dealing with sets of data, strategies that will be used in writing. For example, treatments categorized as inquiry might involve students in finding and stating specific details that convey personal experience vividly, in examining sets of data to develop and support explanatory generalizations, or in analyzing situations that present ethical problems and in developing arguments about those situations. On the average, these treatments are nearly four times more effective than free writing and over two-and-a-half times more powerful than the traditional study of model pieces of writing.

While the results for the various treatments differ greatly from each other, this does not imply that the less effective techniques have no place in the writing curriculum. Indeed, sentence combining, scales, and inquiry all make occasional use of models, but they certainly do not emphasize the study of models exclusively. Structured free writing, in which writers jot down all of their ideas on a particular topic, can be successfully integrated with other techniques as a means of both memory search and invention.

These results have important ramifications for those in positions to make and recommend policy at local, state, and national levels. Indeed, the findings of this study directly contradict the assumptions, policy decisions, and recommendations of publicly funded agencies such as the National Assessment of Educational Progress. In its Winter 1983 newsletter, the NAEP offers eight " 'How to' Tips on Ways to Teach Writing." None of them lead teachers to the most effective mode or focuses of instruction identified above. In fact, all assume that the free-writing focus and the natural process mode of instruction are effective. No suggestion leads to the teacher's planning problems conducive to students' working together on various kinds of composition problems (environmental treatments). No suggestions say anything about the application of criteria, sentence combining, or inquiry (all superior to free writing). The experts, "conversant with the state-of-the-art research" (p. 4), making these recommendations were either not "conversant" with the research on which this paper is based or chose to ignore it.

For over a decade, authorities in the field have been caught up in the "writing as process" model, which calls for exploratory talk, followed by free writing, reading by or for an audience of peers, comments from peers, and revision. The teacher's role is simply to facilitate this process—*not* to make specific assignments, *not* to help students learn criteria for judging writing, *not* to structure classroom activities based on specific objectives as in the environmental treatments, *not* to provide exercises in manipulating syntax, *not* to design activities that engage students in identifiable processes of examining data. In short, this mode, advocated by several subsidiaries of the National Writing Project (e.g., Alloway et al. 1979), studiously avoids the approaches to writing instruction that this report demonstrates to be more effective.

Finally, the results of this study have important implications for research. First, they belie assertions by Emig (1982) and Graves (1980) that experimental research has no value for classroom teachers and that it has no utility for composition researchers. The controlled treatments with similar instructional variables included in this study have comparable (homogeneous) results. It is indeed possible to transfer effective treatments to new classroom settings. More important, it is possible to determine the effectiveness of treatment variables through experimental designs. To cast such research aside in favor of an exclusive reliance on case study methods as Emig and Graves recommend is folly. Researchers concerned with effective instruction in composition can make a happy marriage of the best case study and experimental methods, using careful observations to identify variables and experimental designs to test them.

Second, the results of this study suggest a number of directions for future research. The relative effectiveness of the variables identified should be a continuing question for researchers. This review could not examine the interaction of mode and focus of instruction because too few studies were available, but this appears to be a promising area. For example, although we know that the environmental mode appears significantly more effective than other modes, we do not know how it interacts with the various focuses of instruction. We do know that the focus on models for the purpose of learning the characteristics of good writing is less effective than three other focuses. If the mode of instruction were systematically varied with the focus on models, what would be the results? By definition, the natural process mode could not be used for teaching models because it excludes the imposition of forms from sources external to the learner. However, models might be used with presentational, individualized, or environmental modes. If models were studied in the presentational mode of instruction, which is the case in some of the studies included here, the teacher would ask students to read the model and would then explain the parts, qualities, or rhetorical strategies that it exemplifies. Eventually, students would write one or more compositions reflecting those same characteristics. If models were studied in the individualized mode, teachers would work with one student at a time, examining a model with a student, explaining its qualities and characteristics.

If models were the focus of instruction in the environmental mode, students might examine one model under the direction of the teacher but would proceed to the examination of others in small groups, assisted perhaps by a set of questions to guide their analysis. They might then report their ideas to the whole class. Disagreements would be examined and would prompt further explanations and analysis by the students, with the teacher acting as a moderator. This study encountered only one such treatment of models.

In the same way, other focuses of instruction might be varied across modes of instruction. Thus, researchers might ask whether sentence combining or sentence construction (Faigley 1979) is more effective when the mode of instruction is primarily presentational or when it is environmental, with students working in small groups to determine the most effective constructions, given certain substantive and rhetorical constraints. Similarly, one might ask whether inquiry is as effective when the teacher leads analysis of all data sets by explaining and asking questions or when the students themselves, working collaboratively in small groups, examine data and develop their own analyses, making use of specific strategies.

I am currently conducting a study that includes presentational and environmental modes each with a focus on models in one set of classes and a focus on inquiry in another. In the presentational/mode classes, students examine several examples of extended definitions with teachers providing analytical comments and teacher-led whole class discussions of each. In the environmental/model classes, students examine the same model compositions but do so in small groups with the aid of guide questions and then present their findings to and discuss them with the whole class.

In the presentational/inquiry classes teachers will lead students through sets of material, each set representing some problem of definition. One set of material, for example, consists of several scenarios, each briefly describing an action that may or may not be considered courageous. If it is not, the students are asked to explain why and, if possible, to develop a criteria for discriminating such actions from truly courageous actions. In the presentational classes, teachers will lead discussions of each set of scenarios. By contrast, in the environmental classes, students will work on the same problems, but in small groups, determining their own criteria.

Such experimental work should eventually provide clear information on the effects of the interaction of mode of instruction and focus of instruction.

Beyond that, a second promising area for research appears to be the interaction of variables within the dimension of instructional focus. Models and scales, for example, are both used to teach criteria that presumably aid not only in evaluating texts but in generating them. Successful revision must require that the reviser bring criteria to bear on the product to be revised. In the Sager (1973) study, sixth-grade students were provided with prompts implying criteria to use as guides in revising. A useful study might systematically examine the relative effects of these three approaches to teaching criteria (models, scales, and revision) and then proceed to examine their interactions.

This meta-analysis of research in teaching writing provides some tests of basic assumptions about the teaching of writing and suggests promising directions for practice. More important, however, will be answers to the many questions it raises for future research, answers that should go far in developing more adequate theories of teaching composition.

Although a great deal of research remains to be done on such questions, practitioners, policymakers, and researchers can ill afford to ignore the differences in treatment results that this analysis reveals. The experimental research of the past two decades indicates clear directions. If we wish our schools and colleges to teach writing effectively, we cannot retreat to the grammar book or rely on the presentation of rules and advice, or expect students to teach themselves how to write effectively simply by writing whatever they wish for varied groups of their peers. We must make systematic use of instructional techniques that are demonstrably more effective and continue our efforts to evaluate them.

Note

The research reported in this paper was supported by a grant from the Spencer Foundation and will be part of a book-length review of research on the teaching of composition.

References

Applebee, A. N. *Writing in the Secondary School* (Research Report No. 21). Urbana, Ill.: National Council of Teachers of English, 1981.

Braddock, R., R. Lloyd-Jones, and L. Schoer. *Research in Written Composition.* Champaign, Ill.: National Council of Teachers of English, 1963.

Bridwell, L. S. "Revising Strategies in Twelfth Grade Students' Transactional Writing." *Research in the Teaching of English* 14 (1980): 197–222.

Buckley, M. H., and O. Boyle. "Mapping and Composing." In *Theory and Practice in the Teaching of Composition: Processing, Distancing, and Modeling,* edited by M. Myers and J. Grey. Urbana, Ill.: National Council of Teachers of English, 1983.

Burton, D. L. "Research in the Teaching of English: The Troubled Dream." *Research in the Teaching of English* 7 (1973): 160–89.

Christensen, F. *Notes toward a New Rhetoric: Six Essays for Teachers.* New York: Harper & Row, 1967.

Cooper, C. R., and L. Odell, eds. *Research on Composing: Points of Departure.* Urbana, Ill.: National Council of Teachers of English, 1978.

Emig, J. "Inquiry Paradigms and Writing." *College Composition and Communication* 33 (1982): 64–75.

Giaconia, R., and L. Hedges. "Identifying Features of Effective Open Education." *Review of Educational Research* 52 (1982): 579–602.

Glass, G. V. "Integrating Findings: The Meta-analysis of Research." In *Review of Research in Education,* vol. 5, edited by L. S. Shulman. Itasca, Ill.: F. E. Peacock, 1978.

Graves, D. H. "Research Update: A New Look at Writing Research." *Language Arts* 57 (1980): 913–19.

Hedges, L. V. "Distribution Theory for Glass's Estimator of Effect Size and Related Estimators." *Journal of Educational Statistics* 6 (1981): 107–28.

Hedges, L. V. "Estimating Effect Size from a Series of Independent Experiments." *Psychological Bulletin* 92 (1982): 490–99. (*a*)

Hedges, L. V. "Fitting Categorical Models to Effect Sizes from a Series of Experiments." *Journal of Educational Statistics* 7 (1982): 119–37. (*b*)

Hillocks, G., Jr. "The Responses of College Freshmen to Three Modes of Instruction." *American Journal of Education* 89 (1981): 373–95.

Huber, P. J.: *Robust Statistical Procedures.* Philadelphia: Society for Industrial and Applied Mathematics, 1977.

Mellon, J. C. *Transformational Sentence-combining: A Method for Enhancing the Development of Syntactic Fluency in English Composition* (Research Report No. 10). Urbana, Ill.: National Council of Teachers of English, 1969.

Myers, M. "Approaches to the Teaching of Composition." In *Theory and Practice in the Teaching of Composition: Processing, Distancing, and Modeling,* edited by M. Myers and J. Gray. Urbana, Ill.: National Council of Teachers of English, 1983.

O'Hare, F. *Sentence Combining: Improving Student Writing without Formal Grammar Instruction* (Research Report No. 15). Urbana, Ill.: National Council of Teachers of English, 1973. (ERIC Document Reproduction Service No. ED 073 483)

Parker, R. P. "From Sputnik to Dartmouth: Trends in the Teaching of Composition." *English Journal* 68 (1979): 32–37.

Sager, C. "Improving the Quality of Written Composition through Pupil Use of Rating Scale." Unpublished doctoral dissertation, Boston University, 1973.

Wesdorp, H. *SCO Rapport: De didactiek van het stelen: Een overzicht van het onderzoek naar de effecten van diverse instructie-variabelen op de stelvardigheid.* Amsterdam: University van Amsterdam, 1982.

Studies in Meta-analysis

[The doctoral dissertations are on University microfilms, unless otherwise noted.]

Adams, V. A. "A Study of the Effects of Two Methods of Teaching Composition on Twelfth Graders." Doctoral dissertation, University of Illinois, 1971.

Alloway, E., J. Carroll, J. Emig, B. King, I. Marcotrigiano, J. Smith, and W. Spicer. *The New Jersey Writing Project.* New Brunswick, N.J.: A Consortium Project of Rutgers University, Educational Testing Service, and Nineteen New Jersey Public School Districts, 1979. (ERIC Document Reproduction Service No. ED 178 943)

Bata, E. J. "A Study of the Relative Effectiveness of Marking Techniques on Junior College Freshman English Composition." Doctoral dissertation, University of Maryland, 1972.

Belanger, J. F. "Reading Skill as an Influence on Writing Skill." Doctoral dissertation, University of Alberta, 1978. (ERIC Document Reproduction Service No. ED 163 409)

Benson, N. L. "The Effects of Peer Feedback during the Writing Process on Writing Performance, Revision Behavior, and Attitude toward Writing." Doctoral dissertation, University of Colorado, 1979.

Calhoun, J. L. "The Effects of Analysis of Essays in College Composition Classes on Reading and Writing Skills." Doctoral dissertation, Boston University, 1971.

Caplan, R., and C. Keech. *Showing-writing: A Training Program to Help Students Be Specific.* Berkeley: University of California, Bay Area Writing Project, 1980.

Clark, W. G. *An Evaluation of Two Techniques of Teaching Freshman Composition* (Final Report, DHEW Project No. 5-8427). Colorado Springs, Colo.: Air Force Academy, 1968. (ERIC Document Reproduction Service No. ED 053 142)

Clifford, J. P. "An Experimental Inquiry into the Effectiveness of Collaborative Learning as a Method for Improving the Experiential Writing Performance of College Freshmen in a Remedial Writing Class." Doctoral dissertation, New York University, 1977.

Clifford, J. "Composing in Stages: The Effects of a Collaborative Pedagogy." *Research in the Teaching of English* 15 (1981): 37–53.

Clopper, R. R. "A Study of Contract Correcting as a Means of Significantly Increasing Writing and English Skills." Doctoral dissertation, University of Maryland, 1967.

Coleman, V. B. "A Comparison between the Relative Effectiveness of Marginal-interlinear-terminal Commentary and of Audio-taped Commentary in Responding to English Compositions." Doctoral dissertation, University of Pittsburgh, 1973.

Davis, K. "Significant Improvement in Freshman Composition as Measured by Impromptu Essays: A Large-scale Experiment." *Research in the Teaching of English* 15 (1979): 45–48.

Eagleton, C. J. "Reciprocal Effects of Eleventh-Graders and Twelfth-Graders as Tutors to Sixth-Graders in Reading, Written Expression, and Attitude Modification." Doctoral dissertation, American University, 1973.

Ebbert, G. M. "A Comparison of Three Instructional Approaches for Teaching Written Composition: Pentadic, Tagmemic, and Control Treatment." Doctoral dissertation, Boston University, 1980.

Edmonds, G. F. "An Evaluation of the Effectiveness of the Writing Component in a Freshman Remedial Program at a Community College." Doctoral dissertation, Walden University, 1979. (ERIC Document Reproduction Service No. ED 178 946)

Effros, C. *An Experimental Study of the Effects of Guided Revision and Delayed Grades on Writing Proficiency of College Freshmen* (Final Report, DHEW grant OEG-72-0017[509]). West Haven, Conn.: New Haven University, 1973. (ERIC Document Reproduction Service No. ED 079 764).

Elley, W. B., I. H. Barham, H. Lamb, and M. Wylie. "The Role of Grammar in a Secondary School English Curriculum." *Research in the Teaching of English* 10 (1976): 5–21.

Faigley, L. "The Influence of Generative Rhetoric on the Syntactic Maturity and Writing Effectiveness of College Freshmen." *Research in the Teaching of English* 13 (1979): 197–206.

Farmer, W. L. "Individualized Evaluation as a Method of Instruction to Improve Writing Ability in Freshman College Composition." Doctoral dissertation, Southern Illinois University, 1976.

Farrell, K. J. "A Comparison of Three Instructional Approaches for Teaching Written Composition to High School Juniors: Teacher Lecture, Peer Evaluation, and Group Tutoring." Doctoral dissertation, Boston University, 1977.

Fichtenau, R. L. *Teaching Rhetorical Concepts to Elementary Children: A Research Report.* Pontiac, Mich.: Oakland Schools, 1968. (ERIC Document Reproduction Service No. ED 026 383)

Ganong, F. L. "Teaching Writing through the Use of a Program Based on the Work of Donald M. Murray," Doctoral dissertation, Boston University, 1974.

Gauntlett, J. F. "Project WRITE and its Effect on the Writing of High School Students." Doctoral dissertation, Northern Arizona University, 1977.

Gray, S., and C. Keech. *Writing from Given Information* (Collaborative Research Study No. 3). Berkeley: University of California, Bay Area Writing Project, 1980.

Gunter, G. O., and H. McNitt. *Effectiveness of an Interest-motivated Approach to Junior College Remedial English Instruction* (USOE Cooperative Research Project No. 2856). York Pa.: York Junior College, 1966. (ERIC Document Reproduction Service No. ED 010 121)

Hillocks, G., Jr. "The Effects of Observational Activities on Student Writing." *Research in the Teaching of English* 13 (1979): 23–35.

Hillocks, G., Jr. "The Interaction of Instruction, Teacher Comment, and Revision in Teaching the Composing Process." *Research in the Teaching of English* 16 (1982): 261–78.

Howie, S. M. H. "A Study: The Effects of Sentence Combining Practice on the Writing Ability and Reading Level of Ninth Grade Students." Doctoral dissertation, University of Colorado, 1979.

Judd, K. E. "The Effectiveness of Tape Recorded Evaluations of Compositions Written by Seventh and Eighth Grade Students." Doctoral dissertation, University of Connecticut, 1973.

Kemp, J. H. "A Comparison of Two Procedures for Improving the Writing of Developmental Writers." Doctoral dissertation, University of Georgia, 1979.

Kerek, A., D. A. Daiker, and M. Morenberg. "Sentence Combining and College Composition." *Perceptual and Motor Skills* 51 (Suppl. 1) (1980): 1059–1157 (monograph).

Kernan, M. N. "The Effects of a Human Development Program on Performance in College Freshman Writing Classes." Doctoral dissertation, University of Pittsburgh, 1973.

Lareau, E. H. "Comparison of Two Methods of Teaching Expository Composition and Evaluation of a Testing Instrument." Doctoral dissertation, Lehigh University, 1971.

Loritsch, R. H. "A Comparative Study of Traditional and Self-paced Methods of Teaching Freshman English Composition at the Northern Virginia Community College." Doctoral dissertation, George Washington University, 1976.

McCleary, W. J. "Teaching Deductive Logic: A Test of the Toulmin and Aristotelian Models for Critical Thinking and College Composition." Doctoral dissertation, University of Texas at Austin, 1979.

Mayo, N. B. "The Effects of Discussion and Assignment Questions on the Quality of Descriptive Writing of Tenth Grade Students." Doctoral dissertation, Memphis State University, 1975.

Miller, R. L. "An Evaluation of an Experimental Written Composition Program for Second Grade." Doctoral dissertation, University of Nebraska Teachers College, 1967.

Murdock, M. L. "Independent Study versus Lecture-Discussion in Teaching Freshman Composition." Doctoral dissertation, University of Maryland, 1973.

Olson, M. C., and P. DiStefano. "Describing and Testing the Effectiveness of a Contemporary Model for In-service Education in Teaching Composition." *English Education* 12 (1980): 69–76.

Pechar, G. M. "An Evaluation of an Oral Proofreading Technique Used to Teach Grammar and Composition." Doctoral dissertation, University of Kansas, 1976.

Pedersen, E. L. "Improving Syntactic and Semantic Fluency in the Writing of Language Arts Students through Extended Practice in Sentence-Combining." Doctoral dissertation, University of Minnesota, 1977.

Pisano, R. C. "The Effectiveness of an Intervention Study in Critical Thinking Skills Designed to Improve Written Composition in Eleventh and Twelfth Graders." Doctoral dissertation, Rutgers University, 1980.

Reedy, J. E. "A Comparative Study of Two Methods of Teaching the Organization of Expository Writing to Ninth-Grade Pupils." Doctoral dissertation, Boston University, 1964.

Rosen, M. "A Structured Classroom Writing Method: An Experiment in Teaching Rhetoric to Remedial English College Students." Doctoral dissertation, New York University, 1973.

Sanders, S. E. "A Comparison of 'Aims' and 'Modes' Approaches to the Teaching of Junior College Freshman Composition Both with and without an Auxiliary Writing Lab." Doctoral dissertation, University of Texas at Austin, 1973.

Sbaratta, P. A. "A Flexible Modular System: An Experiment in Teaching Freshman Composition." Doctoral dissertation, Boston University, 1975.

Smith, D. I. "Effects of Class Size and Individualized Instruction on the Writing of High School Juniors." Doctoral dissertation, Florida State University, 1974.

Swenson, D. H., C. P. Freeman, R. Supnick, and J. T. Segal. "Reducing the Number of Teacher-graded Papers in the Teaching of Informational Business Writing." Paper presented at the annual meeting of the American Business Communication Association, Phoenix, 1981. (ERIC Document Reproduction Service No. ED 209 666)

Thibodeau, A. L. "A Study of the Effects of Elaborative Thinking and Vocabulary Enrichment Exercises on Written Composition." Doctoral dissertation, Boston University, 1963.

Thibodeau, A. E. "Improving Composition Writing with Grammar and Organization Exercises Utilizing Differentiated Group Patterns." Doctoral dissertation, Boston University, 1963.

Troyka, L. Q. "A Study of the Effect of Simulation-gaming on Expository Prose Competence of College Remedial English Composition Students." Doctoral dissertation, New York University, 1973.

Vinson, L. L. N. "The Effects of Two Prewriting Activities upon the Overall Quality of Ninth Graders' Descriptive Paragraphs." Doctoral dissertation, University of South Carolina, 1980.

Wagner, B. J., S. Zemelman, and A. Malone-Trout. *The Chicago Area Writing Project Assessment.* Elmhurst, Ill.: School District 205, 1981.

Walker, J. P. "A Study of the Comparative Effectiveness of an Experience-centered and a Knowledge-centered Method of Teaching Composition." Doctoral dissertation, George Peabody College for Teachers, 1974.

Waterfall, C. M. "An Experimental Study of Sentence-Combining as a Means of Increasing Syntactic Maturity and Writing Quality in the Compositions of College-age Students Enrolled in Remedial English Classes." Doctoral dissertation, Utah State University, 1977.

West, W. W. "A Comparison of a 'Composition Equivalencies' Approach and a Traditional Approach to Teaching Writing." Doctoral dissertation, Syracuse University, 1966.

Widvey, L. I. "A Study of the Use of a Problem-Solving Approach to Composition in High School English." Doctoral dissertation, University of Nebraska, 1971.

Wienke, J. W. *Strategies for Improving Elementary School Students' Writing Skills,* 1981. (ERIC Document Reproduction Service No. ED 209 679)

Witte, S. P., and L. Faigley. *A Comparison of Analytic and Synthetic Approaches to the Teaching of College Writing.* Austin: University of Texas, 1981. (ERIC Document Reproduction Service No. ED 209 677)

Wright, N. J. "The Effects of Role-Playing on the Improvement of Freshman Composition." Doctoral dissertation, Texas A & M University, 1975.

Critical Issues in the Development of Literacy Education: Toward a Theory of Learning and Instruction

NANCY L. STEIN
University of Chicago

> Six blind men were given the task of describing an elephant. The first fellow touched its broad and sturdy side and declared that an elephant was like a wall. The second felt the tusk and described the animal as a spear; another felt the trunk and said it was like a snake, and another felt its knee and compared it to a tree. The fifth blind man felt its ear and insisted that the elephant was like a fan, and the sixth having felt its tail, declared that, to the contrary, an elephant was like a rope.
>
> An Indian Folktale

It is unusual to begin a commentary with a folktale, but in the case of discussing the development of literacy in the American schools, such a folktale seems quite appropriate. Among the essays gathered here, Sylvia Scribner's essay, in particular, seems to capture the mood of the folktale by illustrating the difficulty of arriving at one definition of literacy to which all individuals would adhere. The use of three different metaphors to describe literacy illustrates that people often have very different beliefs about the value and function of literacy. Furthermore, these different beliefs often preclude the development of an integrated viewpoint concerning how children should be educated, especially in the domain of verbal literacy. The ability to read and write can be perceived as one of the most valuable skills a person can acquire, these abilities can be perceived as useless, or acquiring literary skills can be perceived as very threatening, depending on the particular reference group to which a reader or writer belongs.

The critical component underlying the support of literacy programs across many different groups appears to be intimately connected with the fulfillment of personal goals for those who are involved in the literacy process. The more a program incorporates the needs and values of the individuals who participate in a reading or writing program, the more successful the program will be in advancing the literacy skills of various groups. This principle has been advocated not only by Scribner but also by several other investigators (see, e.g., Heath 1983) who have argued for the necessity of understanding a particular culture and its value system before advocating any particular type of approach to the development of literacy.

While this point of view is valid, especially if we are to succeed in educating a large number of individuals coming from different social and cultural communities, we are left with many unanswered questions concerning the definition and development of literacy education in this country. In this overview, I discuss some of the more pervasive problems and, where possible, make suggestions for a beginning resolution to some of the difficulties.

Definitions of Literacy

The first issue concerns the definition of literacy to be used in the school systems. Should the definition of literacy extend beyond the teaching of decoding skills? This is an important question to many individuals because of the possible conflicting value systems that are communicated through the type of texts used to teach reading. Some individuals believe that the solution to the problem of different value systems is to get the schools to concentrate on the basics. Here, the basics refer to the teaching and advancement of rapid decoding skills, isolated from tasks requiring meaning and value inferences. Although this position represents a nonexistent possibility, this is where many

---

NANCY L. STEIN is an associate professor in the Departments of Education and Behavioral Sciences at the University of Chicago. Her primary work focuses on the development of language and thought, especially in reference to theories of story understanding and story telling. Her recent studies focus on the development of writing and comprehension skill in relation to theories of learning and instruction. She is a co-author of *Learning and Comprehension of Text*, in collaboration with Heinz Mandl and Tom Trabasso.

of the debates concerning reading education begin. The slogan "Back to the Basics" is sometimes used to represent the belief that the teaching of reading primarily involves the teaching of decoding skills or the translation of written elements into language, to use Charles A. Perfetti's terminology.

Although many individuals would like to think of reading as a process primarily bound up in the decoding and recognition of words, the development of skilled reading is a more complicated process. As Perfetti shows in his essay, decoding skills (e.g., an awareness of certain letter-sound correspondences, an awareness of certain letter patterns) *are* essential for the growth of reading skill to rise above a certain level. In this regard, it is interesting to note that deaf children who are taught to read have difficulty attaining levels of reading skill beyond the third grade (Conrad 1979). One hypothesis for the lack of deaf children's success is that they have no direct access to acoustic information and therefore have difficulty acquiring the relevant linguistic knowledge necessary for skilled reading to occur. Thus, we see that direct and explicit attention to linguistic knowledge (e.g., decoding skill) is essential. Initial reading could probably be taught with a primary emphasis on the decoding aspects of the reading process, and indeed textbook publishers have concentrated on developing a list of subskills that are related to the development of the linguistic knowledge underlying the acquisition of reading skills.

As Perfetti points out, however, the development of skilled reading also depends on knowledge of word meanings and the ability to recognize words. As reading skill begins to develop, access to word meaning becomes an integral part of the reading process. In fact, the skilled reader uses many types of knowledge to increase the speed with which the written code is translated into language. This means that both linguistic and semantic knowledge are continually and interactively used. Because semantic knowledge is continually accessed during reading, one of the major emphases of the reading process becomes an effort after meaning. The reader is continually trying to make sense of the material being read. The end result is the construction of a meaningful, coherent representation of the text being read.

Difficulties in teaching reading often arise because publishers of basal reading series (the primary source of decoding and comprehension instruction for many school systems) adopt too narrow a view of the definition of skilled reading. For example, there are some reading programs that overemphasize the decoding aspect of teaching children to read. These reading programs often focus on a systematic introduction of letter-sound correspondences, an introduction to vowel and consonant sounds, presentation of reoccurring linguistic patterns, and so forth.

Initially, this type of approach is quite helpful to the novice reader, because attention to the linguistic aspects of words is quite difficult for some young children. However, many basals that emphasize decoding are not sensitive to the fact that children do read for meaning even during the early stages of reading acquisition (see Judith Langer's article). The texts that appear in many basals are frequently not well formed. As such, children lack the possibility of discovering a coherent meaning structure (Beck, McKeown, McCaslin, and Burkes 1979; Stein 1979; Stein and Trabasso 1982). Moreover, these basal reading series give little thought to the comprehension instruction that should accompany teachers' manuals (Durkin 1984). Thus, reading for meaning becomes an arduous task for many children.

On the other hand, there are basal reading series that do attempt to attend to meaning. These series include more meaningful literature in the curriculum. The content of these basals is often interesting, and the structure of the text material is well formed. However, many of these meaning approaches do not contain a systematic method of teaching the development of good decoding skills, and the comprehension activities are often not adequate for teachers to use the materials in a meaningful and instructive fashion.

In the last few years, textbook publishers have become much more aware of the many different processes that underlie the act of reading (see Anderson, Osborn, and Tierney [1984] for an edited volume addressed specifically to publishers of basal reading series). Many publishers are revising their basals in an attempt to include both a systematic approach to the development of decoding skills and an approach to text comprehension that deals more systematically with the structure and meaning of text material. In considering the meaningful nature of text processing, however, another ugly problem rears its head.

Selection of Curriculum Content

The inclusion of texts that are coherent in structure immediately raises the issue of the content that should be included in a text. When children engage in the construction of meaningful representations of texts, they also make inferences about the value of the information presented in the text. Abstracting value and moral information is inherent in the process of comprehension regardless of the subject matter being addressed. By the very fact that certain types of information are being presented to children, a value judgment has been made that this type of information is suitable for them and worthy of learning.

Thus, it is virtually impossible to escape learning about some type of value system during the educational process.

The realization that values are an inherent part of reading comprehension deflates many of the current arguments over how reading should be taught. There are several groups of individuals across the country who believe that reading skills can be taught as a procedure and can be separated from the content that one is using to learn how to read. Examples of the stances developing are seen in such statements as "We don't want to be bothered with issues of content, just tell us how to teach reading" and "We can't use your method of reading because it not only tells us how to teach, but it tells us what to teach!"

From my previous discussion and from Perfetti's discussion of the reading process, it becomes obvious that part of the skilled reading process is focused on the process of constructing meaning from text material. Thus the definition of literacy, by its very nature, includes a meaning component and leads directly to some of the problems addressed in Sylvia Scribner's essay, as well as by several other investigators (Anderson 1984; Heath 1982; Resnick and Resnick 1977). The basic question concerns the system of values to be represented in written materials included in the different subject areas that form school curricula. Given the existence of different value systems in our country, what should be the basis of the selection of curriculum material?

Different solutions to this problem have been attempted. Some groups of educators have attempted to form curriculum committees, sometimes at the state level, for the sole purpose of reviewing material to be included in school curriculums. Both the states of California and Texas have such committees. California has even provided a manual listing the standards for evaluation of instructional material with respect to social content. And Texas has formal procedures for the approval of all material used in the classroom.

The problem with committees such as these is that they often delete materials from the curriculum that other individuals think is valuable literature. For example, in completing a reading list appropriate for high school students, some committees have deleted books such as *Huckleberry Finn* by Mark Twain and *To Kill a Mockingbird* by Harper Lee. The reason given was that each book portrayed some type of ethnic group in a negative light. Studs Terkel's *American Dreams: Lost and Found* received the same type of scrutiny by a group of working-class parents who did not want their children exposed to such a book. The problem, said many of the parents, was that Terkel presented many working-class parents in a negative light, especially with respect to the language and behavior exhibited by many of the protagonists in Terkel's book.

The intensity of the debate about the appropriate curriculum materials reflects a sharp division in the value systems that exist in our country. For example, some groups are concerned that children become aware of the appropriate Christian values and the conservative political philosophy that influenced the development of our country. Individuals adhering to this perspective believe that curriculum materials should be constructed to represent only one set of values. Norma and Mel Gabler, two individuals who have had enormous influence on the adoption of curriculum material in the state of Texas, exemplify this viewpoint. Their belief is that curriculum material should be severely constrained and should reflect only "positive" approaches to many of the social problems faced by students. This means that references to negative feelings and to expressions of aggression or hopelessness should not occur in any curriculum material. Also, the role of women, the function of the family, and the importance of religion are topics where only certain viewpoints can be represented.

There are other groups, however, who believe that presenting alternative viewpoints is an essential element of schooling. These groups of individuals would advocate that students read as widely as possible in order to understand the different types of values and motives underlying human action. In fact, one of the goals of education for these groups of people is to allow the formation of a perspective that fosters the development of understanding and toleration of different points of views. In contrast to a constrained curriculum content approach, this group encourages students to compare and contrast different viewpoints, in terms of the values inherent in each point of view. For example, many high schools encourage the study of another culture by their students in order to facilitate a more accurate representation of both their own culture and another one.

If we were to pick one strategy that should be used in educating children, which one would it be? To answer this question appropriately, it would be important to have some data concerning the natural interaction that takes place in the classroom, apart from the types of curriculum materials that are introduced in basal readers and trade books. From many observational studies and from teacher reports, one of the first things that becomes apparent to young children in kindergarten and first grade are the differences and similarities among themselves and their classmates (Suls and Miller 1977). Children have very definite preferences for friends at an early age (Asher and Renshaw 1981; Corsaro 1981), have specific standards for the development of friendship, are aware of how different moral and social codes operate (Shweder, Turiel, and Much 1981), and make comparisons between themselves and others on many different dimensions.

The difficulty with social comparison processes is that many times children make incorrect harmful inferences about others different from themselves. Thus, the emphasis in many schools has been on discovering what those inferences are and attempting to provide information that would correct misinterpretations and allow children to understand one another in a more accurate and tolerant fashion. The fact that social comparisons are almost a given in any type of classroom leads one to the conclusion that different types of viewpoints *have* to be considered in an explicit, consistent fashion. Whether basal readers include different perspectives or not, teachers and students will have to construct some type of understanding of other people and their value systems. An approach that corresponds to real-world learning already occurring in the classroom would be extremely important.

Supporting the introduction of different value systems in the curriculum does not mean that there cannot be an integrated, more unified approach to the construction of curriculum materials. There are certain principles and systems that unite people in this country. Because of the rapid change occurring in some of the social structures in this country, an overabundance of attention has been focused on the changes and difference among people. However, there are formal and informal political and social structures that are common to all people, simply because they have participated in a shared American experience. These common goals are rarely emphasized and brought up for classroom discussion, especially in comparison with the attention given to the differences in value systems.

To begin a more systematic restructuring of the curriculum, one of the first necessary steps should be an evaluation of curriculum materials, especially in terms of the specific content and ideas now included. Although there are profound disagreements as to what the content of curriculum material should be, there has not been an effort by any group to come up with a taxonomy of ideas and concepts worth communicating. Although individual teachers and some school districts may undertake such an analysis to organize their approach to teaching, a content analysis has not been completed on a broad systematic basis. Basal readers have been evaluated in terms of the ease of comprehending the structure of texts (Beck et al. 1979). These types of readers have also been evaluated in terms of the amount of actual comprehension instruction disseminated to teachers for each unit in the text (Durkin 1984). The missing component in all of these analyses is a method for understanding how the nature of the specific content of the material influences comprehension and the development of literacy.

Because of the missing content analysis, we really do not know in detail how curriculum materials in different parts of the country differ from one another or what the amount of actual overlap is in content material across geographic and social boundaries. This type of research needs to be implemented, with a taxonomy of ideas and concepts being created as the evaluation of material proceeds. Furthermore, a more systematic basis for including or excluding curriculum content needs to be constructed.

Because certain types of content arouse the ire of different interest groups, a more systematic examination of the effects of presenting certain types of ideas needs to be carried out. Many of the beliefs concerning the detrimental effects of various types of materials and values may or may not be well founded. Advocates of different approaches to the development of literacy often have little knowledge about the context in which teachers introduce certain books or the functions that underlie the use of various pieces of literature. Since the development of reading and writing skills assumes a central part of schooling in our society, it would seem imperative that a more detailed analysis of written materials be undertaken. The main objective would be to focus on the *goals and ideas* being communicated in various types of texts. The necessity of completing a content analysis of curriculum material is not only important in resolving some of the major differences underlying notions of curriculum reform but the role of specific content knowledge is thought to be a powerful factor regulating the development of skilled reading and writing. As we shall see later in this article, there is much debate about whether general thinking skills can be taught without rapid access to a large amount of specific knowledge in a given area.

The Development of Skilled Reading and Writing

Now, for the moment, suppose that we could come to some agreement about the types of materials to be included in the school curriculum. The next questions concern the process by which children learn the knowledge valued by society. What factors are critical in ensuring that children learn to acquire knowledge, especially from text material? And what factors are important in acquiring good writing skills?

To answer these questions, it is necessary to understand that there are constraints that operate during the process of understanding text material. One of the fundamental dimensions that guides the process of understanding and learning is the amount and structure of knowledge already acquired by a reader or learner. In their essays, Isabel L. Beck and Margaret G. McKeown, Alan C. Purves, and Judith A. Langer all acknowledge the importance of prior knowledge in determining comprehension, and a plethora of studies has been completed in the last 10 years to document the importance of assessing prior knowledge in predicting how well text material will be understood (see Langer 1981; Mandl, Stein, and Trabasso 1984; Pearson and Gallagher 1983; Stein 1983).

Three points are worth acknowledging in discussing the role of prior knowledge in the comprehension process. First, much of the prior knowledge necessary for understanding text material is acquired outside of school and through modes other than reading and writing. Second, there are many types of knowledge used to comprehend text material, as Purves, in his essay, and Stein and Trabasso (1982; Stein 1983) illustrate. Third, there are definite constraints on how information is encoded and organized.

The latter point is worth emphasizing because often we tend to think that the end point in the development of skilled reading is a state of expertise where the reader can take in any type of material and construct an unambiguous meaningful representation of the text, independent of its content and structure. This is not the case. Even the skilled reader has difficulty processing certain types of material (see Rumelhart 1980; Schank and Abelson 1977; Simon 1969; Stein 1983). For example, it would be virtually impossible for a skilled reader to remember very much of a story that was sequenced in a random fashion, where the events did not correspond to any sense of real time order (Stein and Nezworski 1978). Also, adults have difficulty remembering two episodes presented in an interleaved fashion (Mandler 1978).

Although these are relatively simple examples, they do illustrate that understanding is very dependent on the form in which material is presented (Stein and Trabasso 1982; Trabasso, Secco, and van den Broek 1984) and is somewhat independent of the skill of the reader. There are certain ways of organizing and structuring texts that are preferable and more comprehensible to all age groups and skill levels (Stein, Kilgore, and Policastro 1984).

Because of the importance attributed to text structure and organization, many individuals have attempted to illustrate how certain types of texts can be rewritten to increase memory and comprehension during reading. Isabel L. Beck and Margaret G. McKeown's essay is a good example of one such effort. By removing linguistic ambiguities from a text, by clarifying the relationships among certain events in a story, and by adding information that would make certain concepts comprehensible to children, Beck, McKeown, and their colleagues (Beck, McKeown, Omanson, and Pople 1984) have demonstrated that both comprehension and memory for stories can be increased. Comparing commercial stories to their revised versions, Beck et al. (1984) showed an increase in both recall and skill in answering probe questions.

Their findings raise some very interesting questions, however, with respect to other research on text structure and organization. First of all, increases in recall of their revised stories occurred primarily for the central or "most important" information in a text. Recall of detail or noncentral information was not improved. Second, the major increases in recall were found in groups of skilled readers as opposed to groups of nonskilled readers. In terms of recalling central information, skilled readers recalled 17 percent of the central events in the original basal version and 33 percent of the events in the revised version. Less skilled readers recalled 12 percent of the central events in the original version and 17 percent in the revised version.

In answering probe questions, differences were found when the original and revised texts were compared. However, these differences resulting from the type of text material presented were not very large. Skilled readers answered 65 percent of all questions accurately when given the original version; they answered 72 percent of all questions in the revised versions. Less skilled readers answered 54 percent of the questions for the original version and 61 percent of the questions for the revised version.

Several things are of interest in the Beck et al. (1984) study. Rewriting texts does increase the amount of material remembered, but the increases both in recall and comprehension are fairly small. In fact, the increases in correct answers to probe questions is about 7 percent for both groups of readers. This amounts to about one question in terms of increasing children's understanding of text information. Also the primary increase in recall occurred in the skilled reading group. The less skilled readers did not improve that much and only recalled less than one-fourth of the events mentioned in the story. Thus, although rewriting these stories did increase comprehension, with respect to both memory and understanding, the children participating in the Beck et al. (1984) study still have much to understand about the stories presented.

Several reasons might underlie the limited amount of improvement. First, the students' level of conceptual knowledge about each of the passages may not have been very great. As Beck and McKeown argue in their essay and as I have illustrated before, the amount of prior knowledge children have about the concepts and content included in a text is critical.

In the Beck et al. (1984) study (see Beck and McKeown's essay for a synopsis of the study), the types of concepts introduced in each of the stories were relatively sophisticated. For example, one of their stories, "The Raccoon and Mrs. McGinnis," concerned a woman who wanted to build a barn for her animals. The woman thought that by wishing on a star she would somehow be able to get the barn that she desired. At the end of the story, the woman gets a bag of money and uses it to build a barn. She thinks that wishing on a star made her wish come true. The circumstances leading up to the woman getting the bag of money, however, were very different from the way she envisioned them.

When the woman went inside her house, two men came and stole her animals. When the men were escaping with the animals, they kept hearing odd noises in the background. In reality it was a raccoon that Mrs. McGinnis fed every night. As the story progresses, the men hear more noises. On hearing one set of odd sounds, the men look directly into a tree where the raccoon is hiding. Since it is dark, all they see is the mask around the raccoon's eyes. The men think the raccoon is another robber, fear that the "masked bandit" will shoot, drop a bag of money they have been carrying, and flee from the scene.

When the men flee, the animals go back to Mrs. McGinnis's house, the raccoon picks up the money bag, and then he, too, goes back to Mrs. McGinnis's house. When he arrives at the house, he drops the bag of money on Mrs. McGinnis's door step and looks for food. When he finds no food, he climbs up his tree and goes to bed. In the morning Mrs. McGinnis finds the money bag.

One of the main points that could underlie the telling of this story is that the explanation for many events are not what we think they are. We tend to construct reasons for the occurrence of events, often without examining the accuracy of these reasons. There is no information given in the story, in the form of a moral, that would necessarily lead an elementary school child to this conclusion as being the primary reason for reading the story. The publishers have not considered in detail what types of information they want students to learn from such a story.

Had a moral been included in the story, the series of coincidental events presented would still be difficult to understand, even for older children. Elementary school children can distinguish between acts that are accidental and purposeful in nature. However, the context in which they are asked to do so must be made explicit, as Beck et al. (1984) show. Before revising this text, Beck and her colleagues report that children often assumed that the raccoon played an intentional role in helping Mrs. McGinnis's build her barn. By specifying explicitly that this was not the case, many children began to understand the underlying conceptual nature of the story.

There are still problems with the structure of the story, however, even if the concept of intentionality is made explicit. The problems are both structural and content related. First, even Beck et al.'s revised version is not a well-formed story, according to the conceptions of an ideal form laid out in many theories of story understanding (Mandler and Johnson 1977; Rumelhart 1977; Stein and Glenn 1979). In the revised version, the raccoon is the first character introduced into the story line, even though Mrs. McGinnis assumes the first central role in the story. Second, in describing the raccoon's actions in relation to the two bandits' actions, the events in the story are interleaved. That is, the goals, plans, and actions of each set of characters are described in a piecemeal fashion, where one character's actions are interleaved with the other character's action.

Although this technique might appear to be interesting and literary in nature, the presence of interleaving decreases comprehension by a significant amount (Mandler 1978; Schnotz 1984). This finding holds for adults as well as children. In fact, Schnotz (1984) has shown that only when adults become very knowledgeable and familiar with a topic can they begin to remember information in an interleaved fashion.

What all of this discussion points to is the massive amount of reworking and revision that will be necessary if basal readers are to be more comprehensible to children. What we have found in revising basal stories is that most of the stories and texts cannot be changed by the use of simple revision strategies. The main reason is that not enough attention has been focused on the conceptual underpinnings of each selection included in the basal reader. (See the Beck and McKeown essay for similar comments concerning prereading activities and the Langer article for similar comments regarding reading comprehension tests.)

As three different papers in this collection illustrate (Beck and McKeown, Purves, and Langer), comprehension of text is contingent on many factors. Both structural information and content play a crucial role and account for part of the variance in determining comprehension. Purves shows the diverse nature of the understanding process in his analysis of what it takes for a reader to understand the sonnet "On First Looking into Chapman's Homer" by John Keats. The importance of his analysis, along with Beck and McKeown's analysis of basal readers, is that a rigorous task analysis is necessary for almost any piece of prose to be included in the curriculum.

In the past five years, much of the research in the field of discourse comprehension has focused on the structural dimensions underlying text comprehension (see Meyer [1984] and Stein and Trabasso [1982] for reviews of work in both story and expository text comprehension). Although we do not know all of the structural dimensions regulating comprehension, we know that certain types of text organization facilitate comprehension whereas other types of text structures decrease comprehension.

One of the reasons that these research findings are difficult to translate into classroom learning is that text comprehension is dependent on more than structural-organizational factors. Understanding is also dependent on how much knowledge students have about the specific content included in a text. At the moment, we lack a theory of domain specific content that would provide some idea of how people organize specific types of knowledge. The success of any instructional program is contingent upon how specific knowledge is organized and encoded, and without such a theory, comprehension and writing instruction become a rather haphazard operation.

The Development of a Theory of Learning and Instruction

Our lack of knowledge about the role of specific content in both the comprehension and composition processes has serious consequences for all phases of instruction. Perhaps a concrete example will illustrate the importance of such knowledge. In her essay, Judith Langer outlines several factors that she considers to be important in a successful instructional program. Most of these factors underlie many existing theories of learning, independent of the bias inherent in a particular theory. For example, almost all theories (whether they are behavioristic or cognitive in nature) start with the assumption that what is being taught must be directly related to what the student already knows. The assumption here is that learning occurs by allowing students to incorporate new information into existing structures (Bartlett 1932; Piaget 1967; Skinner 1964).

Assumptions underlying the notions of operant conditioning correspond to Langer's notions of the necessity for structure and the withdrawal of "support." So do many of the instructional assumptions underlying current notions of learning vis-à-vis cognitive models of learning (Simon 1980; Tuma and Reif 1980). Many of the instructional studies completed, both recently (Bloom 1976, 1984; Palinscar and Brown, in press) and in the past (Cronbach 1966, Shulman and Keislar 1966) have shown that the type of structure present in a learning situation is significant in predicting whether or not learning occurs. George Hillocks's meta-analysis essay of strategies that work in composition instruction is another indication that some type of specific structural organization and support is necessary for successful instruction.

Langer's notion of "student ownership" corresponds to the idea that learning requires an active role in order to ensure that the new information is well integrated into a student's existing mental structures. Almost all studies of the learning process, whether they are cognitive or behavioristic in orientation, show that many trials and different contexts are necessary for students to retain and use information. These studies also show that much "rehearsal" is necessary for students to be able to truly integrate new information into what is already known. Students can "memorize" and regurgitate much new information because they create some type of meaningful structure to help them retain the information. Use of new information over a broad range of situations, however, takes much more than memorization. The contextual knowledge in which information is used tends to change the structure and use of the information. Thus the student has to be aware of how the context affects the acquisition and storage of information in order to be able to use it in new situations.

The problem in applying Langer's principles to a learning situation is that, most of the time, teachers and researchers are missing information about the two most critical states related to learning: the initial state of the learner and the projected end state that should result as a function of learning (Glaser 1980). Thus, even if teachers knew that the learning task had to be related to what children already know, they would first need to devise some method of determining what their students know about a particular task.

At the moment, the procedure of determining students' prior knowledge is not well organized. Although teachers' manuals emphasize the importance of activating prior knowledge, the manuals contain no theoretically based method for determining the contents of this knowledge. Also missing from the manuals are clear objectives about the material to be learned. Few, if any, lessons give the teacher an idea of how children's knowledge is to be changed by participating in an exercise. And virtually no basals tell the teacher what to do if the children do not understand the prereading tasks.

A teacher who was aware of Langer's principles underlying good learning but who had little awareness of the initial state of her pupils' knowledge would have a very difficult time teaching children anything. In fact, the example Langer includes in her essay, concerning a teacher who wanted her students to write about China, serves as an illustration of this problem. It is interesting to note that Langer's teacher did not attempt to delve into the students' knowledge base in any consistent fashion, nor did she attempt to direct students in term of specific goals set forth in a lesson on China, nor did she attempt to assess the transitional process associated with learning.

Part of the difficulty inherent in the comprehension and writing processes is a lack of awareness that a student's mental structures are undergoing change and that "learning" is occurring. Teachers and publishers of basals often get so bound up in the act of reading and writing that they forget that the real purpose underlying these activities has to do with learning.

If learning is considered the primary objective in a reading and writing curriculum, then several dimensions have to be considered. First, a clear outline of the end goal has to be stated. This entails describing in a fair amount of detail the concepts that are to be learned. Both Glaser (1980) and Resnick (1984) propose that a systematic task analysis be completed on the relevant material. Second, a description of the initial state of the learner must be assessed, in terms of the end goals of instruction. This task is normally completed by relating what the student already knows to the concepts described in the task analysis. An assessment of the initial knowledge state is important because different instructional strategies might be used for different levels of initial knowledge states (Rumelhart and Norman 1978). And third, a rationale for getting the student from the initial state to the final state has to be given.

Although these dimensions are simple to outline, achieving the desired end result is quite difficult (Glaser 1980). Not only do instructors need knowledge of the beginning and end states of the learner, they also need knowledge of the process by which the learner will proceed from state A to state B. As Hillocks's meta-analysis shows, some of the more intuitive strategies used in comprehension instruction are not the most effective. Understanding and describing the initial knowledge state of a student does not necessarily guarantee that learning will occur. A necessary step in ensuring effective instruction is an analysis of what goes on in the head of the learner (Norman 1980) when certain instructional practices are used. To date, we have very little research completed in this area.

Hillocks's meta-analysis of instructional treatments in composition research is a first step toward progress in this area. His review of composition research accomplishes two goals. First, he has constructed a taxonomy of both modes and focuses of instruction that have actually been used in experimental writing studies in the last 20 years. In reading his essay, we are able to get a rough estimate of the relative effectiveness of several different types of instruction. A consequence of his review is that it makes us more aware of the difficulty of ensuring instructional effectiveness without comparing different modes and focuses of instruction. What Hillocks shows us is that the more intuitive and naturalistic approaches to writing instruction are not necessarily the most effective in teaching complex writing skills, even though the naturalistic approach approximates much of the instruction being advocated by many different researchers across the country.

More important, Hillocks's analysis provides us with a useful description to begin the construction of a taxonomy of learning and instructional objectives that have *not* been explored in the studies included in the meta-analysis. It should be apparent to the reader that the ways in which past studies have been carried out have confounded many of the variables important to the process of learning. Thus, it would be difficult for a teacher or textbook publisher to ensure that a particular mode or focus would be effective without exploring in more detail the specific content being communicated to students.

To illustrate the problems with the taxonomy that resulted from past studies, I have given an explicit example of the problematic nature of the variables contained in the taxonomy. Then, I have constructed an alternative taxonomy that includes a more systematic description of the variables important to the learning process. Bear in mind that my alternative taxonomy is constructed using some of the principles of information processing and knowledge acquisition underlying models of comprehension and composition. Hillocks's taxonomy, by necessity, was constrained to those studies available in the literature.

In characterizing the mode of instruction used in the meta-analysis, the role of teachers, in terms of whether they lecture to students or choose to interact with them is intimately bound to the type of materials they present. For example, in the presentational mode of instruction outlined by Hillocks, teachers (or experimenters) most often use models or materials to explain or illustrate the particular concept that is to be learned. Specific assignments or exercises are then given where the student is instructed to imitate a pattern or follow certain rules to create a text. Feedback comes primarily from the teacher.

On the other hand, the environmental mode uses materials to engage the students with each other in processes that have been specified in an a priori fashion. The teacher, rather than lecturing, uses small groups and specific tasks to illustrate the specific dimensions under consideration. Students work on certain tasks in small groups before proceeding to independent tasks constructed in a similar fashion. Principles are taught but not simply announced, as they are in the presentational mode.

The problem with making generalizations about the modes of instruction used in past studies is that each mode contains several different components that do not necessarily have to be linked together. For example, we could easily devise an instructional treatment that the current taxonomy could not describe. More important, the hypothesized treatment could be more effective than either the presentational or environmental mode of instruction. Furthermore, we could devise techniques where teachers in the presentational mode were by far more effective than those in the environmental mode. This could easily be done by presenting different types of content materials and examples in a lecture than are classically presented in presentational mode studies. The point is that a lecture can be as concrete, organized, interesting, and flexible as the lecturer chooses it to be. The quality and content depend on who is teaching, what is being taught, and how the information is being disseminated.

In past experimental studies, there has been little effort to determine the relative contributions of the content of instruction as separated from the process by which the material is presented to students. The fact that Hillocks's mode of instruction combines how materials are structured with the type of interaction that occurs in the classroom illustrates that most researchers have not been active in discovering the proportion of instructional variation that can be accounted for by the content being presented separate from the process of instruction.

Bloom (1984) and his students have attempted to explore this issue in a beginning attempt to make group comprehension instruction as effective as one-to-one tutoring, which is found to be a very effective instructional strategy. In constructing different methods of instruction, two of Bloom's students (Anania 1981; Burke 1983) compared three methods of instruction: conventional, mastery learning, and tutorial. Conventional instruction corresponded to regular classroom learning (class size about 30), where tests were given only for the purposes for determining students' marks. Mastery learning corresponded to regular classroom learning (same class size), where the same tests were given to students but with a different purpose underlying the test. The tests were used to allow the teacher to give corrective feedback to students and to determine the extent to which students mastered the concepts under consideration. Tutorial instruction involved a one-to-one interaction between student and teacher or between three students and a teacher. Similar types of mastery learning evaluative procedures were used in a one-to-one tutorial situation.

The results of both the Anania (1981) and Burke (1983) studies were as follows. Students participating in the tutorial instruction were about two standard deviations above the group receiving regular classroom instruction. The average tutored student outperformed 98 percent of the students receiving normal classroom instruction. The students receiving group instruction in the mastery learning condition were about one standard deviation above the students in the normal instruction group, outperforming 84 percent of the students in the normal instruction group.

Other changes were apparent in the three instructional groups. The mastery learning and tutorial instruction groups differed from the normal instruction group on both the level of summative achievement and the amount of time spent on task. Both mastery learning and tutorial instruction groups achieved more and spent more time on task. Thus, the method of group instruction can be increased in effectiveness if corrective feedback is given to students concerning their performance. A lecture-type presentation is effective if it is combined with some type of feedback during instruction. Again, the focus is on the type of information being communicated to students rather than the process of presentation.

Traditionally, tutorials and small-group instruction in comprehension activities tend to be most effective because the tutorial process can be more sensitive to the nature of the learning process. In learning tasks, students will use what knowledge they have available to construct an understanding of new information. As I mentioned previously, however, the type of prior knowledge used in acquiring new information constrains the student in terms of the quality of inferences made about the new material. Often, children will make some correct inferences about how the new information is to be remembered and organized, but more often than not some inferences made are incorrect in terms of the instructional objectives.

In an effort to teach new concepts, there are procedures adopted by the teacher to remedy some of the difficulties experienced in the learning situation. For example, an analysis of the prototypic dimensions of the concept are usually given. Then an effort is made to teach students attributes that are not relevant to the concept. Concrete examples of both instances and noninstances follow. And then an effort is made to relate the particular concept to other concepts frequently used in association to the central concept (Frayer, Frederick, and Klausmeier 1969; Winston 1973).

For these procedures to work, however, a teacher must know if the student processed the material in the predicted way. The nonexamples used in concept formation tasks are most often included in order to correct any misinterpretations students have made about the relevant attributes of a concept. Usually nonexamples are "near misses," instances that have some of the attributes in common with a concept but do not include all of the necessary features. However nonexamples used in concept formation tasks can be confusing or ineffective in teaching concepts. Often, students have made errors not predicted by the teacher or the constructor of the learning task. Thus, individual corrective feedback becomes essential if students have made a unique set of wrong inferences about a particular concept.

One of the reasons for the success of the environmental mode in writing instruction may be that the sequence of activities almost always provides an opportunity for children to receive feedback about the nature of the inferences made during concept acquisition. Students can receive feedback from their peers or the teacher or by reviewing how the task is structured. The three sources of information provide a richness that many other types of teaching do not. The richness of feedback is important, especially when the teacher or task instructor does not know very much about the nature and source of errors students will make during the learning process.

There is the real possibility, however, of devising an instructional procedure that uses acurate information about the kinds of typical errors made in learning new tasks. Several existing computer programs are designed to do just this (see Henry Jay Becker's essay for examples of these programs; also see Goldstein 1980). The difference between these computer programs and many school concept acquisition tasks is that, in building a program designed to teach a concept, much more effort is advanced in learning the nature of errors during concept formation than in most school learning environments. Thus, the important focus becomes one of the specific knowledge (e.g., the nature of the corrective feedback) given during instruction rather than one of the method of delivery.

Similar problems are inherent in the tasks used in the different *focuses* of instruction. Two major dimensions are included in the notion of focus; one is related to the nature of the content to be learned, and the other concerns the type of task used during the process of instruction. In the studies included in Hillocks's meta-analysis, these two factors are not explored in a systematic fashion. No one study varied the tasks used to teach writing while holding constant the type of content or concept to be learned. More important, there were no studies that made any distinctions within the types of content knowledge that could be taught.

In recent analyses of problem-solving behavior and story-understanding skills (Brown, Bransford, Ferrara, and Campione 1983; Glaser 1984; Larkin 1980; Mandler 1983; Stein 1983), distinctions are made between two types of knowledge: declarative and procedural. Declarative knowledge represents the types of factual knowledge that is acquired during the course of development. Procedural knowledge represents the schemes or structures used to access and organize factual knowledge. In other words, procedural knowledge is representative of knowing how to do something, whereas declarative knowledge is representative of knowing that something is true in reference to a particular concept (Mandler 1983).

A second distinction can be made within the declarative knowledge domain, especially in reference to the development of writing skills. We can get students to focus on three different types of knowledge during the writing process: linguistic knowledge, genre-specific knowledge, and domain-specific knowledge. Linguistic knowledge includes knowledge of syntax, spelling, and punctuation. Genre knowledge focuses on the knowledge that defines different forms of discourse (e.g., stories, descriptions, opinion essays, concept definition texts, and procedures). Content-domain knowledge refers to the specific information used to write different types of prose. Divisions in content knowledge can correspond to categories of knowledge about people, places, objects, physical events, and so forth. Another way of conceptualizing domain-specific knowledge is according to subject matter (e.g., mathematics, physics, chemistry, social studies, including history, anthropology, psychology).

To discover whether or not a particular focus of instruction is successful, we would have to vary knowledge factors in a more systematic way. Although Hillocks reports that the inquiry focus was the more successful in ensuring improvement in composing skill, we do not know exactly what was involved in using this focus. Also we do not know what would have happened had the inquiry method been used to teach genre knowledge versus domain-specific knowledge.

Another hidden factor in the focus of instruction is that of *process*. Some rely on discovery learning methods, whereas others contain procedures for guided discovery of the important concepts, and others make explicit exactly what is to be learned. There has not been any effort to take different types of tasks, such as a scales task, vary the amount of explicit instruction given during the procedures, and measure the effectiveness of the instructional strategy.

To remedy some of the conceptual difficulties inherent in past studies, I have reconstructed a working taxonomy that can be used as an analytic tool to discover the many different factors inherent in both the mode and focus of instruction. Table 1 presents descriptions of the three major dimensions of the taxonomy: the mode of instruction, the focus of instruction, and the process of instruction.

Included in the "mode of instruction" are five dimensions: goal setting, initiator of the writing task, presence of corrective feedback, source of the feedback, and the evaluation of the writing process and finished product.

TABLE 1

Taxonomy of Factors Important to Instruction

MODE OF INSTRUCTION

A. Goal setting:
1. Specific objectives: Setting goals to master specific types of material
2. General goal: Setting a general goal (e.g., to increase writing fluency or speed) where many different types of discourse and content are acceptable
B. Initiator of writing task:
1. Teacher initiated
2. Student initiated
3. Collaboration between student and teacher
C. Presence of corrective feedback:
1. Corrective feedback is given during the process of instruction before the final written product is evaluated
2. No corrective feedback is given prior to the final writing process
D. Source of feedback:
1. Teacher
2. Student
3. Peers
4. Interaction among any of the two or of the three parties
5. None
E. Evaluation of finished product:
1. Teacher
2. Student
3. Peers
4. Interaction among any two or three of the parties
5. No overt evaluation

FOCUS OF INSTRUCTION

A. Linguistic knowledge:
1. Declarative knowledge:
a. Focus on syntax, both intra-sentential and inter-sentential
b. Focus on spelling
c. Focus on punctuation
2. Procedural knowledge:
a. Syntax
b. Spelling
c. Punctuation
B. Structural and genre knowledge:
1. Declarative knowledge about various types of discourse
2. Procedural knowledge about how to produce various types of discourse
C. Knowledge specific to content domain:
1. Declarative knowledge about a particular domain of knowledge
2. Procedural knowledge for producing or gathering knowledge within a domain

(*Table continues on next page.*)

TABLE 1 (*continued*)

PROCESS OF INSTRUCTION

A. Explicit instruction:

This type of instruction involves a situation where a teacher explicitly defines the types of information to be learned. There is little guesswork involved. Teachers will normally lay out clear definitions of terms and generate clear examples to instantiate specific concepts under consideration.

B. Guided instruction:

This type of instruction involves the creation of materials, whereby the student has to infer the necessary content or structure. The tasks are constrained so that students will discover the important information and be able to make the correct set of inferences concerning the material to be learned.

C. Discovery learning:

This type of learning involves the student taking almost complete responsibility for discovering the material to be learned. There is no formal or informal presentation of the relevant criteria to be learned, except, perhaps, by presentation of a model. No mention is made, however, as to what makes the model correct. The student has to figure out or discover the principles inherent in the model.

Goal setting refers to the type and specificity of the goal to be accomplished during the writing process. Every writing task has some type of objective underlying its inception, even if the goal is to allow students to have "fun" writing about certain topics. Writing tasks do vary, however, in terms of the specific requirements proposed. Some writing tasks emphasize fluency and speed of writing; therefore, just about anything produced will be acceptable, as long as the student writes on a daily basis for an extended period of time. Other writing tasks require students to master specific genre knowledge or to learn about a specific content domain. Here, the standards of acceptable compositions are narrowed.

The initiator of the task refers to the person who chooses the particular writing objective to be accomplished. In many programs, the students not only control the choice of topic and discourse structure but they also control the time and place that writing occurs. In other programs, the objectives are controlled more by the teacher. In some programs, there is a mutual decision-making process involved in choosing the objectives, time, and place associated with writing.

The dimensions underlying the nature of corrective feedback pertain to whether or not corrective feedback occurs during the instructional process before the final act of writing. Two options are available. Either corrective feedback is given or it is not. The nature and quantity of feedback can vary, but these dimensions have more to do with the nature of structure the teacher wishes to impose on the task. The structural and organizational dimensions contained in Hillocks's modes of instruction have their own separate category: the process of instruction. The role that process plays in instruction will be discussed later.

The two remaining dimensions included in the mode of instruction refer to who gives corrective feedback and who evaluates the final written product. There are five options underneath each dimension: teacher, student, peers, combinations of the three, and no feedback or evaluation. The listing of these dimensions includes all possible combinations.

The "focus of instruction" in this taxonomy includes the different types of knowledge that can be imparted in writing instruction. Three substantive divisions are made: linguistic knowledge, genre knowledge, and knowledge specific to a content domain. These divisions are similar in nature to the ones Alan Purves in his essay presents in his taxonomy of knowledge underlying successful reading achievement. The difference is that an extra dimension is added: a distinction between declarative and procedural knowledge. Within each of the content domains, we can include information about each level of knowledge, either in the form of facts or in the form of a procedure related to retrieving or generating the particular type of declarative knowledge.

The emphasis on the type of structure inherent in a task and the choice of task has now been allocated to a different category: "process of instruction." In this category, the dimensions inherent in communicating concepts are described. Basically, the instructional process varies in the degree of explicitness that is presented in communication. Some instructional strategies contain explicit information about the nature of the content and organization of a concept to be learned. Hillocks's presentational mode and scales focus could be thought of as containing explicit reference to the particular concepts to be learned. It should be noted, however, that these two types of treatments present declarative knowledge to the learner (e.g., specific factual knowledge about the dimensions of a concept).

Other instructional modes and focuses are not as direct in their presentation of declarative knowledge. Instead, what these modes and focuses include are tasks that allow the student to derive some of the declarative knowledge underlying a particular concept. To succeed at this task, some type of procedural knowledge has to be included in the instructional process. Thus, the student is given some type of knowledge but not all types. The student has to derive the rest, either with the help of peers, the teacher, or the structure of the task.

In some learning tasks, students are given no information about the factual or procedural knowledge base underlying concept attainment. They may be presented with some material, but the type of knowledge and strategy used to complete the task are left primarily to the students' initiative. This type of instruction is generally labeled "discovery learning," and the principles regulating this type of instruction have been explored in some depth (see Shulman and Keislar [1966] for a review of discovery learning).

What advantages are inherent in this taxonomy? By using this delineation of variables, we can begin to separate the process of instruction from the content of instruction. A major issue underlying instructional studies concerns the relative roles that knowledge and process play in acquiring new concepts. Since each of the modes and focuses described by Hillocks in his essay have several different factors associated with them, we cannot conclude beyond a reasonable doubt that a particular mode and focus will always be more effective than the others.

What we can do, however, is begin to explore the relative effectiveness of each of the factors outlined in the reconstructed taxonomy. We know from several sources (Brown et al. 1983; Larkin 1980; Simon 1980) that procedural knowledge is thought to be just as important as declarative knowledge in ensuring instructional effectiveness. There are some who would argue that it is the lack of procedural knowledge that prevents children from fully developing new concepts (Bransford 1984).

Because we are just becoming sensitive to the powerful role that different types of knowledge play in the comprehension and composition process, few studies have actively examined or explored the importance of this dimension. The results from several instructional studies (Glaser 1984; Pearson 1983) suggest that the role of specific content knowledge is a more powerful indicator of performance that the acquisition of broad, general problem-solving strategies. In fact, it is not clear that general problem-solving strategies can be acquired and separated from domain-specific knowledge (Glaser 1984; Pearson 1983).

This issue is important in examining the composition process because, although certain focuses and modes of instruction were more effective in a specific sense, we do not know how well the learning in certain modes or focuses would transfer to other tasks. By distinguishing among different types of knowledge and by looking at the process of instruction, we can begin to examine the issue of generalization of skills.

The reconstructed taxonomy would also help in the evaluation of curricula and computer programs designed for classroom use. As Becker shows in this essay, there are more dreams associated with the use of computers in the schools than the realities would warrant. The costs are prohibitive (at least for the moment), and the amount of time students spend on a computer is minimal.

Even if every student had access to a computer, the available instructional packages are often very poor substitutes for good instruction. Many of the people writing computer programs know little about the content area under consideration and even less about the nature of learning. Additionally, the objectives underlying the construction of programs have not been worked out in a planned way so as to map onto the curriculum actually being used in a classroom. The problems of computer programs are similar in nature to the ones described for commercial basal reading series.

If we are to be successful at advancing the development of literacy in American schools, much more effort must be made to understand the nature of the learning and instructional process. The amount of work to be accomplished is rather large. In the past 10 years, there has been an extraordinary amount of research completed on all aspects of the literacy process. We have learned about some of the fundamental problems associated with the acquisition of literacy skills. The reviews presented here attest to the rich diversity of research and to the fundamental principles being derived from much of this work.

A necessary step in developing instructional procedures for reading and writing activities will require a cooperative effort among many groups. The diverse nature of the belief system existing in our country requires that a primary goal in the next 10 years should be the development of some type of social policy where efforts at literacy development are not destroyed because of a disagreement over values and content areas. There are many important problems about the nature of learning that need resolution. Attention to the ideas and concepts to be learned is central to this efforts. Destructive disagreements are not.

Similar comments can be made about the types of research that are ongoing in the literacy domain. Many of the studies tend toward naturalistic observation of a relatively homogeneous population (Graves 1983), others are comparative in nature (Heath 1983), and others are experimental (Bloom 1984; Stein and Trabasso 1982). Some studies are descriptive, while others are explanatory and theoretical in nature. Each type of study makes a unique contribution to the field. Observational studies are often necessary when we do not have very good intuitions about the reality of a phenomenon. Comparative studies are essential, especially when there are different world views about the nature of learning. And experimental studies are central in order to determine the causal relationship among certain variables. Naturalistic

199

studies do not provide good information about causal relationships among events, whereas experimental studies are more forceful in this regard. On the other hand, sometimes the relevant knowledge to be studied is not known, and then observation is critical.

Even though all of these different types of studies are critical, those who are involved in certain types of studies often have little respect for individuals doing different types of work. People devoted to naturalistic observation are highly critical of those who are involved in experimental research. The lack of "relevance" associated with certain types of experimentation is often given as a reason (see Graves [1983] for an example of this type of belief). And yet it is the systematic study of the writing process that will allow a test of hypotheses central to learning and instruction (see George Hillocks's essay).

Experimenters have difficulty with naturalistic observations studies because often an investigator will draw major conclusions regarding the writing or comprehension process without any good supportive evidence. There is an inherent belief among many that simply describing a phenomenon is the same thing as explaining why and how it occurred. The problem is that describing a phenomenon often has little relationship to the factors that caused the event. Experimenters are more concerned with the causal and explanatory properties of a phenomenon.

Sometimes, it is difficult to get at the nature of explanation. In terms of the writing process, much has to be discovered before we can seek explanations. Astute observations about the classroom or the role of cultural factors in determining the development of literacy are invaluable. Many times our knowledge of an area is sparse and ill-defined, and in these situations observation is critical. In fact, most good experimental studies combine pilot work (systematic observation) with the evolution of the experiment.

If we consider the process of the evolution of knowledge about a domain, then both types of work become an integral part of the field. The problem is to convince people in each camp of the other's worthiness. In the case of literacy development, this will be essential. A first step in development of good curricula will entail an evaluation of the concepts and ideas to be taught. Good descriptions of current curriculum material in terms of the goals, functions, and content will be necessary. Explorations of the learning and instructional processes are also needed. A reevaluation of certain beliefs about effective instruction and learning will be necessary. What we wish were true and what actually works are often very different. By integrating a variety of approaches in the area of literacy development, we should slowly be able to devise a more planned and considered approach to reading and writing.

References

Anania, J. "The Effects of Quality Instruction on the Cognitive and Affective Learning of Students." Ph.D. dissertation, University of Chicago, 1981.

Anderson, R. C. "Role of the Reader's Schema in Comprehension, Learning, and Memory." In *Learning to Read in American Schools*, edited by R. C. Anderson, J. Osborn, and R. J. Tierney. Hillsdale, N.J.: Lawrence Erlbaum Associates, 1984.

Anderson, R. C., J. Osborn, and R. J. Tierney, eds. *Learning to Read in American Schools*. Hillsdale, N.J.: Lawrence Erlbaum Associates, 1984.

Asher, S. R., and P. D. Renshaw. "Children without Friends: Social Knowledge and Social Skill Training." In *The Development of Children's Friendships*, edited by S. R. Asher and J. Gottman. New York: Cambridge University Press, 1981.

Bartlett, F. C. *Remembering: A Study in Experimental Social Psychology*. Cambridge: Cambridge University Press, 1932.

Beck, I. L., M. G. McKeown, E. S. McCaslin and A. M. Burkes. "Instructional Dimensions that May Affect Reading Comprehension: Examples from Two Commercial Reading Programs" (Publication 20). Pittsburgh, Pa.: University of Pittsburgh, Learning Research and Development Center, 1979.

Beck, I. L., M. G. McKeown, R. C. Omanson, and M. T. Pople. "Improving the Comprehensibility of Stories: The Effects of Revisions that Improve Coherence." *Reading Research Quarterly* 19 (1984): 263–77.

Bloom, B. *Human Characteristics and School Learning*. New York: McGraw-Hill Book Co., 1976.

Bloom, B. "The Search for Methods of Instruction as Effective as One-to-One Tutoring." *Educational Leadership* 41, no. 4 (1984): 4–18.

Bransford, J. D. "Schema Activation and Schema Acquisition: Comments on R. C. Anderson's Remarks." In *Learning to Read in American Schools*, edited by R. C. Anderson, J. Osborn, and R. J. Tierney. Hillsdale, N.J.: Lawrence Erlbaum Associates, 1984.

Brown, A. L., J. D. Bransford, R. A. Ferrara, and J. C. Campione. "Learning, Remembering, and Understanding." In *Handbook of Child Psychology*, vol. 3, edited by J. H. Flavell and E. M. Markman (P. Mussen, series editor). New York: John Wiley & Sons, 1983.

Burke, A. J. "Students' Potential for Learning Contrasted Under Tutorial and Group Approaches to Instruction." Ph.D. dissertation, University of Chicago, 1983.

Conrad, R. *The Deaf School Child*. London: Harper & Row, 1979.

Corsaro, W. A. "Friendship in the Nursery School: Social Organization in a Peer Environment." In *The Development of Children's Friendships*, edited by S. R. Asher and J. Gottman. New York: Cambridge University Press, 1981.

Cronbach, L. J. "The Logic of Experiments on Discovery." In *Learning by Discovery: A Critical Approach*, edited by L. S. Shulman and E. R. Keislar. Chicago: Rand McNally and Co., 1966.

Durkin, D. "Do Basal Manuals Teach Reading Comprehension." In *Learning to Read in American Schools*, edited by R. C. Anderson, J. Osborn, and R. J. Tierney. Hillsdale, N.J.: Lawrence Erlbaum Associates, 1984.

Frayer, D. A., Frederick, W. C., and Klausmeier, H. J. "A Schema for Testing the Level of Concept Mastery" (Working Paper No. 16). Madison: University of Wisconsin, Wisconsin Research and Development Center for Cognitive Learning, 1969.

Glaser, R. "Instructional Psychology: Past, Present, and Future." *American Psychologist* 37 (1980): 292–305.

Glaser, R. "Education and Thinking: The Role of Knowledge." *American Psychologist* 39 (1984): 93–104.

Goldstein, I. "Developing a Computational Representation for Problem Solving Skills." In *Problem Solving and Education,* edited by D. T. Tuma and F. Reif. Hillsdale, N.J.: Lawrence Erlbaum Associates, 1980.

Graves, D. *Writing: Teachers and Children at Work.* Exeter, N.H.: Heinemann Educational Books, 1983.

Heath, S. B. *Way with Words.* New York: Cambridge University Press, 1983.

Langer, J. "From Theory to Practice: A Pre-Reading Plan." *Journal of Reading Behavior* 25 (1981): 152–56.

Larkin, J. H. "Teaching Problem Solving in Physics: The Psychological Laboratory and the Practical Classroom." In *Problem Solving and Education,* edited by D. T. Tuma and F. Reif. Hillsdale, N.J.: Lawrence Erlbaum Associates, 1980.

Mandl, H., N. L. Stein, and T. Trabasso. *Learning and Comprehension of Text.* Hillsdale, N.J.: Lawrence Erlbaum Associates, 1984.

Mandler, J. M. "A Code in the Node." *Discourse Processes* 1 (1978): 14–35.

Mandler, J. M. "Representation." In *Handbook of Child Psychology,* vol. 3, edited by J. H. Flavell and E. M. Markman (P. Mussen, series editor). New York: John Wiley & Sons, 1983.

Meyer, B. "Text Dimensions and Cognitive Processing." In *Learning and Comprehension of Text,* edited by H. Mandl, N. L. Stein, and T. Trabasso. Hillsdale, N.J.: Lawrence Erlbaum Associates, 1984.

Norman, D. "What goes on in the Head of the Learner." In *Learning, Cognition, and College Teaching: New Directions for Learning and Thinking,* edited by W. J. McKeachie. San Francisco: Jossey-Bass, Inc., 1980.

Palinscar, A. S., and A. L. Brown. "Reciprocal Teaching of Comprehension." *Cognition and Instruction,* in press.

Pearson, D. P., and M. C. Gallagher. "The Instruction of Reading Comprehension." *Contemporary Educational Psychology* 8 (1983): 317–44.

Piaget, J. *Six Psychological Studies.* New York: Random House, 1967.

Resnick, D. P., and L. B. Resnick. "The Nature of Literacy: An Historical Exploration." *Harvard Educational Review* 47 (1977): 370–85.

Resnick, L. "Comprehension and Learning: Implications for a Theory of Instruction." In *Learning and Comprehension of Text,* edited by H. Mandl, N. L. Stein, and T. Trabasso. Hillsdale, N.J.: Lawrence Erlbaum Associates, 1984.

Rumelhart, D. E. "Schemata: The Building Blocks of Cognition." In *Theoretical Issues in Reading Comprehension,* edited by R. J. Spiro, B. C. Bruce, and W. F. Brewer. Hillsdale, N.J.: Lawrence Erlbaum Associates, 1980.

Rumelhart, D. E., and D. Norman. "Accretion, Tuning, and Restructuring: Three Modes of Learning." In *Semantic Factors in Cognition,* edited by J. W. Cotton and R. Klatsky. Hillsdale, N.J.: Lawrence Erlbaum Associates, 1978.

Schank, R. C., and R. P. Abelson. *Scripts, Plans, Goals and Understanding.* Hillsdale, N.J.: Lawrence Erlbaum Associates, 1977.

Schnotz, W. "Comparative Instructional Text Organization." In *Learning and Comprehension of Text,* edited by H. Mandl, N. L. Stein, and T. Trabasso. Hillsdale, N.J.: Lawrence Erlbaum Associates, 1984.

Shulman, L. S., and E. R. Keislar. *Learning by Discovery: A Critical Approach.* Chicago: Rand McNally and Co., 1966.

Shweder, R. A., E. Turiel, and N. C. Much. "The Moral Intuition of the Child." In *Social Cognitive Development,* edited by J. H. Flavell and L. Ross. New York: Cambridge University Press, 1981.

Simon, H. A. *Sciences of the Artificial.* Cambridge, Mass.: MIT Press, 1969.

Simon, H. A. "Problem Solving and Education." In *Problem Solving and Education,* edited by D. T. Tuma and F. Reif. Hillsdale, N.J.: Lawrence Erlbaum Associates, 1980.

Skinner, B. F. "Behaviorism at Fifty." In *Behaviorism and phenomenology,* edited by T. W. Wann. Chicago: University of Chicago Press, 1964.

Stein, N. L. "How Children Understand Stories: A Developmental Analysis." In *Current Topics in Early Childhood Education,* edited by L. Katz. Norwood, N.J.: Ablex, Inc., 1979.

Stein, N. L. "On the Goals, Functions, and Knowledge of Reading and Writing." *Contemporary Educational Psychology* 8 (1983): 261–92.

Stein, N. L., K. Kilgore, and M. Policastro. "The Development of a Story Concept." Unpublished manuscript, University of Chicago, 1984.

Stein, N. L., and M. T. Nezworski. "The Effects of Organization and Instructional Set on Story Memory." *Discourse Processes* 1 (1978): 177–93.

Stein, N. L., and T. Trabasso. "What's in a Story: An Approach to Comprehension and Instruction." In *Advances in Instructional Psychology,* edited by R. Glaser. Hillsdale, N.J.: Lawrence Erlbaum Associates, 1982.

Suls, J. M., and R. L. Miller. *Social Comparison Processes.* Washington D.C.: Hemisphere Publishing Co., 1977.

Trabasso, T., T. Secco, and P. van den Broek. "Causal Cohesion and Story Coherence." In *Learning and Comprehension of Text,* edited by H. Mandl, N. L. Stein, and T. Trabasso. Hillsdale, N.J.: Lawrence Erlbaum Associates, 1984.

Tuma, D. T., and F. Reif. *Problem Solving and Education.* Hillsdale, N.J.: Lawrence Erlbaum Associates, 1980.

Winston, P. "Learning to Identify Toy Block Structures." In *Contemporary Issues in Cognitive Psychology,* edited by R. L. Solso. Washington, D.C.: Hemisphere Publishing Corp., 1973.

Index